THE POWER PROBLEM

THE POWER PROBLEM

HOW AMERICAN MILITARY DOMINANCE MAKES US
LESS SAFE, LESS PROSPEROUS, AND LESS FREE

CHRISTOPHER A. PREBLE

CORNELL UNIVERSITY PRESS

ITHACA AND LONDON

Library
University of Texas
at San Antonio

A VOLUME IN THE SERIES CORNELL STUDIES IN SECURITY AFFAIRS,
edited by Robert J. Art, Robert Jervis, and Stephen M. Walt.
A list of titles in this series is available at www.cornellpress.cornell.edu.

First published 2009 by Cornell University Press

Printed in the United States of America

Library of Congress Cataloging-in-Publication Data

Preble, Christopher A.
   The power problem : how American military dominance makes us less
safe, less prosperous, and less free / Christopher A. Preble.
       p. cm. — (Cornell studies in security affairs)
   Includes bibliographical references and index.
   ISBN 978-0-8014-4765-5 (cloth : alk. paper)
   1. United States—Military policy.   2. National security—United States.
3. Hegemony—United States.   4. Power (Social sciences)—United States.
I. Title.   II. Series: Cornell studies in security affairs.

   UA23.P6825   2009
   355'.033073—dc22   2008052553

Cornell University Press strives to use environmentally responsible suppliers
and materials to the fullest extent possible in the publishing of its books.
Such materials include vegetable-based, low-VOC inks and acid-free papers
that are recycled, totally chlorine-free, or partly composed of nonwood fibers.
For further information, visit our website at www.cornellpress.cornell.edu.

Cloth printing   10 9 8 7 6 5 4 3 2 1

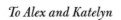

To Alex and Katelyn

Madeleine Albright, our ambassador to the UN, asked me in frustration "What's the point of having this superb military that you're always talking about if we can't use it?" I thought I would have an aneurysm. American GIs were not toy soldiers to be moved around on some sort of global game board.

Colin Powell, *My American Journey*

CONTENTS

ACKNOWLEDGMENTS

This book began as a series of hand-written notes scrawled in the margins of my heavily worn copy of Thucydides' *The Peloponnesian War*. I had been induced to read some unfamiliar passages in preparation for a discussion of the Battle of Salamis, hosted by the Liberty Fund of Indianapolis. The conversation was lively and well-informed, and I was privileged to be surrounded by a diverse group of intellectuals from many different backgrounds.

I couldn't help shake the sense that our contemporary policies could learn much from the Athenians' experience. Although Greek history makes only a passing appearance in this manuscript, the ideas that I struggled with—including the purpose and limitations of military power, the role of allies in starting or preventing wars, and the moral obligations of a government to its people, and of a people of one place to the people of another—are not so different than those with which Pericles and Alcibiades, Cleon and Nicias, and Thucydides himself, wrestled nearly 2,500 years ago.

Thucydides likely toiled alone. I, by contrast, am fortunate to have been assisted in this project by many friends and colleagues.

To my compatriots at the Cato Institute, I have many debts to discharge. My colleagues in the Defense and Foreign Policy Department were instrumental. Justin Logan and Ted Galen Carpenter read all of the chapters, in most cases several drafts of the same chapters, and provided essential feedback every time. My newest colleague, Ben Friedman, read several chapters, and was a crucial sounding board for some of my ideas pertaining to force structure. Malou Innocent, Ionut Popescu, and Charles Zakaib provided invaluable research assistance at various stages, as well as insightful commentary on several of the chapters. Gene Healy provided detailed feedback on the entire manuscript in his never-ending quest to make me a better writer. I am also grateful to Stanley

Kober, Peter Van Doren, Jagadeesh Gokhale, Jerry Taylor, and Cato Chairman Bill Niskanen for their comments and suggestions.

We have an outstanding intern program at Cato (full disclosure: I began my career in public policy many years ago as a Cato intern), and it has been my privilege to work with a number of these promising young people, including Kaylin Wainwright, Kevin Ross, Charles Rice, Brian Garst, and Jonathan Winegar-Mendez. My special thanks go out to Paul Meinshausen and Jessica Wright for their hard work and thoughtful contributions in the final weeks that enabled me to finish the manuscript on time.

I wish to thank Ed Crane and David Boaz, who have provided steady leadership at Cato for nearly three decades. In a city that treats non-conformity with utter disdain, Cato has managed to maintain its independence and creativity, and those of us who are fortunate enough to work there are all better off for it. Ed and David deserve much of the credit for making the Institute what it is today.

Many others assisted me along the way, including Doug Bandow, Winslow Wheeler, Steve Teles, Steve Klemencic, Brian Goodhart, Chris Leavitt, and Fred Sheehy. I am grateful for the patient encouragement of my Mom and Dad. Special thanks go out to J. D. Wooten for volunteering his valuable time to help out, especially with chapter 1, and to Eric Lupfer for his help in turning my idea into a proposal. Barry Posen invited me to discuss the themes contained within this book, and he and the rest of the staff at MIT's Security Studies Program provided instant feedback that helped me to hone some of my arguments.

I am grateful to Robert Art, Robert Jervis, and Steve Walt, the editors of the Studies in Security Affairs series, and to Roger Haydon at Cornell University Press. I have long admired the quality of Cornell books, now I know first-hand why the press has such a stellar reputation. I am grateful to Roger for his interest in this book from the outset, and for his timely and insightful comments on early chapter drafts that had more than their fair share of rough edges. Bob Jervis offered a number of crucial suggestions that I strived to incorporate into the final manuscript. Thanks also go out to Karen Laun and Irina Burns for their copyediting, and to Judith Kip for preparing the index.

I cannot begin to thank, so I will only begin to do so, my wife Krista. She is my best friend, my trusted partner, and the love of my life. I have always benefited from her steady encouragement. Her perceptive questions and gentle criticisms have helped me to sharpen my arguments over the years. I am particularly grateful for her willingness to take on added responsibilities at home, despite her already very busy schedule. This additional help while I was writing the book allowed me to get the ideas on paper, and to do so under deadline.

Speaking of responsibilities at home, and of loving family, there are my children—my son Alex, and my daughter Katelyn—to whom this book is dedicated. As I was finishing the manuscript, we told my daughter—who was just learning to read—that someday, if she continued to pay attention to her homework, she might be able to read Daddy's book. She was characteristically blunt: "Why would I want to read Daddy's book?" Here's hoping that someday she'll want to.

THE POWER PROBLEM

INTRODUCTION

This book is about U.S. power, specifically U.S. military power: what it is, how it is measured, and how it should be used. It considers how much that power costs, and what benefits we as Americans derive from it. It ponders why our power sometimes doesn't work, why our power has not contributed to our strength as a nation, and why in some cases it has actually undermined us. It explores how our possession of great power, and our willingness to use it in Bosnia, Kosovo, Afghanistan, and Iraq, has prompted others to appeal for us to intervene in Liberia, Darfur, Burma, and Georgia.

Such calls for us to use our power persist despite its obvious shortcomings. Our enormous power did not deter or intimidate the 9/11 attackers. Saddam Hussein did not capitulate to our demands. North Korea repeatedly ignored U.S. warnings to cease and desist with its nuclear weapons production; our threats against Iran have been unavailing.

Some see our current predicament, with the United States held in low regard around the world, and with Americans deeply dissatisfied with the direction of our foreign policies, as essentially a marketing problem. They believe that if we more neatly package what we are doing, if we bind ourselves to multilateral institutions, if we pay more heed to the wishes of others, then Americans and non-Americans alike will again welcome the use of U.S. military power in more places around the world.[1]

This book takes a very different view. We cannot convincingly tame our power such that some others will not fear us, resent us, and, in extreme cases, resist us. Meanwhile, we don't have nearly enough power to run rough-shod over others, dominating the world by threat and intimidation as past empires did. Indeed, we shouldn't want to, even if we could. In our quest to achieve and sustain global dominance, we would distort our sense of self, that which makes us Americans.

The United States has been corrupted by its great military power, which has shifted the delicate balance between the executive branch and the other two branches of government. It has driven once reliable international partners to criticize our conduct, even as many of those same critics have come to see, not always correctly, that their security is contingent upon our willingness to use our power on their behalf. We have occasionally forgotten that national power involves so much more than military strength. We have lost sight of the purpose of military power, confusing military strength—the physical capacity to wage war—with power, which Merriam-Webster defines as the "ability to act or produce an effect." Put another way, strength is the possession of physical capabilities; power is the ability to use what you have. We are able to use our military strength, but by doing so we often lose sight of its purpose, and our willingness to use our vast military can even warp our national purpose.

In many ways, then, our military power has become a problem, and this problem is the basis for this book's controversial argument:

We should reduce our military power in order to be more secure.

Solving the power problem begins with seeing military power for what it should be: namely, a means to an end, an end stipulated in the U.S. Constitution, but based on centuries of experience and history. Our military exists to secure economic, social, and cultural freedoms for all Americans. The Framers of the Constitution created a government to serve "We the People of the United States." This new government's object was to "provide for the common defence" and "secure the blessings of Liberty to ourselves and our posterity." In recent times, however, we have deployed the sharp end of that government's power—our military—in support of those who are not parties to our unique social contract.

To the extent that we've always believed in a purpose for our power that reached beyond our shores, Americans have traditionally defined power largely in economic and cultural terms. The Founders intended the new nation to be a light unto the world, a beacon of hope to show others the way. But they strongly resisted the urge to force their views on others. In the earliest days of the Republic, they lacked the power to do so, but that was not entirely by accident. Rather, the Framers of the Constitution deliberately constrained the new government's power, especially the power to go to war, because they believed that such power would alter what they saw as the proper balance between the different branches of government, and, even more important, between the government and the people. George Washington—the Founder who could legitimately claim the title of military hero—saw military power as purely an instrument of politics, and he feared, as he said in his Farewell Address, "those overgrown military establishments which, under any form of government, are inauspicious to liberty."[2]

Another general-turned-president, Dwight David Eisenhower, similarly feared the effect that massive military spending and a permanent sense of crisis and warfare would have on the nation's character. Eisenhower anticipated that it was our peaceful engagement on a global scale—our dynamism, the collective energy of tens of millions of individuals each pursuing his or her own path— more so than our military might, that would ultimately enable us to prevail in the long struggle. And history would prove him right. In commerce, in trade, in culture, in the arts, all of these elements of national greatness helped us to win the Cold War. This is obvious when one considers what the Soviet Union produced. In addition to thousands of nuclear warheads, the Soviets built powerful rockets, fast submarines, and agile aircraft to deliver these weapons. But they also built ugly, lumbering automobiles that only the elites could afford to buy; they grew too little food to feed themselves; their supermarkets were filled with empty shelves, their department stores with worthless trinkets and shoddy consumer goods. The most important lesson of the Cold War, then, was that true strength was not merely a function of military power.

In the two decades following the collapse of the Soviet Union, some Americans have forgotten that lesson. Still, to the extent to which many Americans have come to see our military power as an end in itself, a sign of our national greatness, some of this is to be expected. Simple patriotism takes pride in keeping score, from Olympic gold medals to the number of American Nobel Laureates. With respect to our military, we celebrate the vast gulf separating us from others. We are dominant militarily, literally second to none, and not even second to everyone else combined. The total amount that we spend on our military every year in the United States is roughly the same as the sum total of all defense expenditures by every other country on the planet.

But money only tells part of the story. Decades of research and development in defense industries and technologies have created an array of weapons and gadgets that are unmatched anywhere in the world. Even aircraft and ships designed in the 1980s, and built in the 1990s, are superior to what other countries can put in the air or out to sea today.

Our military advantages go even farther than that. The men and women who operate these marvelous gadgets—the soldiers, sailors, airmen, and Marines of the U.S. armed forces—constitute yet another intangible advantage, one that other countries have long struggled to match. Our military personnel are well-trained and adaptive. They are capable of tackling problems not taught in school. In other words, they think. Because they are volunteers, they are highly motivated. Although some might be induced to join primarily by the financial benefits, none expect to become rich. They regularly face long periods of separation from family and friends, and, increasingly in the post-9/11 environment, they face the very real prospect of severe injury, permanent disfigurement, or death, and yet they never fail to answer the call of their civilian leaders.

Even still, these men and women struggle to bring order to Iraq, a nation the size of California, and fight valiantly against a determined foe in Afghanistan, one of the poorest countries on the planet. Our best and brightest are killed and injured by bombs fashioned from the crudest combination of old and aging equipment.

The problems that our troops are encountering in Iraq, Afghanistan, and elsewhere are not new, and they are connected to a deeper power problem: our insufficient attention to the need to prioritize when and whether we should intervene militarily. Our inability or unwillingness to do so grew out of the erroneous belief that a military strong enough to prevail during the Cold War could—and should—be used to solve a number of the world's problems. Former secretary of state Madeleine Albright expressed this sentiment rather well when she said to the then joint chiefs of staff chairman Colin Powell: "What's the point of having this superb military that you're always talking about if we can't use it?"[3]

Powell reported that he "nearly had an aneurysm" when he heard this, and that is hardly surprising. Powell's concerns about a lack of discrimination on the part of policymakers, and not just those in the Clinton administration, reflected his genuine concerns about the morale and well-being of the military institutions he so loved. He headed the U.S. military at a time when military spending was being cut by one-third, and he was anxious to ensure that his "superb military" wasn't turned into a "hollow force"—a military that appeared strong on the outside, but that was diminished on the inside by low morale, inadequate training, and substandard equipment.

At a more fundamental level, Powell was incensed by the implication that U.S. soldiers were geopolitical pawns that policymakers in Washington could move around some "global game board."[4] If policymakers were to be asked why the U.S. military has been used so often in recent years, they likely would not justify their actions on the grounds that the disappearance of our main rival allowed us to get involved where once we might have hesitated. It is certainly true that after 1989 we gained confidence in our own security such that we were willing to countenance new challenges. U.S. leaders prefer, however, to invoke our liberalism, the universal appeal of our ideals.[5] Rather than focus on the considerable freedom of action afforded to the United States by the collapse of the Soviet Union, the Bush Senior and Clinton administrations portrayed the United States as the vanguard of an ineluctable march toward human liberty and peace. It was not merely that the United States *could* be a force for good, but rather that the United States was the *engine* of all that was good.

The United States, in this context, became the world's "indispensable nation." Likely coined by the historian James Chace, the phrase was later picked up by Madeleine Albright and ultimately Bill Clinton. The bipartisan enthusiasm for indispensableness carried into the George W. Bush administration, and persists to this day despite the enormous costs incurred as a result of the war in Iraq. Bush administration officials cast the discussion of the U.S. role in the world in moral terms, much as it was during the Clinton administration; namely, that our great prosperity and power confer unique obligations on the American people. "I believe the United States is *the* beacon for freedom in the world," President George W. Bush told Bob Woodward. "And I believe we have a responsibility to promote freedom that is as solemn as the responsibility is to protecting the American people, because the two go hand-in-hand."[6] One cannot gainsay what President Bush believed; it is genuinely disturbing, however, that he or any president could equate his presumed responsibility to "promote freedom" to his Constitutional obligation to protect the American people as though the two were synonymous. They are not.

But Bush was hardly alone. His sentiments echo those of some of the most outspoken defenders of our current foreign policies who say that our willingness to use the U.S. military might be driven by a sense of our obligation to humanity, but that advancing our values is synonymous with securing our interests.

Oftentimes, however, foreign interventions are not intended to advance U.S. interests; the interventions are, as their advocates suggest, "gifts" intended for the benefit of others. But because our government's enumerated powers do not include the right to give such gifts—paid for by U.S. taxpayers—Washington often attempts to justify such acts on the grounds that U.S. interests *are* at stake, even when they are not. The interventions in Bosnia and Kosovo in 1995 and 1999, respectively, reflect this approach, as did calls for U.S. military intervention in Liberia in 2003, or in Sudan in 2006, on the absurd notion that these were crucial fronts in the "war on terror."

Another aspect of our power problem is our outsized expectations for what military power can do. It is a dangerous folly to look to the military as a way to cure the world's ills; military intervention often makes a horrible situation even worse. Seemingly successful missions often mask a deeper reality that might not become apparent for years. The 1991 Persian Gulf War claimed far fewer American lives than most experts had predicted, but left behind thousands of U.S. troops in Saudi Arabia. Osama bin Laden seized upon the presence of these personnel as a pretext for his campaign of violence around the globe. He even managed to stoke sufficient anger and resentment within the hearts of a few young men—fifteen of them Saudis—to convince them to commit suicide and mass murder on September 11, 2001. Meanwhile, the presumed need to finish the job left undone in the first Gulf War, namely the removal of Saddam Hussein from power, was the rationale for the subsequent military campaign that the nation is still struggling to bring to a close.

It does not always take years to accurately assess the costs of military intervention; many are longer, bloodier, and more frustrating than anticipated, and the costs are almost immediately apparent. The current Iraq mission certainly fits into the latter category, as did the Vietnam War four decades earlier. Even short and relatively small-scale operations can prove extremely costly for those involved—the 1982-83 intervention in Lebanon culminated in a suicide bombing in Beirut that killed 241 Marines; the mission in 1992-93 in Somalia collapsed after a firefight in Mogadishu that left eighteen Army Rangers dead—and no less frustrating for Americans back home than wars that drag on for years.

We have too often forgotten that for every seemingly easy military intervention, there are many difficult ones, and we can never know when we initiate a mission how it will turn out. But we have forgotten other even more important lessons over the years. For example, we have not accurately assessed the costs of the power that we have. Some of these costs are easily calculated in dollars and cents, but most defy simple arithmetic.

Because I call for reducing our military power, critics might accuse me of being "anti-military," a particularly damning charge during a time of war. But this misses a crucial distinction between my approach and that of other strategists. I would match our military power to our national security needs, and define those needs far more stringently than has been done over the past two decades. By contrast, the Bush Senior and Clinton administrations cut funding for personnel and equipment, but at the same time sent our troops on a number of dangerous missions that were not essential to U.S. national security.

The pattern continued under the next administration. Although George W. Bush dramatically expanded military spending after 9/11, he expanded the military's missions even more. In other words, the gap between means and ends has actually grown over the past eight years. Some experts predict that it will take over $190 billion to recapitalize and reset the U.S. military to pre-Iraq War levels, over and above what we are already projected to spend on the military in the years ahead.[7] Meanwhile, lackluster recruitment and difficulties in retaining experienced personnel have forced the military to accept people into the service who only a few years ago would have been turned away. The long-term effects of these policies might not be apparent for years.

After the end of the Cold War, we became a nation of perpetual war in part because we could do war so very well. Or so it seemed. But perhaps now, finally, we are beginning to appreciate the limits of our power. If there is any good to come of our recent struggles, it may be that we have a moment to reassess the nature of our power, its benefits, its costs, its virtues, and its limits. To that end, at this critical juncture in the nation's history, it is essential that every weapon system, every proposal to increase the size of the force, every plan for deploying our military abroad or for expanding operations already under way, be scrutinized anew. We need a new grand strategy, not merely a refinement or a revision of our old one. Our new grand strategy needs to take account of our strengths, and address our weaknesses. Above all, it should be based on an appreciation that even the most powerful country in the world must make choices. Our military is second to none, and our men and women in uniform are well-trained, extremely qualified, and highly motivated. But they cannot be everywhere, and they cannot do everything. If our new grand strategy attempts to resolve the current mismatch between means and ends by recruiting more soldiers and buying more hardware and equipment, we won't have solved our power problem. We will only have made it worse.

This book and its controversial thesis are structured around two simple and related questions. First, "What should our vast military power get us?" As I show, it should focus and capitalize on a state of physical security not enjoyed by many other nations today; this is very important. Indeed, this physical security is the precondition that provides all Americans with an opportunity to live their lives and pursue their dreams. We should do nothing to undermine this feature of our power; where necessary, we must enhance it.

The benefits that we derive from a strong military comprise only one side of the ledger. On the other side are the costs. To the second central question of this book—"What does our great power cost us?"—the answer seems simple enough: a lot. The dollar costs are relatively easy to measure. Congress debates, deliberates, compromises, and passes legislation funding the Departments of Defense and Homeland Security, as well as the intelligence agencies. Since the start of the Iraq War, Congress has also passed a series of supplemental spending requests intended to support the war effort there and in Afghanistan.

As far as the process goes, it could be said that the debate over the Pentagon's budget is remarkably transparent, but it is not as transparent as it may seem. For starters, the sheer size of the official Department of Defense budget (more than $515 billion in 2009) enables a number of large and costly projects to escape careful scrutiny. A few non-profit organizations—including Taxpayers for Common Sense, the Center for Defense Information, the Project on Government Oversight, and my employer, the Cato Institute—will critique aspects of the Pentagon's budget, sometimes even down to the line-item level, in an attempt to ensure that taxpayer dollars are being wisely spent. And there are a few conscientious members of Congress who are willing to do the same, asking hard questions about what the members of our military need, as opposed to what they want, or what others want for them. But for every organization willing to challenge aspects of the defense budgets, there are five or six making the case for still more spending. And for every congressman willing to ask "What's in it for the U.S.?" there are dozens asking simply, "What's in it for *us*—my constituents and me?" Will the base be kept open? Will the ship be built in my district? Will the aircraft assembly line employ men and women who might vote for me the next time around? It is this type of thinking that has allowed the defense budget to grow, on average, at a rate of more than 12 percent every year since 2001. By way of comparison, non-defense discretionary spending during the same period has grown 8 percent each year.

There are other costs that are harder to measure. Often, the existence—or even the perception—of great military power encourages arrogance and overconfidence. Meanwhile, our capacity for waging war in far-flung places, and disconnected from any consideration of U.S. national interests, encourages individuals and groups to come to Washington to appeal for assistance. The Reform Party of Syria wants us to get rid of Syrian President Bashar Assad. The Georgians want to be members of NATO, and in the meantime they have received U.S. military assistance. We came to the aid of Muslims in Bosnia and Kosovo. Why not Muslims in Chechnya? We delivered food to starving Somalis in 1993, and then intervened militarily to prevent our aid from being diverted to warlords. Why, then, did we not stop a far greater humanitarian crisis in Rwanda? Or why has the United States not sent military forces to the Darfur region of Sudan, where a genocide has claimed an estimated 200,000 lives?

Although we do not always intervene, our impulse to do so is understandable. Our sense of obligation to come to the assistance of those in need is deeply grounded in a number of religious traditions. Christian theologians point to a passage in the New Testament, Luke 12:48, that translates over the ages to a simple affirmation: From those who have been given much, much will be required. Pop culture has adapted this timeless message in the popular Spider-Man comic books and movies, where Peter Parker is haunted by the admonition "with great power comes great responsibility." U.S. leaders from both major political parties, representing views from across the ideological spectrum, regularly invoke the theme of the country's great responsibilities to explain why we exert ourselves so often, and why we need an enormous military to fulfill those presumed obligations.

However, as our experience in Iraq has shown, our desire to do good is not always matched by our capacity to do good. We do have great power, but we are not omnipotent. No one is. You could say that is another lesson of the Bible.

Is there an alternative? Or are we doomed to spend vast sums of money on our military, and then be forced—either out of a sense of honor or shame (or both?)—to use this power on behalf of others? Must we sustain such a policy toward the use of force even if, in the process, we destroy ourselves?

I am an optimist. I believe we can recover from this state of affairs. I believe that we can move beyond the United States being the sole superpower, expected to intervene in all places, and at all times, to our more rightful role as *a* world leader. But the change should come from within. It is unlikely to be forced upon us from the outside—or, if it is, we won't like the way it plays out. We should begin reducing our power in conjunction with a concerted effort to induce our friends and allies around the world to play a greater role.

My approach to U.S. foreign policy is very different from that favored by policymakers in Washington, both Democrats and Republicans, and I am under no illusions that it will be easy to change course. Conversely, I am not the only one to note the sizable gap that has opened up between policymakers and the public with respect to U.S. foreign policy, and my point of view is consistent with the attitudes of most Americans.[8] While Washington dreams up new ways to apply U.S. military power, those Americans living outside of the Beltway are becoming increasingly frustrated by international crises that have not been solved—and might have been made worse—by the application of that power. And they are highly resistant to suggestions that this power should or must be deployed in even more places.

What the public actually believes has been regularly mischaracterized in the media, and seems to borrow heavily from the dominant Washington mind-set that to question the current course of U.S. foreign policy makes someone an "isolationist"—an odious epithet that has been deployed with considerable success for over 100 years.[9] For example when a *New York Times*/CBS News poll taken in July 2006 found that, by a nearly two-to-one margin, "Americans did not believe the United States should take the lead in solving conflicts in general," the *Times'* writers explained that this reflected "a strong isolationist streak in the nation."[10]

To the extent that there *is* an isolationist streak in U.S. politics, it often takes on ugly forms. It manifests itself in the xenophobia, nativism, and outright bigotry, which maintains that the United States can remain strong only by deporting 12 million undocumented immigrants and building a twenty-foot high wall along the Mexican border. Isolationism also manifest itself in protectionism, a false belief that U.S. manufacturers and workers can operate independent of the global marketplace, and that producers and consumers alike would both be better off if we were isolated.

Some might embrace the characterization "isolationist," despite its pejorative connotations, celebrating their opposition to immigration and international trade, and calling for the United States to withdraw from international organizations. Still others would vociferously reject the isolationist label, even as they advance policies not so different from self-described and genuine isolationists. The net effect, for example, of protectionist trade policies (sometimes dressed up in the euphemism of "fair trade") that seek to impose labor and environmental standards on foreign manufacturers would be to dramatically reduce the import of foreign-made goods into the United States, and would likely, as a second-order effect, reduce U.S. exports as other countries retaliate.

But it isn't accurate to say that most Americans are isolationists, nor that a different foreign policy, one more focused on self-defense and exhibiting restraint abroad, reflects isolationism. Americans crave a different kind of engagement with the world. A poll conducted for the UN Foundation's Better World Campaign divided the electorate into five segments based on responses to a series of questions about U.S. foreign policy. The survey found the strongest support for burden sharing with friends and allies and the least support for "going it alone" or "isolationism."[11] Among the top messages favored across the ideological spectrum there is widespread dissatisfaction with the current course of U.S. foreign policy, and a hunger for alternatives that would allow the United States to remain engaged in the world, but at less cost, and with other countries doing their fair share.[12] Concern about strategic overstretch, doubts about the utility of U.S. military might to solve the world's problems, and fear that U.S. military intervention abroad might be contributing to—rather than solving—our insecurity here at home, reflects a rational calculation about costs and benefits that too few politicians and opinion leaders seem willing to contemplate. ⁁ The threats facing us are not so urgent that we must maintain a vast military presence scattered across the globe, and the international economic system is not so fragile that it would come crashing down if Washington were less inclined to deploy U.S. military power abroad.

If the problem is that we use our military too often, then the solution seems simple enough—intervene less often. Keep the powder dry, the pistol holstered, the sword within its sheathe; or, in a variation on Teddy Roosevelt's famous dictum, carry that big stick, but rarely wield it.

This was also Colin Powell's preference. He was troubled by Madeleine Albright's enthusiasm for military intervention at a time when the military was slowly shrinking. Powell instead favored a relatively large military that was rarely used.

Alas, if only it were that simple. Powell did not consider, or at least did not appreciate, how hard it is to control the impulse to use great power. Our military capability implicitly confers an obligation on all Americans to become involved in foreign disputes, even those that have no credible connection to U.S. national security. To stand aside when great injustices take place seems immoral, doubly so when we perceive that we have the ability to do something about it. This impulse to do something—anything—is made all the more urgent, therefore, by the sense that we *always* have the ability to act. If we choose not to do so, it implies indifference, or, worse, sympathy for the perpetrators of crimes over the victims.[14]

That Americans are not comfortable standing aside while problems fester and grow, even problems that do not affect us directly, is a reflection of our nation's admirable can-do spirit, but can be a dangerous trait when it comes to matters involving the use of force. We need a new approach to military intervention grounded in a realization that even well-managed wars unleash a host of unintended consequences.

Solving our power problem requires a more selective form of engagement than we've practiced in recent years, more selective even than that favored by proponents of "selective engagement." Robert Art, the leading advocate of such a grand strategy, is correct to identify a set of criteria that should govern when and whether to use military force abroad. However, his criteria are not selective enough, and could well result in the use of such forces in nearly as many places, and nearly as many times, as occurred during the high point of interventionism in the first fifteen years after the end of the Cold War.[15] In this book, I call for solving our power problem by adopting a more stringent form of selective engagement. Beyond self-defense, which should be the primary focus for all militaries in all countries, we should apply a different set of criteria to constrain our use of the U.S. military when our own physical security is not threatened. We should deploy forces abroad only when there are vital U.S. security interests at stake; when there is a clear and attainable military mission; when there is broad public support; and when there is a clear understanding of what constitutes victory, and therefore when our forces can leave.[16]

Even if we could come to agreement on when and whether we should use the U.S. military, we would still be faced with an equally pressing question: What do we truly *need* in terms of military capacity? I contend that we need enough to ensure our peace and security. We must be able to deter any state foolish enough to threaten the American homeland. We must be on alert against non-state actors who seek to harm American citizens, and are not so easily deterred.

We can do all of these things with a military that is smaller than the unwieldy behemoth that has lumbered since the end of the Cold War. A few hundred, and certainly less than one thousand, nuclear weapons are more than sufficient to deter any state stupid enough to attack us directly. Today the U.S. arsenal includes nearly 5,000 nuclear warheads. If the nuclear deterrent proved insufficient—and it hasn't for the past sixty years—our Navy and Air Force would be sure to give a good fight to anyone who dared to challenge us directly, and this would still be true even if we scaled those forces back to a posture suited for self-defense. Meanwhile, our conventional forces, the Army and Marine Corps, could be much smaller if we weren't planning to engage in more Iraq-style missions, and they could be augmented by the Army Reserves and the National Guard in the case of genuine emergencies. Indeed, if our physical security, our homeland, our lives, fortunes and sacred honor were under assault, if foreign armies set foot on U.S. soil for the first time since 1815, we can rest assured that *every* American capable of carrying a gun (and we have 200 million of them!) would make the foolish aggressor pay.

The above scenario is fanciful, even absurd, but that is the whole point: it is sheer lunacy to think that any country, any nation-state, any tin-pot dictator with a palace or villa to call home, would dare to attack the United States. Such an attack would result in his (or her) certain destruction, along with the destruction of family, friends, associates, and countrymen.

As for the threat posed by terrorist groups and other non-state actors, 280 modern warships, 8,000 military aircraft, 30,000 tanks and armored personnel

carriers, and more than 1.4 million men and women at arms did not deter nineteen angry young men from flying airplanes into buildings on 9/11; twice or
three times that number of ships, planes, and tanks would have been equally
irrelevant. If anything, our reliance on massive military force often has the effect
of increasing the terrorist threat. If U.S. counterterrorism efforts rely on conventional Army and Marine Corps units stationed abroad—especially in pre-
dominantly Muslim countries—al-Qaeda and other violent groups will feed
on the anger and resentment generated by this presence to grow their ranks.

Similarly, with respect to the remote but serious risk that terrorists might
gain control of a nuclear weapon, it is logical for policymakers to pay close attention to locking down loose nuclear materials. Whereas diplomacy and cooperation with other countries to discourage further nuclear proliferation and to
enhance the security of existing arsenals might pay dividends, military action is
likely to be counterproductive.

The past seven years reveal the limited utility of military power in reducing
the threat of terrorism, but they also show what works. Effective strategies for
countering terrorism, and of doing so in a manner that does not generate more
terrorism, begin by putting the problem into the proper perspective. To portray the terrorists as posing an existential threat to the United States, or more
broadly the West, dramatically exaggerates their power and influence. Indeed,
recent research has concluded that the threat of jihadi terrorism is already on
the wane.[17] Because acts of terrorism often kill or injure the very people that
terrorists seek to influence, the strategy carries within it the seeds of its own
destruction.

The *Atlantic Monthly*'s James Fallows concluded that al-Qaeda's "hopes for
fundamentally harming the United States now rest less on what it can do itself
than on what it can trick, tempt, or goad us into doing."[18] In short, terrorist aims
may be grandiose, but their capacity for achieving these aims is severely limited.
The most effective counterterrorism strategies capitalize on our strengths and
exploit their weaknesses to let them lose. This argues strongly for a strategy of
containment, which further requires a tight focus on the most urgent threats,
and an equally strong commitment on the part of policymakers against exag-
geration or overreaction.[19]

It will not be easy to solve the power problem, but we can take the necessary
steps on our own initiative. And we must take *all* of the appropriate steps. We
must not change our force structure and reduce our troop levels without also
changing our strategy; to do the former without the latter, as was done after

the Cold War, would be worse than doing nothing. Instead, we must rethink our government's obligations to its citizens—not the other way around—and understand the role that the military can and should play in meeting these obligations. The money that the United States invested in its military during the Cold War, and the money that we have continued to invest in it ever since, will pay dividends for many years to come. If we gradually reduce our military power and use it less often, other countries can be expected to step forward. As other nations build capacity to defend themselves, they will gradually acquire the capability, and with it the will, to act independent of us. And if we are right in our belief that many other nations of the world truly share our values, in other words if we actually believe what we proclaim, then solving our power problem will result in greater security—at home and abroad—without requiring us to change who we are.

CHAPTER ONE

THE U.S. MILITARY—DOMINANT, BUT NOT OMNIPOTENT

To the extent that our power problem is a military problem, we must begin by understanding what our military is, where it is, and what it does. Just as important, we have to understand how and why the U.S. military became the preeminent force of its kind in the world today, and likely the most capable in all of human history.

Our military covers the four corners of the earth, and controls the skies and space. It patrols the oceans, not merely the surface, but the air above and the depths below. We face no peer competitor, few near-peer competitors, and not even very many competitors. All the catapults, longbows, muskets, and machine guns ever manufactured lack the sheer destructive power of even a single thermonuclear weapon in our possession. We are dominant even when compared against any plausible combination of contemporary powers.

Our nuclear arsenal, the world's largest, is deployed on submarines at sea, on the tips of intercontinental ballistic missiles poised at the ready in silos underground, and is available for deployment on Air Force B-52 and B-2 bombers, based at air fields around the United States.[1] But the destructive capacity of our vast nuclear arsenal only begins to describe the extent of our dominance. Consider the conventional military striking power within the four services that comprise our military.[2]

The U.S. Navy counts over 280 ships and submarines in its active fleet, ranging in size from the newest aircraft carrier, the USS *Ronald Reagan* (CVN-76), more than three football fields long, to the tiny PCs—patrol coastal ships—five of which could fit comfortably end-to-end on a carrier flight deck. If the U.S. Navy were an air force, it would be one of the largest in the world: it operates more than 1,100 aircraft, ranging from fighter jets to helicopters that ferry people and material to and from the ships in the fleet. As of the beginning of 2008, there were 340,000 men and women serving on active duty in the U.S. Navy.

The men and women in the U.S. Air Force, 336,000 in active service as of early 2008, support a diverse force, from large and small fixed-wing aircraft to 500 Minuteman III intercontinental ballistic missiles. The service's pride and joy are its top-flight fighters like the stealthy F-22 Raptor and the fast and agile F-15 Eagles and F-16 Falcons. It also counts nearly 200 long-range bombers, plus an array of attack, refueling, and transport aircraft.

The U.S. Marine Corps operates helicopters and fixed-wing aircraft, as well as Abrams tanks and armored vehicles. As of early 2008, there were just over 186,000 men and women in its ranks, scheduled to climb to 202,000 within a few years. Marines are mobile and adaptable. They can deploy by land, sea, or air, sometimes in conjunction with the Corps' sister-service, the Navy, but Marines can also operate independently.

Finally there is the Army, the largest of the four services, which counted just over 593,000 soldiers in active service as of early 2008, including nearly 71,000 active reservists. Army personnel fly Black Hawk helicopters, drive Bradley fighting vehicles and Abrams tanks, and operate a host of other platforms and weapon systems. Most of the time, however, our soldiers perform less "kinetic" missions: serving as de facto mayors in Iraq and Afghanistan, and as de facto diplomats just about everywhere else.[3]

Numbers only begin to tell the tale of our military dominance. Our troops are arguably better trained, more motivated, and more adaptable than any other military in the world. They also have the best equipment. The combination of our well-trained and highly motivated personnel operating state-of-the-art technology should enable us to sustain our military dominance over any potential rival well into the future. But we aren't taking any chances. The Pentagon's budget in 2008 devoted over $76 billion to "research, development, testing, and evaluation," more than Germany, the United Kingdom, France, Russia, or Japan each spent on their entire defense budgets.[4]

If the military were the most important indicator of U.S. power, we could reasonably claim that we are the biggest, the baddest, and the best country on the planet. But it is more than playground bravado that makes the military the most respected institution in the United States.[5] Americans are justifiably proud of our men and women in uniform, and of the military writ large. They are also, to an extent that many don't realize, tightly connected to the military.

While the number of active duty personnel in the U.S. military is relatively small, barely one half of one percent of our total population, there are approximately 24 million living veterans, more than 10 percent of all adults. In addition, three-and-a-half million Americans receive veterans' disability benefits, including widows and surviving dependents.[6]

Furthermore, the military reaches into many other Americans' lives. For starters, it has a physical presence in all fifty states and in all U.S. territories. Hawaii is a favorite destination or stop-over point for our military personnel: 17 percent of the state's population are either serving on active duty, or have served sometime during their lives. The military controls over 4 million acres in California alone. Texas hosts three large Army bases—Fort Bliss, Fort Hood, and Fort Sam Houston—plus nearly 100 other military facilities. The largest Army base in the world is Fort Bragg in North Carolina. The Air Force maintains major bases in the North (Elmendorf and Eielson in Alaska), South (Maxwell in Alabama, and Eglin in Florida), East (Andrews in Maryland and Dover in Delaware), and West (Hickham in Hawaii, and Fairchild and McChord in Washington State)—and all points in between.

The military's physical footprint, vast though it may be, is considerably smaller than it was during the height of the Cold War. Still, it might have shrunk even more since 1991. After all, its principal adversary ceased to exist then, and the total number of military personnel on active duty fell by about 33 percent during the 1990s. Five rounds of cutting and realignment by the Base Realignment and Closure (BRAC) Commissions will eventually result in the closure of nearly 120 major facilities, and major realignments to another 88.[7]

Although the Army and Marine Corps are expected to grow by more than 10 percent over the next five years, the country still does not need anywhere near the number of military facilities that we maintained during the height of the Cold War. For now, politicians posture about their ability to "save" a base from closure, despite the fact that a number of communities that feared economic ruin following a decision to close a local base have been able to turn the land to constructive use.[8]

The pace of closures or realignment overseas has been equally desultory, and is often met with resistance—just as in the United States—from locals who might suffer economically. Nearly two decades after the end of the Cold War, the U.S. military remains firmly ensconced around the globe, continuing a decades-long posture designed with the ostensible object of deterring or defeating the Soviet Union.

The actual number of overseas military facilities is the subject of some debate, a crucial factor being the criteria one uses to differentiate bases from facilities and other smaller properties owned or leased by the U.S. government. Another criteria is boots on the ground. As of the end of 2007, and not including the deployments to Iraq and Afghanistan, the United States had 1,000 or more troops in eleven different countries. All told, the Department of Defense reported that it had over 267,000 soldiers, sailors, airmen, and Marines deployed ashore in over 100 countries.[9]

Another way to determine the nature and scope of the U.S. military's activities in a given country, and the relationship between the United States and the host government, is to review the relevant Status of Forces Agreement (SOFA). However, not all of these agreements are publicly available—some are classified—and U.S. officials have disagreed on the number of SOFAs in effect. For example, U.S. ambassador to Iraq Ryan Crocker testified before Congress in April 2008 that the United States had approximately eighty SOFAs worldwide, but this number conflicted with a *Washington Post* op-ed, coauthored by Secretary of State Condoleezza Rice and Secretary of Defense Robert M. Gates, which put the number at "more than 115."[10] Regardless of what metric one uses to measure the U.S. military's presence, however, it obviously casts a very wide shadow.

This process did not happen overnight. The history of the rise of the United States from a loose collection of disparate communities tucked along the Atlantic coast of North America to the world's foremost global power—and arguably the most powerful country of all time—has been told elsewhere, and well, but certain aspects of this spectacular and curious rise deserve special attention here.[11] Of particular note is of how attitudes toward military power and the role of force in the nation's foreign policies have changed over time, but especially in the two decades since the end of the Cold War. Our post–Cold War strategy—founded on the presumption that the United States is and must be the world's sole superpower, and that it must possess a vast military geared toward defending a variety of client states and protectorates—represents a significant departure from deeply rooted U.S. traditions. To understand the extent to which this is true requires a look back at where we started, and how we arrived at the state we are in today.

A (Very) Brief History of the U.S. Military

During the long periods of peace during the nineteenth century, and the shorter periods in the early twentieth century, the United States maintained a small standing army, mobilized additional personnel to fight the few wars declared by Congress, and then sent most of the men home when the war was won. This pattern was established during the earliest days of the Republic, and was driven by the Founders' ambivalent view of military power. "The vast majority of America's landowning aristocracy had an almost congenital distrust of standing armies, which their ancestors for generations had identified with despotism," writes Bruce Porter in *War and the Rise of the State.* "They glorified instead the yeoman militiamen, linked to the land and closely tied to local interests."[12] But this philosophy came up against a bitter truth. On the one hand, the Founders realized that their ability to prevail militarily against the British during the Revolution had been instrumental to securing their independence. On the other hand, the presence of British troops in their midst was among the list of particulars that Thomas Jefferson cited in the Declaration of Independence for wanting to be free of the mother country in the first place.

During the Revolution, George Washington successfully prevailed upon his fellow patriots to create a national army, which engaged the British from time to time in pitched battles, and not always to great effect. But there were other engagements throughout the Revolutionary War fought according to the model employed at Lexington and Concord in April 1775; namely of local militias using guerilla tactics against the more-disciplined professional militaries employed by the British.

The Founders' deep skepticism toward standing armies manifested itself in the U.S. Constitution, which granted Congress the power "to *provide and maintain* a Navy," but stipulated that armies would be *raised* and *supported* as needed, essentially implying that there would be *no* standing army.[13] This was not so radical a provision at the time. Most countries in the late eighteenth century chose to rely on a small number of professional soldiers, including mercenaries for hire, that would then be augmented by individual citizens as conditions required. For countries such as England, for example, which had a relatively small population resting comfortable and secure on an island abundant in natural resources and protected from foreign invasion by water on all sides, there was no great need for *any* army. Although Washington generally disdained militias, he nonetheless warned his countrymen in his Farewell Address to "avoid the necessity of...overgrown military establishments."[14]

Critical to avoiding the need for such "overgrown military establishments" was the Constitution's provision that Congress, not the executive, would have the authority to declare war. James Madison explained the rationale in a letter to Thomas Jefferson: "The constitution supposes, what the History of all Governments demonstrates, that the Executive is the branch of power most interested in war, and most prone to it. It has accordingly with studied care vested the question of war in the Legislature."[15] "This system will not hurry us into war; it is calculated to guard against it," explained James Wilson to the Pennsylvania Ratifying Convention. "It will not be in the power of a single man, or a single body of men, to involve us in such distress."[16] Madison later saw this provision as perhaps the most important one of the entire document. "In no part of the constitution is more wisdom to be found, than in the clause which confides the question of war or peace to the legislature, and not to the executive department."[17]

Such sentiments strike many today as naive, and there were no doubt some in the late eighteenth century who believed much the same thing. But by fortunate circumstances as much as by design, an ideology founded on—in Thomas Jefferson's immortal words from his first inaugural address—"peace, commerce, and honest friendship with all nations; entangling alliances with none," survived and thrived in North America.[18] For much of the first 140 or so years of the nation's history, Americans were rather successful at staying out of unnecessary wars, and therefore didn't much need a large military, as the Framers of the Constitution had hoped. And when Congress saw fit to declare war, as it did on a few occasions from the War of 1812 to World War II, it did so while at the same time making provisions for raising the necessary numbers of men and materials.

It was not simply ideology, and a commitment to adhering to the letter and spirit of the Constitution, that enabled this pattern to persist for so long. The United States was also blessed by a dearth of powerful enemies. In the span of twenty years at the dawn of the nineteenth century, the United States had convinced three European powers to largely quit its portion of North America. Jefferson bought off the French with the Louisiana Purchase, the Americans prevailed over the British in the War of 1812, and the Spanish ceded Florida in the Adams-Onís Treaty of 1819. Just a few years later, President James Monroe declared on December 2, 1823, that the European powers were not to interfere in the affairs of the independent nations in all of the Western Hemisphere. In return, the Monroe Doctrine pledged that the United States would remain neutral in disputes between the European states.[19]

Monroe's bold stand against further colonization in the Americas would not have stood if tested; the U.S. government lacked any formal authority to be the guarantor of independence for the new nations in our hemisphere, and the still small country lacked the power to back up Monroe's claim to such authority had any European power sought to challenge it. But few did. Exhausted by the Napoleonic Wars, fearful of domestic disturbances that might overturn the established social and political order, and with eyes set on conquest in Africa and

Asia, Europe pretty much left the Americas alone.[20] The good fortune for the United States was that the young nation developed during a peculiar period in human history, and that it had a few wise leaders who had the sense to take advantage of this splendid isolation to build an enduring nation-state. The greatest threat to the Republic in the nineteenth century came not from foreign states but rather from the Civil War that remains the costliest war in our history.

As far as foreign adventures go, there were a few exceptions, to be sure. Congress declared war on Mexico in 1846 and on Spain in 1898. From the former, the nation acquired California and Texas, and parts of five other states, which most Americans perceive as a good thing. From the latter, the United States acquired the Philippines, which most Americans think was a generally bad thing.

Indeed, the bitter experience in the Philippines soured one of the most fervent advocates of the Spanish-American War. In 1897, Theodore Roosevelt had told a friend "I should welcome almost any war, for I think this country needs one."[21] Of the annexation of the Philippines that came with victory over Spain, Roosevelt predicted, "[I]f we do our duty aright...we will...greatly benefit the people of the Philippine Islands, and above all, we will play our part well in the great work of uplifting mankind."[22] Yet, as John Judis notes, Roosevelt's enthusiasm for expanding the nascent empire cooled considerably after he became president in September 1901. Urged to seize the Dominican Republic, TR quipped, "I have about the same desire to annex it as a gorged boa constrictor might have to swallow a porcupine wrong-end-to."[23]

That even so outspoken an advocate of American Empire as Roosevelt had learned to regret foreign conquest bespeaks a broader U.S. mind-set. Throughout U.S. history, we can see a pendulum swing of enthusiasm for, swiftly followed by disgust with, war. Such shifting attitudes reflected Americans' collective ability to learn—and then over time forget—the high costs of combat. Nearly every generation in U.S. history had some experience with some war. In each case, ambition and optimism about the likelihood of quick success was eventually replaced with humility and pessimism, an appreciation of the costs, and of the possibility of failure. Once these lessons sunk in, Americans generally returned to the core underlying philosophy, espoused by the Founders, that free nations possess small professional militaries and strive to avoid foreign wars, even as they were happy to profit from foreign trade and to otherwise serve as an example to the world by upholding the highest ideals of liberal governance.

These attitudes persisted even as the United States became involved in far larger wars, in far-distant lands, in the first half of the twentieth century. World War I claimed 116,000 American lives, World War II more than three-and-a-half times that number. The nation had barely completed its demobilization after Germany, and later Japan, surrendered when it found itself at war again, this time in a former Japanese colony against a new enemy, the People's Republic of China. Nearly 7 million Americans served in the military during the Korean War, without Congress ever having actually declared war.

By 1960, the United States seemed to have settled into a permanent state of near-war. This prospect greatly disturbed President Dwight David Eisenhower. He shared the Founders' concerns that a constant state of war would alter the nation's character in profound ways. As he prepared to leave the White House after two successful terms, Eisenhower took to the airwaves to warn his countrymen to be on guard against a "military-industrial complex" acquiring "unwarranted influence" in the halls of power. He continued:

> We must never let the weight of this combination endanger our liberties or democratic processes. We should take nothing for granted. Only an alert and knowledgeable citizenry can compel the proper meshing of huge industrial and military machinery of defense with our peaceful methods and goals, so that security and liberty may prosper together.[24]

Eisenhower correctly recognized that whereas U.S. economic interests had once broadly favored peace, there were, by the time he left office, crucial segments of industry, as well as particular regions of the country, that had become heavily dependent on the sales of arms and equipment to the U.S. military.

Eisenhower reminded his countrymen that the "conjunction of an immense military establishment and a large arms industry" was a new development in the nation's history. He implored them to be on guard against it even as its influence was "felt in every city, every state house, every office of the Federal government." That such a vast and permanent arms industry was necessary, and Eisenhower believed that it was, did not mean that the country should merely accept it as given. On the contrary, he explained, "we must not fail to comprehend its grave implications. Our toil, resources and livelihood are all involved; so is the very structure of our society."[25]

We would learn only after the Cold War had ended how right Eisenhower had been. When the Soviet Union ceased to exist, the United States enjoyed a modest peace dividend, cutting defense spending by more than 26 percent; by 1999 defense spending as a share of GDP had fallen to 3.0 percent in 1999, its lowest level since 1940.[26] Some companies transitioned away from the manufacture of arms; others simply disappeared. Some of the monies that had once gone to the military were redirected elsewhere: to reduce the federal deficit, provide for modest tax relief, and similarly modest increases in total non-defense spending.

One might have expected far deeper cuts in military spending. After all, the great threat of Soviet communism was gone, and nearly everything that the U.S. military had been preparing to do during the Cold War had been overcome by events. But building weapons is a lucrative business, and it did not become considerably less lucrative during the 1990s for those companies that survived the first few rounds of cuts. Political pressures and bureaucratic inertia—precisely the military-industrial complex that Eisenhower had warned of three decades earlier—kept military spending much higher than dictated by necessity. Instead, the U.S. military machine remained largely intact, albeit as a leaner, more focused version of its prior self. Equally important, the United States kept many of its overseas bases and retained and even expanded security commitments under alliances ostensibly created to contain a now defunct Soviet empire.

Whereas Americans had once armed for war and then returned to peaceful pursuits when the wars ended, the creation of a permanent armaments industry during the Cold War had created similarly permanent political constituencies that objected to cuts in the military, or at least to cuts in the particular part of the military that happened to affect them directly. Every weapon system had its defenders in Congress. Every community could come up with a dozen reasons for why *their* base shouldn't be cut.

A better proxy for judging the effect that the end of the Cold War had on the U.S. military was not the size and nature of the peace dividend that Washington doled out but rather the change in policymakers' attitudes toward the use of force. In the first ten years of the post–Cold War era, the U.S. military was engaged in about the same number of major operations as it had been in the forty-five years since the end of World War II. Because military spending had been cut, and the number of men and women in uniform had come down, our troops who remained in the service bore the brunt of this increased propensity to intervene.

The collapse of the Soviet empire facilitated this new approach to military intervention. Unconstrained by the fear, rampant during the Cold War, that even small-scale wars might spiral into a full-on confrontation with the other superpower, the United States was suddenly free to engage in military interventions that only a few years earlier would have seemed if not impossible then at least highly risky. The generals, admirals, and armchair strategists contemplated how they might choose to use the still enormous military left behind by the Cold War.

The Era of Intervention

As it happened, they didn't have to sit around thinking for long. The dispatch of 27,000 U.S. troops to Panama in December 1989 to remove General Manuel Noriega from power was a decidedly small-scale affair, consistent with other Cold War–era interventions in the Western Hemisphere—such as Lyndon Johnson's dispatch of troops to the Dominican Republic in 1965 and Ronald Reagan's invasion of Grenada in 1983. Within just two weeks, Noriega was in U.S. custody, and a civilian government was in power.

But the first truly post–Cold War mission, one made possible both by the recent disappearance of the Soviet Union and by the continued existence of a U.S. military that had not gotten much smaller after the end of the Cold War, was the 1991 Gulf War. Within days of Saddam Hussein's invasion of Kuwait on August 2, 1990, President George H. W. Bush moved military assets already deployed near the region to deter Saddam from moving further, especially toward the oil fields in Saudi Arabia. By January 1991, more than 500,000 American troops stood poised on Iraq's borders, and when Hussein didn't capitulate to U.S. demands to withdraw, the U.S. military drove his forces out of Kuwait in the matter of a few days.

It was doubly appropriate that the Chairman of the Joint Chiefs of Staff General Colin Powell would be seen as one of the main architects of the Gulf War plan, for he represented what the post–Cold War military was, and would become. Coincidentally, Powell had earlier served as a principal aide to Defense Secretary Casper Weinberger in 1984. In this capacity he had had a hand in the shaping of the so-called Weinberger Doctrine that had sought to apply the bitter lessons learned from Vietnam and the ill-fated mission in Lebanon in 1983 to the conduct of U.S. foreign policy. Weinberger hoped to constrain policymakers who might be inclined to use the military in a reckless or promiscuous manner, and also to ensure that the military, once unleashed, would have a clear and unambiguous objective, and the tools—including, strong public support—to see the mission to completion.

Elements of the Weinberger Doctrine could clearly be seen at play during the Gulf War. Although the public remained ambivalent up to the start of the Gulf War—ambivalence reflected, in part, by the fact that the war resolution passed in the Senate by a vote of just 52 to 47—sustaining public support once the war began wasn't a problem: the ground combat phase didn't last as long as even one polling cycle. As for the Weinberger Doctrine's provision that the U.S.

military would use overwhelming force in pursuit of a swift, decisive victory, that also seemed clear.[27]

However, the apparent ease of the Gulf War victory masked a deeper truth: it had been considerably less destructive to Saddam's regime than U.S. military commanders and the Bush White House conveyed. Hussein remained in power, and he used his still intact Republican Guard to brutalize his enemies inside Iraq, crushing a Kurdish uprising in the north, and the Shiites in the south.

Desert Storm did, however, serve as a rallying point for the now all-volunteer military, which had struggled since Vietnam to reinvent itself. For hundreds of thousands of military personnel who returned from the Gulf War to a hero's welcome, that fifteen-year struggle had paid off and the problems and images of disconsolate draftees, drug abusers, and common criminals perpetrating horrible atrocities—the searing images from that earlier disastrous war—now seemed behind them, shattered by a swift victory over a loathsome foe.

The Gulf War proved beyond a shadow of a doubt that the U.S. military was without peer. With the threat of global communism gone, and the United States still clearly capable of deploying its troops abroad, U.S. policymakers contemplated future interventions. And just as the Gulf War taught many lessons—some accurate, some not—so too would each of the interventions of the 1990s inform and misinform subsequent decisions on when and whether to use force.

The outgoing President Bush launched the first of these interventions in late 1992 as a mission to ensure that food aid would reach hundreds of thousands of people dying of hunger in Somalia. By the summer of 1993 the mission, now under the new President Bill Clinton, had morphed into a crusade to crack down on rival warlords, chiefly General Mohammed Farah Aideed. When a U.S. Black Hawk helicopter was shot down in early October while assaulting one of Aideed's positions in the Somali capital of Mogadishu, the bloody firefight that followed resulted in eighteen U.S. Army Rangers killed, and another seventy-six wounded.

By any objective measure, the Black Hawk Down incident was no military disaster. Whereas the gruesome pictures of American bodies being dragged through the streets elicited shock and outrage, the men on the ground performed bravely, holding off a far larger force for hours, and enabling the majority of U.S. troops to evacuate safely.[28] But the setback had a huge impact because it elicited a harshly negative public response. Americans had never been strongly supportive of the Somalia mission, and they turned decisively against it when even a few U.S. servicemen came home in body bags.[29] The lesson drawn from this incident—that the public would not support military operations if American lives were at stake—was not entirely correct, but the enduring presumption of extreme casualty-aversion shaped how President Clinton conducted foreign policy for the balance of his presidency.

The lingering impact of the Somalia mission was clear the following year, when Clinton opted not to intervene to halt the genocide in Rwanda that claimed the lives of as many as 800,000 people, most of them members of Rwanda's Tutsi minority.[30] Members of the Clinton administration were aware of the killings, but the president explained at the time that other commitments around the world—including the anticipated dispatch of troops to Haiti, which did occur later that year—precluded U.S. involvement. Privately, U.S. officials expressed concerns that a UN mission in Rwanda would fail, prompting another U.S. bailout as had occurred in Somalia.[31]

The following year, however, wracked by guilt over his decision not to act in Rwanda, and seeing parallels with what was occurring in Bosnia, Clinton chose to get involved, compelling the three main ethnic factions there—the Croats, the Bosnian Muslims, and the Serbs—to negotiate a peace settlement.[32]

When Yugoslavia crumbled in the early 1990s, the three groups had vied for power and control of territory, in the process carving Bosnia into a hodgepodge of non-contiguous ethnic enclaves, all of which were utterly incapable of defending themselves. Occasionally, these enclaves became nothing more than free-fire zones for atrocities.

Not surprisingly, a key component of the agreement hammered out in Dayton, Ohio, was chief U.S. negotiator Richard Holbrooke's pledge that a sizable international presence—including U.S. troops—would be sent to Bosnia to stand between the warring factions. There was only one problem: few Americans supported the dispatch of U.S. troops for such a mission, and the Congress, now under GOP control for the first time in four decades, voted to prevent public monies from going to support peacekeeping operations.[33]

Clinton ignored the Congress and dispatched the troops anyway. In a backhanded wave to an ambivalent public, he declared that all U.S. forces—the Dayton Agreement stipulated that 20,000 of the 60,000 NATO troops were to be U.S.—would be withdrawn within "about a year." But it seems clear that the president never really intended to adhere to any such timeline. A year later he announced that 8,500 U.S. troops would remain for another eighteen months, and by December 1997 he had dropped all pretense of a deadline, arguing instead that U.S. forces would remain until certain criteria or "benchmarks" were met.[34] For the balance of his presidency, these criteria apparently were not met: there were over 4,000 U.S. troops in Bosnia at the end of 2000.[35]

The lesson here—that Congress supposedly had no authority to shape, much less halt, the dispatch of U.S. military personnel into foreign war zones—had been shown on numerous occasions during the Cold War, when U.S. presidents regularly deployed the U.S. military without so much as notifying the Congress. The lesson would be repeated again in Kosovo in 1999. But a deeper lesson—that neither the Congress, nor the UN Security Council, could constrain a U.S. president's desire to use force—would have far-reaching ramifications in the years ahead.

The problem signs were apparent early on. The most strenuous objections to U.S. actions in the Balkans came from Russia. Whereas Moscow had given tacit approval to U.S. intervention in Panama, voted in favor of the Gulf War at the UN Security Council, and sat silently while U.S. forces entered Haiti and Somalia, U.S. military action in Bosnia, and later in Kosovo, elicited strong and vehement opposition.

U.S.-Russian relations had been tested after the end of the Cold War as the United States expanded NATO toward Russia's borders with the addition of former Warsaw Pact nations—Poland, Hungary, and Czech Republic. The Kremlin's objections to U.S. actions in the Balkans had deeper roots. They were partly grounded in a historical and cultural bond between Christian Orthodox Russians and Serbs. There were broader geopolitical issues at stake, as well. The Kosovo bombing campaign was the second of two occasions in the span of six months—the first being the Desert Fox strikes on Iraq in December 1998—in which the Clinton administration had explicitly circumvented the Security Council to launch military action. Some foreign observers feared the implications of a U.S. hegemon unconstrained by either international law, or by the will of its own people and Congress, and wondered where it might lead.

Such warnings, which presaged later concerns about U.S. unilateralism toward Iraq, should have given Americans pause. But few paid any heed. In subsequent years, members of the Clinton administration hailed the Kosovo intervention as a great victory. However, most were reluctant to concede that they had established a precedent for the use of force that President George W. Bush would gladly embrace when, in late 2002, he moved forward with plans to remove Saddam Hussein from power in Iraq.

The disparate lessons drawn from the peripatetic interventions of the 1990s did not shape a dramatically new grand strategy for, in truth, there was no strategy, or at least not much of one. The United States—now as the sole superpower in a unipolar world—was free to pick and choose where to become involved.

As such, the occasions in which the U.S. military was deployed abroad had an ad hoc quality about them. They seemed purely reactive to world events, not part of a broader U.S. campaign to shape the world order to suit its interests. What's more, they seemed oddly discriminating, albeit according to criteria that defied simple explanations. There had been interventions in the Western Hemisphere, and also in Europe, Africa, and Southwest Asia. The U.S. military had gone into Somalia in 1992, and into Kosovo in 1999, it had ventured into Haiti in 1994, and into Bosnia in 1995. But the United States had stayed out of Rwanda. It had refused to step into the middle of the dispute between Eritrea and Ethiopia. It had passed on intervention in the Central African Republic in 1996, in Albania in 1997, and in Sierra Leone in 1999. Possessing enormous military power, the United States could decide to get involved—or not—based on a number of different factors. It might be the domestic political mood, or an especially effective media outreach campaign. Sometimes, a particular interest on the part of the president alone was sufficient, and these feelings were subject to change.[36]

The public, by and large, showed little interest. Eisenhower had hoped that an "alert and knowledgeable citizenry" would challenge policymakers to weigh the costs and benefits of their actions. But the public had turned their attention to parochial matters, hearth and home, and tolerated or ignored the relatively frequent interventions given that they seemed quick, easy, and cheap. Americans were inclined to go along with what policymakers in Washington were doing, so long as they believed that those policies would keep them safe at reasonable expense, and so long as it did not needlessly risk the lives of American servicemen and women.

But whether there was, or would be, an overarching strategy to guide our conduct in world affairs remained the subject of considerable debate, albeit largely out of the public's field of vision. The process would grind along through the 1990s, and burst forth into public view only after a new president and a new challenge arrived on the scene.

Benevolent Global Hegemony

In early 1992, aides to the then defense secretary Richard "Dick" Cheney began sketching out the Pentagon's plans for the first decade of the post–Cold War era.

The significance of the Defense Planning Guidance (DPG) that these men produced would become clear only many years later, when a number of them, including I. Lewis "Scooter" Libby, Zalmay Khalilzad, and Paul Wolfowitz, assumed prominent roles in George W. Bush's administration. The DPG was just a draft, but it provides an early glimpse of what would one day become the dominant approach to U.S. foreign policy.

Although never formally released to the public, the basic outlines of the DPG are by now well known, and were widely discussed at the time. The document held that U.S. power was crucial to the functioning of the global order. It stipulated that the United States would be the global hegemon, the undisputed power in all regions of the globe, and would stand prepared to act—preemptively, if necessary—to halt the rise of potential challengers. Any military power, held by any other country—be they friendly, economically advanced democracies, or hostile and impoverished autocracies—would be viewed with suspicion.[37]

The primary objective of U.S. foreign policy, as one draft prepared by Khalilzad explained, was to "prevent the re-emergence of a new rival" capable of challenging U.S. power in any vital area, including Western Europe, Asia, or the territory of the Soviet Union.[38] To accomplish this task, the United States would retain preponderant military power not merely to deter attacks against the United States, but also to deter "potential competitors from even aspiring to a larger regional or global role."[39]

Critics seized on the DPG's impolitic tone, particularly toward U.S. allies. According to the *New York Times,* which published several lengthy stories about the DPG, as well as selected excerpts, the document foresaw "building a world security arrangement that pre-empts Germany and Japan from pursuing a course of substantial rearmament, especially nuclear armament, in the future." The desire to keep Germany and Japan tightly bound to "a U.S.-led system of collective security," the *Times* explained, drove the document's "strong emphasis" "on using military force, if necessary, to prevent the proliferation of nuclear weapons and other weapons of mass destruction in such countries as North Korea, Iraq, some of the successor republics to the Soviet Union and in Europe." Such proliferation, the DPG warned, "could tempt Germany, Japan and other industrial powers to acquire nuclear weapons to deter attack from regional foes. This could start them down the road to global competition with the United States and, in a crisis over national interests, military rivalry."[40]

The Bush White House distanced itself from the draft DPG, but critics pounced all the same. Clinton campaign spokesman George Stephanopoulos cast the document as nothing more than an attempt by the Pentagon to justify huge military budgets well into the future.[41] In the *New York Times,* Leslie Gelb knocked the new strategy as unrealistic because it laid "almost all responsibility at America's doorstep—at the very moment when the public mood and common sense would suggest otherwise."[42] One week later, in another *New York Times* op-ed, historian James Chace questioned whether other countries would provide financial support, as they had done in the Gulf War, so that the United States could continue "to police the world as the Pentagon would have us do."[43]

A subsequent revision, drafted by Libby, shifted the emphasis and softened the tone of the DPG in part to soothe the allies' injured pride. The new draft no longer spoke of preventing "the re-emergence of a new rival" and generally climbed down from the supposition that the United States would be the world's sole policeman. Instead, the new DPG explicitly called for greater burden sharing with allies. "Where our allies interests are directly affected, we must expect them to take an appropriate share of the responsibility, and in some cases play the leading role" it said, even as the United States would "maintain the capabilities for addressing selectively those security problems that threaten our own interests."[44]

Cheney was happy to publish the main strategy document under his name as he handed the reins to the incoming Clinton administration, but he didn't seem particularly troubled by the rough edges of the earlier version that had generated so much controversy. Cheney told Khalilzad, "You've discovered a new rationale for our role in the world."[45]

So he had. The reasons offered by the United States for its global military posture in 1992, and the massive superiority that it has maintained since then, have varied somewhat over the course of the last two decades, but the basic premise for U.S. primacy has remained essentially unchanged. Republicans and Democrats alike believe that the United States must act as the lynchpin of the international order, that our global economic interests require the forward deployment of the U.S. military to the four corners of the globe, and that we have an obligation to spread the blessings of liberty to people denied basic human rights.[46]

Those on the left of the political spectrum, the dominant faction within the primacist consensus during the Clinton years, tended to favor multilateralism on its face, but tolerated something less in practice. They spoke chiefly in terms of our moral obligations, and argued that advancing these obligations while occasionally deferring to others and paying homage to international institutions was generally consistent with our national interests.

Perhaps the best exemplar of the neoliberal mind-set was Madeleine Albright. In a glowing profile of Albright written in 1996, when she was serving as ambassador to the United Nations and was widely rumored to be in line for promotion to secretary of state in the second Clinton term, the *New York Times*'s Elaine Sciolino explained Albright's comfort "with the projection of American power." "Whether or not an intervention meets the test of a 'vital national interest,'" the article explained, "is less important for her than whether the United States can do good in the world, using military power if necessary."

"My mind-set is Munich; most of my generation's is Vietnam," Albright explained. "I saw what happened when a dictator was allowed to take over a piece of a country and the country went down the tubes. And I saw the opposite during the war when America joined the fight. For me, America is really, truly the indispensable nation."[47]

It is useful to contrast Albright's confidence that the military could solve the nation's—and the world's—problems with the skepticism of the former chairman of the Joint Chiefs of Staff General Colin Powell. Powell's mind-set was indeed grounded in his personal experience as a young officer in Vietnam; and Powell did indeed favor a more cautious approach to the use of military power abroad than Albright. He was certainly aware that the United States can be a force for good, but he also knew that good intentions do not ensure success. Sometimes becoming involved in the affairs of others works to the detriment of both parties. The collapse of South Vietnam created legions of boat people desperate to flee the pogroms of the communists, but the frustrations with the war itself wounded the morale of the U.S. military—and of American society as a whole.

As noted above, the lessons from Vietnam were translated by the Weinberger Doctrine—reflecting also Powell's views—into principles governing the use of force. In particular, Weinberger and Powell sought to limit the use of U.S. military power unless a particular mission satisfied a set of stringent criteria.[48] President Clinton generally eschewed the Weinberger-Powell Doctrine's criteria during his eight years in office. Critics might say he didn't have any criteria at all. In fairness, however, as noted above, the enthusiasm for military intervention reflected the changes wrought by the collapse of the Soviet Union, and the increased propensity to use force began during the tenure of Clinton's predecessor, George H. W. Bush.

When Albright took over at Foggy Bottom, she moved swiftly to supplant the more cautious approach of Clinton's first term with an eye toward advancing not U.S. national interests, per se, but rather the interests of all humankind. Her comment to Colin Powell, worded as a question—"What's the point of having this superb military that you're always talking about if we can't use it?"—was very much intended as a statement: "We *have* this superb military, and we *intend* to use it."

In that mission, she was aided by other like-minded people in positions of influence, including Richard Holbrooke, who replaced Albright as ambassador to the United Nations, and Samuel "Sandy" Berger, who became Clinton's national security adviser. By 1998, the concept of the United States as the world's indispensable nation appeared to form the organizing principle for much of the Clinton administration's foreign policies. In a widely cited interview on NBC's *Today* show, Albright reiterated and expanded on her strong belief in the unique role of the United States in preserving the global order.

"If we have to use force," she told host Matt Lauer, "it is because we are America; we are the indispensable nation. We stand tall and we see further than other countries into the future, and we see the danger here to all of us."[49]

Not everyone agreed. Even some Democrats were offended by the Clinton administration's approach. Upon hearing President Clinton refer to the United States as the indispensable nation during his second inaugural address, Massachusetts Senator John Kerry asked aloud, "Why are we adopting such an arrogant, obnoxious tone?"[50]

Despite occasional grousing that the Clinton administration's interventions did not advance U.S. security interests, the costs and risks of the United States playing the central role on the world's stage during the mid- to late 1990s seemed to most Americans to be small and eminently manageable.

Albright, and in his second term especially, Clinton, saw the United States as a force for good, and were content to use the U.S. military as a tool for enforcing new global norms. Although the neoliberals might have preferred to work through international institutions that might confer a mark of legitimacy on U.S. actions, they retained the right to pick and choose which institutions to use. So, for example, when it was clear that the UN Security Council would not endorse military action against Kosovo in 1999, the neoliberals simply went around it, using NATO as a cover.[51]

The other wing of the primacist consensus, the neoconservatives, advocated the same unipolar model as the neoliberals, but adopted a slightly different tone. Rather than speak to the moral obligations of the United States to the international community, the neoconservatives contended that it was in our interest to be beneficent. In a similar fashion, they paid little heed—and often simply denigrated—multilateral institutions as irrelevant. But the differences between the neoliberals and the neoconservatives were never so stark as either side liked to pretend; whereas the motto for neoliberal intervention might have reduced

to "multilateral when possible, unilateral when necessary," the neoconservatives merely shifted this around, "multilateral when necessary, unilateral when
possible."[52]

One intriguing sign of the commonality of interests between neoconservatives and neoliberals was what Paul Wolfowitz had to say of Albright in 1996,
before she was appointed secretary of state. "She represents the best instincts
of this Administration on foreign policy," Wolfowitz said. The man whose office had made the unabashed case for U.S. hegemony in 1992 predicted that
Albright's "good solid instincts would go a long way in improving" the Clinton
administration's conduct of foreign policy in the second term.[53] Four years later,
near the end of Clinton's presidency, Wolfowitz professed some puzzlement as
to why the Defense Planning Guidance had generated so much controversy.
The ideas expressed in the DPG represented, in his view, the consensus opinion
of what U.S. post–Cold War strategy should be, and as it had been practiced by
Clinton and Albright.[54]

Indeed it had, and Wolfowitz and Albright were not alone in defending U.S.
primacy during the 1990s. For example, columnist Charles Krauthammer had
called the DPG "an impressive blueprint for the new world order," and scorned
the mere suggestion that the United States would seek to share the burdens of
global governance with others as "merely stupid."[55] Just as the DPG could conceive of no alternative to U.S. primacy, so too had Krauthammer dismissed the
alternatives to global predominance as utterly impractical.[56]

Others echoed the sentiments that the United States, and the United States
alone, could and must act as the world's policeman. "American hegemony is
the only reliable defense against a breakdown of peace and international order,"
wrote William Kristol and Robert Kagan in *Foreign Affairs* in the summer of
1996. They went on to explain that "The enormous disparity between U.S.
military strength and that of any potential challenger is a good thing for America
and the world."[57]

Kristol and Kagan collaborated often in the late 1990s, at the magazine the
Weekly Standard and at the Project for a New American Century, where they
made the unabashed case for what they called "benevolent global hegemony."
They were brash and self-confident, willing to make stark assertions when the
facts painted pictures in half-tones. "Most of the world's major powers," they
claimed, "welcome U.S. global involvement and prefer America's benevolent
hegemony to the alternatives." "The principal concern of America's allies these
days is not that it will be too dominant but that it will withdraw."[58] As for the domestic political environment, Kristol and Kagan predicted that "The American

people can be summoned to meet the challenges of global leadership if states-
men make the case loudly, cogently, and persistently."[59]

Whether all of that was actually true or not was anyone's guess, but Kristol
and Kagan's principal concern, it seemed, was that Americans—and conservatives, especially—would become complacent, so confident in the power of our
ideals that we would not feel the need to promote them openly and aggressively
around the world. In a shocking repudiation of traditional U.S. foreign policy
going back more than two centuries, they castigated conservatives, especially,
for "succumb[ing] easily to the charming old metaphor of the United States as
a 'city on a hill.'" They held John Quincy Adams's admonition "that America
ought not go 'abroad in search of monsters to destroy'" in even lower regard.
"Because America has the capacity to contain or destroy many of the world's
monsters, most of which can be found without much searching," they averred,
"and because the responsibility for the peace and security of the international
order rests so heavily on America's shoulders, *a policy of sitting atop a hill and
leading by example becomes in practice a policy of cowardice and dishonor.*"[60]

Conservatives didn't take up Kristol and Kagan's charge, but, as noted above,
Bill Clinton did embark on a number of foreign policy initiatives during his
second term that occasionally won grudging praise from the neoconservatives,
including Kristol and Kagan, who were competing so intently for the soul of the
Republican Party.

That battle seemed lost when George W. Bush defeated Senator John Mc-
Cain for the GOP presidential nomination in 2000. Kristol and Kagan had
enthusiastically supported McCain, scorning Bush and his coterie of realist foreign policy advisers, led by Condoleezza Rice, a protégé of Brent Scowcroft,
George H. W. Bush's friend and National Security Adviser. From Kristol and
Kagan's perspective, the younger Bush seemed too much like his father, willing
to contemplate good relations with the dictators in China, willing to tolerate
Saddam Hussein remaining in power in Baghdad, willing to cut taxes but not
necessarily willing to—as McCain had done—appeal to Americans' supposedly
innate desire for national greatness.

In a follow-up piece to their earlier *Foreign Affairs* article, published in 2000,
Kristol and Kagan seemed particularly skeptical that George W. Bush—though
they did not mention him by name—would do what they deemed necessary. "The
middle path many of our political leaders would prefer, with token increases in
the defense budget and a more 'humble' view of America's role in the world, will
not suffice," they wrote. "What is needed today is not better management of the
status quo, but a fundamental change in the way our leaders and the public think

about America's role in the world."[61] As it happened, they got their wish in ways that they and other neoconservatives perhaps could not have imagined.

The stage had been set for a return to normalcy after the end of the Cold War; instead, over a ten-year period, we discovered that a new normalcy had been created. Our nation was no longer constrained by the Founders' ideology that had placed great emphasis on humility and leading by example, and which Kristol and Kagan had denigrated as synonymous with "cowardice and dishonor." That pre–Cold War view had been replaced by a new ideology, an ideology that commanded adherents from across the political spectrum, and presumed the United States, and the United States alone, held the key to preserving world order.

We only fully discovered this reality a decade after the Cold War ended, and only because another event—the 9/11 attacks—precipitated a full-on statement of these new principles. The man who had explicitly campaigned on a platform of a humble foreign policy and who doubted that the United States should "go around the world and say this is the way it's got to be," became a leader committed to reshaping world politics.[62]

Speaking before cadets at the U.S. Military Academy at West Point in June 2002, Bush explained, "For much of the last century, America's defense relied on the Cold War doctrines of deterrence and containment. In some cases, those strategies still apply. But new threats also require new thinking." Beyond defeating those who had struck the United States on 9/11, Bush foresaw "an historic opportunity" the "best chance since the rise of the nation state in the seventeenth century to build a world where the great powers compete in peace instead of prepare for war." Specifically, Bush pledged that "America has, and intends to keep, military strengths beyond challenge, thereby making the destabilizing arms races of other eras pointless, and limiting rivalries to trade and other pursuits of peace."[63]

The National Security Strategy (NSS) of 2002, issued in September of that year, echoed many of these sentiments, and deployed language that was similar to that of the Defense Planning Guidance of 1992. "Our forces will be strong enough," the NSS declared, "to dissuade potential adversaries from pursuing a military build-up in hopes of surpassing, or equaling, the power of the United States."[64]

The earliest version of the DPG of 1992 had spoken of "using military force…to prevent the proliferation of nuclear weapons and other weapons of mass destruction in such countries as North Korea [and] Iraq." A decade later, the 2002 NSS explained "in an age where the enemies of civilization openly and actively seek the world's most destructive technologies, the United States cannot remain idle while dangers gather."[65]

Barely six months later, George W. Bush sent U.S. forces into Iraq, and toppled Saddam Hussein's government. The United States was formally committed—rhetorically, at least—to overturning the established political order of most of the states in the Middle East, and had just demonstrated its ability to do so in one of them. Many would question Bush's judgment in launching such a war; none questioned his willingness to make good on his promises, although he always retained the freedom to pick and choose which autocrats would be in the crosshairs.

The advocates of benevolent global hegemony, many of whom now occupied high places in the Bush administration—in the West Wing of the White House, in the offices of the Vice President in the imposing Old Executive Office Building next door, and at the Pentagon—were pleased. No less pleased, to be sure, than Kristol and Kagan, the men who had actually coined the phrase, who were watching from a few blocks away.

George W. Bush's staunchest defenders contend that he reversed course from a humble to a radical foreign policy because the 9/11 attacks awakened him to a new moral purpose.[66] The attacks shocked him as they shocked many Americans, but only he was in a position to truly do something about it. He chose to respond to the attacks with retaliation against the Taliban who had given aid and comfort to al-Qaeda in Afghanistan, but most presidents in a similar position would have done much the same thing. He chose to declare a "war on terror" sensing that an enemy hunkered down in dungy caves, or hidden away in safe houses, would not be sufficiently frightening to awaken the public to a new global mission.

Bush articulated a new approach to U.S. foreign policy based on the sense, assiduously crafted by the advocates of benevolent global hegemony, that we had been victimized on 9/11 not because we were overly aggressive, but rather because we were insufficiently so. Although a competing explanation existed prior to 9/11,[67] and has been expanded upon since,[68] such accounts have been effectively drowned out and shouted down by a competing point of view. The dominant narrative paints the United States as both superhero and victim, capable of reshaping the world, but also supposedly vulnerable to being undone by a band of murderers and thugs who dare only show their face in carefully choreographed video recordings and speak via cryptic audio messages. That the two concepts are contradictory on their face—a country that is supposedly so powerful can't possibly be so weak—has largely escaped scrutiny from a too-credulous public so frightened by the events of 9/11 that they could be convinced of just about anything, no matter how absurd or untrue.

The removal of the Taliban from power after 9/11 could be seen as consistent with the ad hoc interventions of the 1990s—reactive, rather than proactive, and with modest ambitions. But the Iraq War was the first war explicitly fought according to the rationales set forth in the Defense Planning Guidance, and reiterated by the primacist consensus in the years since. The standard for future interventions is set. All that remains to be determined is where the U.S. military will go next.

Our enormous and highly capable military, staffed entirely by volunteers since 1973, deters would-be aggressors from attacking the United States directly. Our military defends long-time allies, many of whom have chosen to divert their resources to mainly peaceful pursuits. And our men and women in uniform, deployed throughout the world on bases on land and ships at sea, are often among the first to arrive on the scene when things go awry. They are the human face of our prodigious power. By offering assistance to victims of disasters both manmade and heaven sent, the oppressed as well as the unfortunate, the individuals who serve in the military exhibit the best features of this country's compassion and generosity. The U.S. military is also poised to ensure the free flow of goods in the global economy, acting as a form of insurance against international crises. Aggressors might aspire to conquer a neighbor and seize its assets, but the United States is poised to make them pay too high a price.

Under the best of circumstances, the mere knowledge that we have the ability to do such things deters other nations from engaging in threatening behavior. But when deterrence fails, the United States is not unlike any other powerful nation in history: we will use that power to punish aggressors and defeat their armies in battle.

But our military power has come up short in recent years. Although the U.S. military scored decisive victories against those individuals in Afghanistan and Iraq who were foolish enough to stand and fight, it has proved incapable of enforcing a rule of law, or delivering security, in many parts of post-Taliban Afghanistan or post-Saddam Iraq. Our vast military power does not work against individuals who would hide behind innocent people in order to launch attacks. It does not deter fanatics bent on suicide. It is vulnerable to crude devices fashioned from primitive military technology. Even the bravest and best-trained infantryman or Marine can be cut down in a moment by a bullet fired from the rifle of a skulking sniper.

In the two decades since the end of the Cold War, and especially since 9/11, Americans have seen the capabilities of our vast military. We know that our men and women in uniform can accomplish remarkable things. But we have also begun to appreciate their limitations, the most important of which being that they cannot be everywhere at once. Our political leaders, and increasingly the president alone, decide where they go, when they go, and how long they stay. In the next chapter, I discuss how much it all costs.

CHAPTER TWO

TALLYING THE COSTS OF
OUR MILITARY POWER

It was necessary to take stock of what we have, to consider where we are, and how we got here. But to look only at what our military provides us, and others, would be to ignore the other side of the balance sheet. Americans spend an enormous amount of money on the military. This chapter examines how much we spend, and where the money goes.

The direct costs that Americans pay in order to develop, maintain, and extend our tremendous military power are relatively easy to calculate. And they are staggering. When one includes both the Pentagon's budget and special funding for the wars in Afghanistan and Iraq, nearly 4.5 percent of the U.S. economy, or $622 billion, was devoted to military spending in 2007. That amounts to $2,065 for every man, woman, and child in the United States. By way of comparison, the average British citizen paid just over $1,000 for defense. The average Frenchman paid around $845. Japan spent about $340 per person on defense; Germany just over $430. The gap grew even wider in 2008 as the costs of the Iraq War mounted, and as military spending in other countries remained stable, or, in some cases, declined. Meanwhile, increased defense spending in Russia and China over the past few years hasn't begun to close the gap in spending on a per capita basis. According to estimates by the International Institute of Strategic Studies, the average Russian paid $495 in 2006; the average Chinese paid a mere $92.[1]

The sum total that U.S. taxpayers spend on national defense actually goes well beyond the budget for the Department of Defense. Consider President Bush's request for FY 2009, officially $515.4 billion.[2] This figure, often referred to as the Pentagon's "base budget," approximates what it will cost to keep the four branches of the military in active service, but misses a number of additional expenditures and budgetary gimmicks that will bring the total spent on the military closer to $800 billion. For example, that figure doesn't include the costs of the wars in Iraq and Afghanistan, and other operations related to the president's Global War on Terror (GWOT). In addition to the Pentagon's base budget, the Bush administration requested $70 billion to fund operations in Iraq and Afghanistan, even though the actual cost in FY 2009 was expected to be at least twice that amount.

A more accurate starting point for understanding what we spend is the "National Defense" category in the president's budget, totaling $608.6 billion. This figure includes the Pentagon's base budget, plus the $70 billion for the GWOT. In addition, there is the $17.1 billion tucked away in the Department of Energy's budget for the care and maintenance of the nation's nuclear weapons, as well as $3.2 billion in defense-related expenditures within other government agencies.

Even the "National Defense" figure misses some of the costs of our military power. National security spending also includes the Department of Homeland Security (proposed budget $40.1 billion in FY 2009) and the Department of Veterans Affairs ($91.3 billion). Meanwhile, the Treasury Department is responsible for military retirement costs totaling $12.1 billion that are not included as part of the official DoD budget.

But wait, there's more. The federal government has been living beyond its means for at least the past seven years, amassing enormous budget deficits that must eventually be closed.[3] In the interest of accurately tracking all national security spending by the federal government, Winslow Wheeler of the Center for Defense Information suggests that we count the national defense portion of the interest on the national debt, which comes to at least $54.5 billion.[4]

Added together, the thousands of line items in the gargantuan federal budget that are purportedly aimed at advancing U.S. national security total nearly $800 billion, or approximately $2,660 for every person living in the United States.

Where does all this money actually go? Many library bookshelves are weighed down with ponderous treatises on the subject, and the discussion here only scratches the surface.[5] I will consider three broad categories: procurement, chiefly of hardware (classified as "Strategic Modernization" within the DoD budget); personnel expenses, including salary and benefits, family housing and facilities, and also recruitment and training costs; and finally the costs of actually waging wars. The first two components of national security spending account for more than 70 percent of President Bush's FY 2009 defense budget, with the balance going to normal operations and maintenance—essentially the costs associated with keeping the military going on a day-to-day basis. The costs of the wars in both Iraq and Afghanistan have totaled more than $750 billion since 9/11, and are expected to accumulate at a comparable rate (between $100 and $200 billion per year) so long as a large number of U.S. troops remain in these two countries. Because these expenditures have largely been paid for through supplemental or emergency spending requests, I will consider them separately.

Buying the Equipment

Military hardware is expensive and highly specialized. Although there is a number of cases in history where military technologies have spawned spin-off products of use to a wider consumer market (some popular examples include the now ubiquitous microwave oven, derived from radar, and the equally ubiquitous Internet, which began as a rudimentary computer network for the Department of Defense), companies that compete for military contracts do so with the understanding that their primary obligation is to one buyer—the U.S. government. Any potential spin-offs are purely coincidental.

The fact that the U.S. government is usually the only customer of interest, combined with the fact that the difficulties of doing business with Uncle Sam discourage most companies from participating in the process, contribute to another key feature of military procurement: it does not function according to market principles.[6] Former secretary of defense Donald Rumsfeld compared the way the Pentagon bought weapons to Soviet central planning, and he pledged to make changes. By and large, however, his program was derailed by the Bush administration's response to the 9/11 attacks, policies that he helped shape. Double-digit increases in military spending removed many incentives that defense contractors and the procurement officers who oversee them might have had to hold down costs.

The Pentagon procurement system's track record in obtaining equipment in a timely fashion and at a reasonable price is so abysmal that it is a wonder that the system ever produces anything of value. Eventually it does, however, and the end product usually meets with expectations; indeed, many of our weapons are truly exceptional. But they are also exceptionally costly.

There is more than enough blame to go around. The firms that design and manufacture items for the military, especially big-ticket items like ships or planes, stake their reputations, and many of their employees' livelihoods, on the expectation that the government will honor its commitment to buy their product. Indeed, in most cases, they hope that the government will buy more, even when the per unit costs skyrocket. But they would prefer not to leave such momentous decisions to chance. Therefore, many of these companies have become particularly adept at playing politics.

Explaining the economic behavior of government actors is one of the central insights of a body of thought known as public choice theory. A related field documents the structural factors that contribute to the growth of government, what political scientist James Payne calls "the culture of spending."[7] Payne and others show that all forms of government spending are subject to the phenomenon of concentrated benefits and diffused costs. Those who pay for government programs—from national security to Social Security and Medicare—vastly outnumber the people who directly benefit from this spending. But the beneficiaries' energy and enthusiasm make up for their relatively small numbers. After all, the beneficiaries have a powerful incentive to keep the dollars flowing. They organize themselves into trade associations, dedicating a small portion of what they receive, or expect to receive, from the government in order to hire experts and paid lobbyists, often former officials, to plead their case. By contrast, individual taxpayers have little incentive to organize comparable advocacy organizations to try to convince Congress not to spend the money.[8] Given the amount of money that they might save from the cancellation of any one program, typically not more than a few dollars per person, most taxpayers have other more pressing concerns (including going to work so that they can pay the taxes). Multiply this scenario hundreds or even thousands of times to account for the myriad programs tucked inside of the federal budget, and one begins to appreciate the scope of the problem.[9]

President Eisenhower appreciated it rather well. As discussed in chapter 1, Eisenhower lamented in his famous farewell address that the combination of disparate interests, from scientists and engineers to military leaders and the captains of industry, had altered the nature of the country's military establishment, and threatened to alter society as a whole.

In an earlier draft of the speech, Eisenhower referred to the "military-industrial-congressional" complex, but he dropped the reference to Congress at the last minute. That omission is unfortunate. For too long, critics of the military-industrial complex have focused on how military officials and business leaders collaborate, ignoring the role that defense workers play in the process of perpetuating an overgrown military establishment. When the men and women who manufacture the implements of warfare have a vested interest in seeing a particular weapon system built, they communicate their interests through elected officials, especially their members of Congress. Congress responds by spreading subcontracts to numerous congressional districts, or by maintaining surplus capacity to preserve a fig leaf of competition between two or more firms. It is logical for workers employed under these contracts to support politicians who steer money to their employers, and punish those who do not. These pressures, both subtle and not so, have a clear effect.

Based on nearly three decades of experience on Capitol Hill and with the General Accounting Office, Winslow Wheeler cataloged the many different ways that members of Congress use military spending to serve narrow pork-barrel interests, specifically by delivering benefits for constituents back home.[10] As we will see, a number of weapon systems survive because members of Congress want it that way. In some cases, defense spending becomes not much more than a thinly veiled jobs program. Unlike spending on public works projects such as roads and bridges that serve a wider domestic constituency, the use of defense spending to stimulate the economy creates powerful, entrenched political constituencies who oppose reductions in military spending, even in times when the strategic situation would facilitate such changes.

There are eighty different major weapons systems listed in the Bush administration's FY 2009 budget, and a detailed examination of each is well beyond the scope of this study. I have chosen to look at five high-profile weapons systems: the F-35 Joint Strike Fighter, the F-22 Raptor fighter aircraft, the Virginia-class submarine, the V-22 Osprey tilt-rotor aircraft, and the Army's Future Combat Systems. The "Strategic Modernization" category represents the largest share of the defense budget (35 percent); these five items reveal the nature of these costs, and especially how the costs tend to accumulate and grow over time.[11]

The F-35 Joint Strike Fighter

According to the then Air Force chief of staff General T. Michael Moseley, the Joint Strike Fighter (JSF) "represents the fruits of lessons learned over a hundred years of flight and aerial combat... and warfighters around the globe are excited about flying it in defense of freedom."[12] And well they should be. The JSF program is one of the most expensive items in the FY 2009 budget, with total costs (procurement plus research and development) reaching $6.7 billion. Different models of the single-engine, single-seat fighter will be used by the Navy, Air Force, and Marines, plus a handful of foreign buyers.

This is not the first time that the military has attempted to develop a multi-service fighter aircraft. But the poor track-record of the Tactical Fighter Experimental project initiated in the 1960s might have discouraged Pentagon planners from trying again.[13] Instead, the leaders of the JSF program tried to learn from their predecessors' missteps. According to Lockheed Martin's executive vice president, Dain Hancock, "the government's management of the Joint Strike Fighter program has set the standard for how to run a development program in the 21st century."[14] By combining common elements in a single platform, JSF designers expected to derive substantial cost savings. Once the plane is put into service, common parts and support equipment are expected to keep operating costs down over the JSF's long life cycle. It is appropriate to emphasize "long." The program was initiated in 1994, but the first operational planes are not expected to be delivered until 2013, at the earliest.

The JSF originated in the early 1990s, when the then defense secretary Richard Cheney canceled the Navy's A-12 Avenger II fighter in 1991, leaving the service without a successor to the venerable A-6 Intruder. Meanwhile, the Air Force had been searching since the mid-1980s for a lower-cost fighter that would be comparable to the F-16 and the Marine Corps was looking for a successor to the AV-8B Harrier, a short takeoff, vertical landing (STOVL) aircraft, which they had been flying since the mid-1980s.

In January 1994, the Clinton administration launched a program aimed at forcing the three services to combine their efforts, and hopefully avoid a counterproductive competition for scarce resources. This proved fortuitous. With the Marine Corps demanding a durable fighter capable of landing on unfinished airstrips and short runways, the JSF program attracted an additional customer: The British Royal Navy. The United Kingdom was seeking a replacement for its Sea Harriers, but such airplanes needed to be able to take off from and land on the Royal Navy's short aircraft carriers. The British joined the JSF project in 1996. Sensing a potential market overseas, the Clinton administration began soliciting still more foreign customers. So far, eight countries have agreed to participate.[15]

Given the large number of potential customers, both by the three branches in the U.S. military and in foreign markets, the JSF contract was expected to be the most lucrative in the history of military aviation. Not surprisingly, the competition to design and build the aircraft was intense. Lockheed Martin and its development partners were awarded the contract in October 2001, beating out a team led by Boeing.

Since then, however, the JSF program has encountered a number of difficulties. The single most important problem has been the plane's considerable cost, estimated at $122 million per plane—more than three times the initial estimate for an aircraft that was explicitly designed with cost containment in mind.

The pattern is familiar to many defense projects, but especially in aviation. Costs accumulated during long periods of research and development almost always exceed early estimates, as new technologies and capabilities are added to the initial design. These accumulated costs then bump up against the budgetary targets for the program, with the result normally being a reduction in the total number of units to be purchased. Spreading research and development expenditures over a smaller number of planes to be purchased within the program increases the per unit costs. Rising per unit costs, in turn, often have a domino effect, where customers reduce the number of planes that they plan to buy, which then has the effect of raising per unit costs still further. Franklin Spinney, a long-time defense analyst in the Pentagon and frequent critic of DoD spending practices, noted other cascading effects. For example, as the costs of the replacement aircraft rise, older, less capable aircraft that are generally more costly to operate are kept in service longer. Budgetary pressures to continue with force modernization are also translated into cuts in other areas, including pilot training. Spinney and others have called these cascading effects the defense death spiral.[16]

The JSF's per unit cost growth has other wide-ranging implications. The JSF program depends on the active participation of a number of foreign countries with far more modest procurement budgets. Canceling or significantly scaling back the project would elicit howls of protest from the other participants who have invested time and effort at the expense of other potentially more promising, and less costly, projects.[17]

The JSF's backers counter that the plane's unique capabilities offset its relatively high cost. Air Force Chief of Staff Moseley boasted that "The F-35's stealthy design was intended to give it the ability to penetrate advanced enemy defenses, day and night, operate with impunity, from day one, day and night, of any future conflict, giving it unmatched survivability."[18]

That may be, but given that the JSF is expected to replace aging equipment, it must demonstrate that it is clearly superior to existing platforms. The Air Force and Navy's current fighters, chiefly the F-15, F-16, and F/A-18s, are highly capable aircraft and they are far less costly than the JSF. The more relevant question, however, concerns not the present but the future. Simply put, how urgent is the need for a next-generation fighter, and should the JSF be that plane? As the second largest line item in the Bush administration's $183.8 billion "Strategic Modernization" budget—behind only missile defense—the JSF's backers have not made a good enough case to silence the critics.

The F-22 Raptor

If the JSF's chief liability is its high cost relative to other alternatives, the F-22 Raptor has this problem in spades. Designed in the 1980s to fight a Soviet enemy, which disappeared in the early 1990s, the F-22 Raptor has been an aircraft in search of a mission since long before its first test flight in September 1997.[19] And it costs nearly three times as much as the JSF. The FY 2009 budget request included $4.1 billion to cover the costs of the last 20 of 183 units that will be delivered to the Air Force. The $65.3 billion spent over the life of the F-22 program bring the average per unit cost to more than $356 million.

Costs have never deterred the plane's advocates. Retired Air Force General Richard Hawley proclaimed in 1999 that the F-22's "combination of maneuverable stealth, [and] the ability to evade detection by enemy radar defenses...will give the pilots of these airplanes unprecedented ability to understand what's going on around them in the battle space."[20] Survivability in air combat will be increasingly important for the Air Force as a small number of F-22s will replace the highly capable but aging F-15s. When the program began, Air Force officials hoped to acquire 750 planes, but rising costs combined with a relatively static aircraft procurement budget progressively reduced the number of F-22s that they could afford.[21]

The Air Force contends that it is unfair to translate all of the program's research and development costs into the price tag of the newest planes rolling off the assembly lines. According to this creative accounting, the "flyaway" costs of prospective purchases, which essentially write off program R&D as sunk costs, will range between $176.8 million and $216.3 million per aircraft. This assumes, however, that this next stage of F-22 production will not encounter any of the cost growth that has plagued the program from the very beginning. At every stage of its development, actual F-22 costs have exceeded projections. Even the flyaway estimates have proved woefully inaccurate. When weighing the prospects of additional F-22 purchases, it seems prudent to assume the high-end estimate of more than $216 million per plane.[22]

The Air Force claims it needs more planes to sustain air supremacy. The F-22's supporters in Congress pressured the Bush administration to buy more of the planes in order to save the jobs of defense workers. Georgia Republican Congressman Phil Gingrey, who represents the district where the F-22 is assembled, warned that Marietta and surrounding Cobb County could become "a ghost town" if the money stopped flowing. Texas Democratic Representative Chet Edwards, whose district includes hundreds of aerospace workers in the Fort Worth area, once described the end of the F-22 program as a "train wreck" that would have a "major impact" on the economy.[23]

Three contractors—Lockheed Martin, Boeing, and Pratt & Whitney—have the most to gain from a decision to extend production. Workers at Lockheed Martin's facility in Marietta, Georgia are responsible for final assembly on the airframe. An estimated 1,500 people are employed in Fort Worth, Texas. Boeing employees in Seattle, Washington build the tail assembly. The F-22's F119 engines are built at a Pratt & Whitney plant in Middletown, Connecticut. In addition, more than 1,000 subcontractors in at least forty-four states are involved in the program.[24]

The Raptor's frame, engines, and control system make it more agile than earlier generation fighters, such as the F-15 and F-16. But the Raptor has a limited air-to-ground capability, and is less durable than its predecessors. And while the F-22's smaller radar cross section and other stealthy characteristics make it harder for enemy radar systems to find and track, and therefore also give the plane an advantage in head-to-head combat against other fighter aircraft, it raises the question: whose fighter aircraft?

The proponents of the F-22 aren't exactly sure, but the aim is to stay ahead of anything that might be developed anywhere in the world during the next half century. "Air supremacy should be the minimum we seek, and air dominance our desired goal," wrote aviation historian Richard P. Hallion on the pages of the *Washington Post*.[25] Pointing to the "1700 combat losses suffered in Vietnam," General Hawley explained: "the Air Force learned that we need a dedicated, high-end, air superiority fighter in order to guarantee air supremacy over future battlefields."[26]

In the absence of any comparable air-to-air threat in the medium- to long term, the F-22's most serious challenge is opportunity cost. Our current fighter inventory is being depleted by age, and experts predict that we will end up with the smallest fighter force since World War II, even if the Air Force obtains the roughly 200 Raptors it wants. The high price tag of the F-22 has crowded out other low-cost alternatives, and the Air Force has been compelled to keep aging aircraft in service because they are unable to replace them in their inventory fast enough, and they have strongly resisted cuts in the size of the overall fighter force.[27] There are also trade-offs in terms of pilot training, which history has shown is the key to success or failure in air combat. Currently, F-22 pilots are receiving only ten to twelve flight hours a month; pilots in the Vietnam War received twice that much, and that was widely seen as inadequate. If the Air Force's obsession with the F-22 cheats pilots of in-flight training, it may rob the United States of air superiority instead of increasing it.[28]

The F-22 is facing only a hypothetical enemy in a future war for air supremacy. Such a war may never occur. Meanwhile, actual foes like the Taliban and al-Qaeda don't have an air force and are not interested in acquiring one. The Air Force tried to send the F-22s to Iraq, but Secretary of Defense Gates denied their request on the grounds that the aircraft is not optimally suited to the battles being fought there.[29] The F-22 hasn't seen action in the skies over Afghanistan either. The F-22's armor is too light even for most small arms fire and this forces it to drop its ordnance at a high elevation.[30] That complicates target identification, and increases the likelihood of civilian casualties and other collateral damage in a conflict in which success is predicated on the precise application of force. Gates has publicly questioned the usefulness of the F-22, noting in testimony before Congress in February 2008 that the plane "is principally for use against a near-peer in a conflict."[31] It is possible that the most expensive fighter plane in history may spend its entire life preparing for a war that never comes, and sitting out the ones that do.

The Virginia-Class Submarine

In its FY 2009 budget request, the Bush administration requested around $3.5 billion for the Navy's Virginia-class submarine, a nuclear-powered, fast-attack submarine that is intended to replace the boats in the Los Angeles class. The USS Virginia (SSN-774), the first vessel in the class, was ordered in June 1998, and commissioned six years later. Three other boats ordered in June 1998 are being delivered to the Navy at a rate of approximately one per year, but the pace is expected to increase beginning in 2010, with two coming online each year from 2010 through 2016, and then three per year from 2017 through 2020. As these boats are commissioned, the Los Angeles-class submarines will be removed from active service; in some cases, LA-class vessels will be retired early to make room for the Virginias.

The Virginia is actually the second prototype designed as a successor to the Los Angeles class. In the late 1980s, Navy leaders pinned their hopes on the USS Seawolf (SSN-21), but only three vessels based on the Seawolf design were actually built, and the total costs of the program exceeded $20 billion, or more than $6.7 billion per vessel.[32] Beyond its enormous costs, the reasons for the Seawolf's demise are fairly obvious. The adversary that the subs were designed and built to defeat, a highly capable Soviet submarine force, ceased to exist in the early 1990s. Clearly, the Virginia-class subs needed a new rationale, and a new enemy, if they were to avoid the Seawolf's fate.

The Virginia's builders and subcontractors, and their advocates in and around the Washington Beltway, responded by throwing in the kitchen sink. They would not fight just one adversary, but several. "The Virginia class is the first U.S. Navy warship designed from the keel up for the full range of mission requirements in the post-Cold War era," proclaims builder General Dynamics on its official Web site.[33] Indeed, the Virginia is being promoted as a new-generation submarine "optimized for maximum technological and operational flexibility" whose "stealth, firepower and unlimited endurance" enable it to accomplish at least seven different missions. These include traditional roles such as seeking and destroying enemy ships in a wide variety of scenarios, and attacking targets ashore with Tomahawk missiles, missions that are adequately fulfilled by the LA-class subs. But the Virginia also includes some features and attributes that will allow it to conduct long-term surveillance and intelligence collection missions, and better assist Special Operation Forces.

In several other respects, the Virginia is not so different from its predecessors. It boasts a quieter propulsion plant, the Holy Grail of submarine construction, but more an evolutionary change than a revolutionary one. Size-wise, the Virginia is about 10 percent larger than the Los Angeles class, and about 10 percent smaller than the Seawolf. And although its top speed and the safe depths to which it can dive are both classified, it is believed to be comparable to its predecessors.

The Navy's enthusiasm for the vessel goes beyond strict considerations of its military utility; the service also wants to preserve a political and economic status quo that is tied to a unique industrial base. The manufacture of submarines is a particularly specialized business, far more specialized, for example, than the building of surface warships. Defenders of the Virginia regularly assert that the U.S. capacity to build submarines would wither and die if the boats were not built.

The industry is clearly nervous. The decline in the size of the nuclear attack submarine force from its Cold War–era high of eighty-seven boats to the current total of fifty-two, prompted the two leading submarine manufacturers, and once fierce rivals—General Dynamics' Electric Boat in Groton, Connecticut, and Northrup Grumman's Newport News Shipbuilding in Virginia—to join forces. The two companies combined their efforts in the Virginia-class program and manufacturing is now divided between them. This practice has the additional advantage of more tightly binding twice as many congressional delegations to a continuation of the status quo. That is good news for the builders, and for the people employed by Electric Boat and Newport News, but potentially bad news for taxpayers everywhere.

The members of Connecticut's congressional delegation have been particularly outspoken in their support for the Virginia, and they haven't been shy about the parochial economic interests at play. Senator Chris Dodd (D-CT) declared that funding for the Virginia class ensures "that our military has the resources it needs to get the job done," and "represents a significant win for our state's economy and jobs."[34] Dodd's colleague Sen. Joseph Lieberman took credit for securing defense projects for his state, and pledged to "continue to fight for this investment, which incidentally will keep high-skilled jobs in Connecticut."[35]

Democratic Congressman Joe Courtney proclaimed it a "great day for southeastern Connecticut and an important victory for our nation's defense infrastructure," when the president signed the 2008 Defense Department budget into law, because the budget included funds to accelerate building of the Virginia class to two per year. Courtney, whose district includes Groton and New London, praised the decision to fund "the most advanced ship to our nation's naval fleet, which will secure our defense jobs in Connecticut."[36] That much seems clear. The role that the Virginia will play in securing the other forty-nine states, however, is still pretty murky.

The V-22 Osprey

The highest acquisition priority for the Marine Corps over the past decade has been the V-22 Osprey, an aircraft that employs tilt-rotor technology to achieve the vertical takeoff and landing of a helicopter, but with in-flight speed and performance characteristics of a fixed-wing turboprop airplane. The V-22s travel at speeds of up to 300 miles per hour, more than twice as fast as most helicopters. They also have longer range and generally greater payload capacity. As advertised, the Osprey is expected to carry twenty-four Marines and all their gear, or up to 10,000 pounds of equipment.

Its advocates predict that it will have an immediate impact on the battlefield. Marine Corps Gen. James Jones declared in July 2002 that "our efficiency in the Afghan scenario would have improved by 65 to 75 percent had we employed the V-22." This greater efficiency would have translated into lives saved, Jones explained.[37] Navy Secretary Donald Winter agrees. "The Osprey can deliver Marines to battle more safely, bring them reinforcements over greater distances in greater numbers, and evacuate wounded ones more quickly" than helicopters explained Winter.[38]

The FY 2009 defense request allocated over $2.7 billion for the V-22, with the Marines paying for the largest chunk—$2.3 billion for the acquisition of thirty units, and projected to purchase that same number over the next four years. All told, current plans call for 458 Ospreys to be built. The lion's share will go to the Marines, but the Air Force intends to purchase as many as fifty CV-22s, the service-specific variant which shares about 85 percent in common with the Marine Corps' version. Maj. Gen. Donald Wurster, Vice Commander of the Air Force Special Operations Command, calls the V-22 "the single most significant transformation of Air Force Special Operations since the introduction of the helicopter....Nearly every mission we have faced in the last 20 years could have been done better and faster with the V-22."[39] The Navy has also expressed an interest in using V-22s for search-and-rescue, logistics, and in support of special warfare operations.

As with any new platform, it has taken many years to move the V-22 from concept, to experimental flight, to flight testing, and ultimately, to deployment in support of our troops. The Osprey program has had more than its share of serious problems and long delays. A contract was first awarded to a joint development team from Bell and Boeing in 1986, the Osprey program delivered the first of six planned prototypes in 1989, and then underwent extensive testing throughout the 1990s.

Of the first six prototypes delivered, two were destroyed in crashes. Engineers reviewed these incidents, one of which killed seven people onboard, and developed four new prototypes that began testing in early 1997. Once again, however, the program suffered a setback. A crash in April 2000 killed nineteen Marines, and four more died in an MV-22 crash in December 2000. These incidents prompted Secretary of Defense William Cohen to commission a panel of experts and retired military officers to review the entire V-22 program. When the panelists delivered their report in April 2001, their list of recommendations ran more than eleven pages long. The aircraft was grounded while these recommendations were acted upon, and did not resume flight testing until May 2002.[40]

Since then, hydraulic failures were noted during testing in 2003, and there were two emergency landings during the tests conducted in 2005.[41] An investigation into an engine fire that occurred in December 2006, more than a year after the aircraft was cleared for full-scale production, led to still more recommended changes to the engine and to the software designed to detect similar incidents in the future. Gen. James Conway, the Commandant of the Marine Corps, took all this in stride, predicting that there would be future V-22 crashes, but that people would have to "accept that when it happens" because that is what "airplanes do over time."[42]

Despite serious concerns about crew safety and comfort—some Marines who have flown in the Osprey have complained of becoming disoriented or airsick[43]—the V-22's supporters in Congress have persisted. Operational units were delivered to the Marine Corps for at-sea flight testing throughout 2004 and into 2005. Finally, on September 28, 2005, the Pentagon's Defense Acquisition Board approved the V-22 program for military use and full-scale production began immediately. The V-22s deployed into a battle zone for the first time in late 2007, in support of operations in Iraq.[44]

The driving impulse behind the V-22 has always been jobs. Prime contractor Boeing's helicopter division in suburban Philadelphia employs voters from at least three different states—Pennsylvania, New Jersey, and Delaware. Bell Helicopter Textron, headquartered in Providence, Rhode Island, has manufacturing facilities in Fort Worth and Amarillo, Texas. According to the *Fort Worth Star-Telegram,* the Pentagon's decision in March 2008 to issue a five-year, $10.4 billion contract for 167 units, "all but guarantees Bell and Boeing years of profitable work and thousands of jobs for their employees."[45] Texas Senator Jon Cornyn declared it "a huge victory for the Amarillo and North Texas communities that continue to support V-22 production and winning the war on terror."[46]

Rep. Pete Geren (D-TX) pushed the V-22 because of the aircraft's merits, but admits that it has important auxiliary benefits. "The economic impact for our country is...hard to exaggerate," Geren explained. "[W]hen this thing does go into full production, we're talking about something that will employ tens of thousands of American....So it's definitely a job issue. It's an economy issue. It's an American technology issue."[47]

Geren's district includes Fort Worth, where the V-22s are built, but he is hardly alone. In addition to the prime contractors Boeing and Bell, the project also boasts hundreds of subcontractors in dozens of states, all of whom have helped to keep the project alive. Members of Congress have repeatedly rescued the V-22 from the chopping block. Indeed, the V-22 is a textbook case of how political logrolling influences defense spending. Critics worry that it is also a textbook case for how congressional interference undermines military effectiveness, and, especially given the Osprey's checkered safety record, endangers lives.

The Army's Future Combat Systems

The largest line item for the U.S. Army within the Strategic Modernization portion of the defense budget is the Future Combat Systems (FCS). As the name implies, this is not a single platform, but really a system of platforms, vehicles, and sensors, all linked together by a sophisticated information network. The FY 2009 budget allocates $3.5 billion ($3.2 on R&D, $300 million on procurement) mainly for the continued research and development of eight manned ground vehicles, two unmanned ground vehicles, two unmanned aerial vehicles, advanced long-range munitions, unattended ground sensors, plus continued development of the underlying information network.

Vice Chief of Staff of the Army Gen. Richard Cody declares that the "FCS promises to save soldiers on the battlefield, [and] allow them to...bring precision munitions to the enemy."[48] The FCS is at the core of the service's transformation plans. The Army is aggressively moving away from a heavy force, organized in divisions, and built to fight a Cold War enemy that ceased to exist nearly two decades ago, toward a light and modular force, organized around much smaller brigade combat teams. These teams will be more quickly deployable than their larger, heavier predecessors, enabling the U.S. Army to respond quickly to global crises.

In its final incarnation, the FCS will equip a third of the troops in the Army. FCS will improve the ability of individual soldiers to work together in complex environments. The networked components and systems will help our troops get to the fight more quickly, and make them more lethal once they get there. For example, the program is investigating new long-range guns and lasers that will be able to engage enemies at a great distance, enhancing our troops' ability to survive in a fire-fight, whereas experiments with composite materials aim to make the vehicles lighter and faster than the current M-1 Abrams tanks and M-2 Bradley fighting vehicles.

Cody and the Army are also counting on FCS to dramatically reduce the "logistical footprint" of troops in the field.[49] For example, the hybrid electric engine to be used in FCS manned ground vehicles is expected to reduce fuel consumption by 30 percent. FCS program officials also expect to reduce water, ammunition, and repair parts consumption by up to 70 percent.[50]

The program itself is still in a very early stage, and critics wonder if its stated goals are achievable, let alone any time soon. Introduced as a concept by Army Chief of Staff Gen. Eric Shinseki in October 1999, the first major contract was not awarded until March 2002, when the Army designated Boeing and Science Applications International Corporation (SAIC) as the program's lead systems integrators.[51]

The FCS program was not expected to achieve initial operational capability—meaning it will be available for use by the men and women in the field—until 2015, but pressure from Congress and from Defense Secretary Gates pushed that timeline up by at least three years. According to guidelines set forth in June 2008, the FCS program was to focus on getting equipment to the field by fiscal year 2011.[52]

For now, however, the FCS is still only a concept, and a costly one at that. At a time when Army personnel are facing decidedly low-tech enemies in Iraq and Afghanistan, the short-term trade-offs seem obvious. The General Accountability Office (GAO), in particular, has closely monitored the program, and has urged Congress to exercise similar oversight.[53] Of particular note were the disparities between the Army's initial projections for the total costs of the program ($91.4 billion) and a number of competing (and far higher) cost estimates. In 2006, GAO estimated program costs at $160.7 billion. A study that same year by the Cost Analysis Improvement Group (CAIG) within the Office of the Secretary of Defense estimated costs between $295 billion and $307.2 billion. The Institute for Defense Analysis reportedly identified even more costs, not captured by GAO or CAIG, but these figures have not been made public.[54]

The program does have a number of vocal supporters. Mackenzie Eaglen and Oliver Horn of the Heritage Foundation disputed widespread criticism that the program's core objectives are contingent upon unproven technologies. They also note that although the program will not equip an FCS Brigade Combat Team for several years, a number of products spun-off from FCS research, including small unmanned ground vehicles and armor upgrade kits, are aiding troops in Iraq and Afghanistan. A series of additional spin-offs are expected over the next few years, with coordination and testing to be performed by an Evaluation Task Force at Fort Bliss, Texas.[55] But GAO director of acquisition and sourcing management, Paul Francis, in testimony to the House Armed Services Committee, disputed Boeing's claims that these were impressive new technologies; Francis called these spin-offs "the harvesting of the low-hanging fruit."[56]

Given the Army's other priorities, and given the costs and risks of the FCS program, even supporters caution that the current development schedule is too aggressive. Congress has set 2009 to decide whether to continue funding the program, but Brig. Gen. James Terry, who oversees doctrine and training for Future Combat Systems at Fort Bliss, told the *Washington Post* that there is no turning back. "We have to head toward the future," he said, adding, "I think the train left the station a couple of years ago."[57]

As noted at the beginning of this discussion, my brief survey of just five major weapon systems within the defense budget cannot begin to capture all of the relevant details. The men and women who design and build them, and the military personnel who use them (or hope to use in the future), might protest that I have focused too much on the costs, and not enough on the unique capabilities that each of these systems provide. That would be a fair criticism. Although I have attempted to accurately portray each system's features and benefits, I have also deliberately chosen to highlight the trade-offs, and especially the costs, relative to the alternatives. I have also discussed the role that politics and congressional logrolling play. I will return to those issues in the next chapter.

The point of this chapter is merely to convey the enormous costs of our military power. Procurement is only one component of these costs, but it is an extremely important one. From the top-line numbers in the FY 2009 budget, U.S. taxpayers will spend $20.7 billion on the five weapon systems discussed here. That is more than all but ten countries spent on their *entire* defense budget in 2006. When one considers the amount of money that we will spend on just these five programs in a single year, and then realizes that there are dozens of other current projects, plus hundreds more over the course of the last thirty years, then we're beginning to appreciate what our military costs are.

And we're just getting warmed up.

Paying the Operators

Although the procurement process is time-consuming and costly, it eventually churns out the warships that ply the seas, the armored vehicles that rumble over the land, the airplanes that police the skies, and the satellites that monitor it all from high above the earth. But this hardware hardly runs itself. We pay people to operate these marvelous gadgets. And attracting, rewarding, and retaining these outstanding men and women often costs more than their high-tech equipment.

The costs start to accumulate long before an individual sits behind a console or in an airplane cockpit. People must first be recruited into one of the services. Recruiters operate in all fifty states, plus U.S. territories such as Puerto Rico and Guam. They visit high schools, set up booths at job fairs, and make hundreds of phone calls. They are aided by a vast marketing machine that includes radio and television advertising, ubiquitous branding campaigns, and slick video games.[58]

Recruiters can get pretty creative. Some partner with local radio stations. Others sponsor bulls at rodeos, or buy advertising space with minor league baseball teams. Every recruiter is trying to meet a monthly quota, and they will do whatever it takes to find qualified applicants, and to sell them on the military.[59] As with any sales job, however, there are far fewer hits than misses. A recruiter can expect to speak with dozens and dozens of people before finding a legitimate prospect. From the handful of prospects, only a few will actually sign up.

People join for a host of different reasons. Many cite their desire to serve their country, and to do something important and exciting. New recruits often mention the comprehensive health care offered to all active-duty personnel and their dependents. Recent immigrants can leverage military service to accelerate the path to citizenship. And most new recruits value the generous assistance that the military provides to help them attend college. A recent report commissioned by the Defense Department concluded that "The most dramatic social force affecting military enlistment is the interest in college attendance," and predicted that this trend would continue and even accelerate in the years ahead.[60] Under the old Montgomery GI Bill, military personnel received more than $73,000 in tuition credits, as well as help in repaying up to $65,000 in college loans, and in July 2008, President Bush signed into law a more generous package of education benefits for veterans who served after September 11, 2001.[61]

However, attracting new recruits is only the beginning. Once they have signed on the dotted line, the new recruits are made into soldiers, sailors, airmen, and Marines at one of nine basic training facilities made famous (or infamous) in films like *Full Metal Jacket*.[62] They then receive still more training in their chosen (or assigned) specialty. Marine Corps basic training lasts for thirteen weeks; the Air Force approximately six weeks; and the Navy between eight and nine. The Army trains new recruits for nine weeks, plus additional schooling in their specialty that can run from six weeks to a year. The Army's Training and Doctrine Command based at Fort Monroe, Virginia operates more than two dozen training facilities around the country. Every year, more than 500,000 people pass through at least one of these schools.[63]

The costs to train our exceptional officer corps are far higher. Most officers earn their commissions either through one of the service academies (West Point for the Army, Annapolis for the Navy and Marine Corps, and Colorado Springs for the Air Force), or through one of many Reserve Officers' Training Corps (ROTC) programs at civilian universities around the country.[64] A relatively small number of individuals obtain their commissions through officer candidate schools (OCS). The costs to turn these former civilians into officers are far lower than in the service academies or through ROTC, because the prospective candidates come to OCS having already completed (and paid for) their undergraduate education.

Once the troops are recruited, fed, clothed, housed, and otherwise equipped, their training continues. Indeed, training occupies a good portion of the average service member's day-to-day life. Other duties include repair and maintenance of equipment, managing supplies and personnel, and responding to specific instructions from their chain of command. The costs associated with day-to-day operations are fairly predictable, especially for a military not actively engaged in one or more wars. These expenses are covered under the "Operations, Readiness and Support" category within DoD's annual budget, totaling $158.3 billion in FY 2009. But when the military is called to fight, the costs rise, often dramatically, as discussed below.

In addition to recruiting and training, the third and largest component of military personnel expenses are for salary and benefits, including health-care coverage for the 2.2 million servicemen and women and up to 7 million dependents. It is widely believed that military personnel earn far less than their civilian peers, but that is only true if one does not accurately account for the non-cash benefits they receive as a condition of their service. The sum total of salary and benefits is roughly comparable to what individuals with similar education and skills earn in the private sector, and in certain instances even higher. For example, a recent Congressional Budget Office study of military compensation found that a twenty-year-old high school graduate with no dependents earned about $33,000 in cash compensation, plus another $28,000 in non-cash and deferred benefits. An average enlistee in pay grade E-6 with twelve years of service received about $96,000 in pay and benefits, and a forty-year-old E-8 earned about $127,000. A comparable GAO study estimated average total compensation among all service members at $115,500.[65]

In addition to competitive salary and benefits, most officers and enlisted personnel are entitled to receive special bonuses when they complete training in certain specialties or when they reenlist. Reenlistment bonuses vary depending on the needs of the services at that time. For example, the Navy offers Selective Reenlistment Bonuses to personnel in Navy ratings that are deemed crucial to combating the "War on Terror"; Navy Divers can receive bonuses up to $45,000 and a Fire Controlman up to $75,000.[66]

In recent years, the Army has employed generous Critical Skills Retention Bonuses (CSRBs) to convince senior noncommissioned officers (NCOs) to remain in the service. The CSRB list published in early 2008 included seventeen different specialties that were eligible to receive a lump sum payment of $100,000, or more, for a six-year reenlistment. The most generous bonuses— $150,000—were being offered to senior NCOs in the Army's Special Forces Command. That is the highest amount ever paid by the Army, but this substantial sum is still far less than it costs to recruit and train a new person.[67]

Bonuses are not usually paid to senior personnel with fifteen or more years of service, on the assumption that such people are "lifers" who were firmly committed to a military career. But that began to change around 2004. In the current environment, the stresses from frequent deployments to Iraq and Afghanistan are driving more and more military personnel to consider a career in the civilian sector. The use of contractors to fulfill duties once performed by the uniformed military has made it harder to retain qualified personnel. The military newspaper *Stars and Stripes* noted dryly that "seasoned leaders are extremely vulnerable to poaching by private contractors."[68] Companies such as Blackwater, Dyncorps, and KBR, Inc. (formerly Kellogg Brown and Root) offer competitive salaries and other benefits to personnel who decide to leave the service, and these companies place particular value on senior NCOs with years of military experience and crucial leadership skills.

The concerns about retention can be heard at the very highest levels of the military. A particular source of worry is the loss of combat-tested junior officers. Even West Point graduates, typically more career-oriented than their peers who obtained commissions through ROTC or OCS, are leaving the Army at a faster rate than before 9/11. The Army reports that it is already short several thousand captains, and that it will need an additional 6,000 by 2012 to coincide with the planned increases in the enlisted ranks. "It is a very fragile situation," admitted Admiral Mike Mullen, chairman of the Joint Chiefs of Staff. "There is this incredibly delicate balance between continuing in two wars [and] making sure we don't break those same forces. If we in fact cross that invisible red line, those [retention] numbers will go south." In a bid to forestall such an exodus, the military began interviewing officers and enlisted personnel nearing the end of their enlistment to determine what combination of bonuses and other quality-of-life improvements might convince them to remain in uniform.[69]

In short, the costs to attract and retain top talent in the military tend to increase when the military must compete more aggressively with civilian employers. They also tend to rise during wartime. Both of these factors are at play in the current operating environment, as discussed below.

Paying (More) When We Go to War

When the United States initiates a war, and puts the U.S. military into the field of battle, U.S. taxpayers incur additional costs, over and above what has already been spent on military hardware, and beyond what is budgeted for feeding, housing, and equipping personnel.[70] The cost of the wars in Afghanistan and Iraq, for example, are supplemental to the base Pentagon budget, and these costs have been subject to particular scrutiny, especially by opponents of the Iraq War.

The most comprehensive work is from Nobel Prize-winning economist Joseph Stiglitz of Columbia University, and his co-author Linda Bilmes, a professor and budget expert at Harvard's Kennedy School of Government. They raised eyebrows in early 2006 when they published a paper arguing that the Iraq War could cost taxpayers as much as $2 trillion dollars, far higher than other estimates at the time. Stiglitz and Bilmes then expanded on their thesis with a book and series of articles published in early 2008. In their evocatively titled book *The $3 Trillion War,* Stiglitz and Bilmes estimated that the costs from the Iraq War would likely fall within a range between $2.7 trillion in direct costs to the federal treasury, to as much as $5 trillion in terms of the total impact of the war on the U.S. economy.[71]

These estimates depend on a series of assumptions, some of which are open to criticism. Stiglitz and Bilmes noted that the price of oil rose dramatically over the course of the Iraq War, and they judged that 25 percent of that rise could be tied to the war. But this is speculative, at best; many factors contribute to the rise in the price of oil over the past five years, and it is impossible to say what impact the war in Iraq has had on oil markets. Further, Stiglitz and Bilmes attempted to account for the costs to the overall economy in lost productivity or diminished earning power for those killed or injured, but they relied on federal government estimates that tend to inflate such costs.

Although critics challenged aspects of the Stiglitz/Bilmes research, two of their central arguments are beyond dispute—and they apply not merely to the Iraq War, but to all wars. First, we spend more money on our military when it is at war than when it as at peace. Second, having waged war, we pay more over the lifetimes of those injured and disabled than we would have paid if they had never fought.[72] These obligations on the federal government's books persist long after the shooting stops. For example, disability payments to World War II veterans peaked in 1993.[73]

In their book, Stiglitz and Bilmes note that of the soldiers who had served in either Iraq or Afghanistan, 224,000 had applied for disability benefits as of December 2007. Among the 1.6 million veterans of either war, including some who have remained in the military, more than 263,000 had "been treated at veterans' medical facilities for a variety of conditions," and another 185,000 had "sought counseling and readjustment services at walk-in 'vet centers.'" Many of our veterans suffer from multiple injuries; "One in four ... has applied for compensation for more than eight separate disabling conditions."[74]

Stiglitz and Bilmes use the Gulf War as a model for estimating the long-term costs of medical care and disability payments to veterans of the wars in Iraq and Afghanistan. Of the 700,000 men and women who served in the Gulf War,

45 percent filed for disability benefits, and 88 percent of these requests were approved. On average, disabled Gulf War veterans receive $6,506 every year; this amounts to $4.3 billion paid out annually by the U.S. government. There are additional disability payments under Social Security. Meanwhile, the cost of providing medical care for the veterans of all our wars averages $5,765 annually per person. With these statistics as a foundation, and then deriving estimates based on different assumptions about the length and intensity of the ongoing wars in Iraq and Afghanistan, Stiglitz and Bilmes predict that total costs over the lifetimes of veterans of these wars, including disability payments and medical care, will range between $422 and $717 billion.[75]

The direct costs to the federal treasury that are paid out as the war rages fall into several categories. The largest component is operations and maintenance (O&M), which covers the repair and refit of damaged equipment, and also accounts for the increased usage of consumables, especially fuel and munitions, that we would not now be paying if the Taliban and Saddam had cried uncle before we launched the wars.

However, a Congressional Budget Office report found that since 2005 a larger share of the supplemental appropriations has gone to "reset" worn or damaged equipment. Some of these constitute major overhauls that repair equipment to "like new" condition, and in other instances equipment upgrades that return items to the field with substantially enhanced capabilities. By 2007 and 2008, DoD had shifted its focus in the supplemental requests yet again, progressively away from "resetting" equipment and toward "reconstituting" the force with new items to replace worn and damaged equipment. During this latter period, therefore, procurement constituted 35 percent of war-related expenditures, up from just 12.7 percent in 2001–5. Meanwhile, although O&M spending increased in real terms, for example, from $57 billion in 2005 to $70 billion and $92 billion in 2006 and 2007, respectively, O&M expenditures declined as a share of all war-related costs.[76]

A third key component of additional wartime spending pertains to personnel. Although the share of personnel costs has declined relative to O&M and procurement, the real costs have remained stable throughout the period from 2001 to 2008. Most war-related personnel expenses are associated with increases in the size of the active duty force. Although we spend hundreds of billions of dollars on our military, that force in terms of men and women in uniform is not so large, particularly relative to all that we ask them to do. When we add more onto their already-full plate, we must augment the active duty force. In the short term, this is accomplished chiefly through the mobilization of reserve and National

Guard units. These individuals draw active duty pay and benefits only when mobilized, and it is therefore easy to account for those additional costs.

But we have grown the active duty Army and Marine Corps, the so-called base force, by 14 percent since 9/11, and we have plans to add still more. Many of the costs of these proposals have been funded through the Iraq and Afghanistan supplementals. Under the current plan, the Army will add 35,000 troops, bringing total Army "end strength" to 547,000, perhaps as early as 2010. The Marine Corps will grow in a similar fashion, by about 5,000 troops each year over a four-year period. At plan's end, the Marine Corps will count 202,000 men and women in its ranks, a nearly 17 percent increase over where they were prior to 9/11.[77]

We pay more during wartime than during peacetime in two other important ways. First, although the regular salaries and benefits of active-duty personnel are paid out of the Pentagon's base budget, we pay military personnel more when they are operating in a war zone. These take the form of Hostile Fire/Imminent Danger Pay (aka combat pay), and Family Separation Allowances paid monthly to any military person who is away from his or her family for more than thirty days. Second, individuals operating in a war zone, including both uniformed military personnel plus other government employees and contractors, pay no federal income taxes. The combination means more take-home pay, which is obviously important for people in the military. But the lost tax revenue relative to what they would have paid from stateside earnings must be counted as a cost of war. Even more significant are the costs paid when reservists are deployed in a war zone. These individuals who are paid active duty salary only when mobilized are also entitled to the war zone tax break.

In short, the costs to recruit new personnel rise during times of war. We pay them more while they are at war. And the military also pays out more in special bonuses to those who reenlist during wartime. All of these costs have risen sharply as the all-volunteer force has been pressed to cope with protracted wars in Iraq and Afghanistan. In 2005, the Army missed its recruiting goals by 8 percent. After that dismal performance, they added one thousand recruiters and upped enlistment bonuses, as noted above. The average signing bonus for new enlistees went from $11,100 in 2005 to $16,500 in 2007. Some can earn as much as $40,000. These and other steps have enabled the service to make its recruiting targets each of the last two years.

These incremental costs are relatively easy to see, but experts also worry that the military has relaxed some of its standards for new recruits, for example by raising the maximum age from thirty-five to forty-two, and granting waivers to some individuals with criminal records. The effects of these changes might not be fully appreciated for years. The Army granted felony waivers to 511 recruits in 2007, double the number from 2006. The Marines also admitted a higher number of convicted felons.[78] Other "moral waivers" are used for potential recruits who have been convicted of minor offenses. All told, 11 percent of all new recruits needed such waivers to be able to join the service in 2007, double the percentage in 2003. Meanwhile, the percentage of high school graduates dropped from 90 to 71 percent, the lowest level in a generation.[79]

The Pentagon has experimented with various other band-aids to cover the twin wounds of lackluster recruiting and lower retention. Fearing the effects of the Afghanistan and Iraq deployments on the force, it began employing stop-loss orders to prevent some military personnel from leaving the service when their terms of enlistment expired. The number of individuals subject to stop-loss rose by 43 percent in 2007, as the Army struggled to support the surge of an additional 30,000 troops into Iraq.[80] Other individuals who have completed their service obligations have been returned to active duty. These provisions are included in a service member's contract with the government, but have been rarely invoked since the all-volunteer force was created in 1973. Some military officials concede that their actions are "inconsistent with the fundamental principles of voluntary service."[81]

Stop-loss orders, or other similar measures, can only postpone a time of reckoning, however. The military cannot compel members to remain in the service forever. Military spouses can opt out of the system by divorce, and an alarming number have done so in the past few years. Meanwhile, new potential recruits, and their parents and spouses, are asking the inevitable question: "How long will I be expected to serve?" Honest recruiters tell them the truth: "It depends."

As bad as the situation has been for the active-duty Army, the Army Reserve has faced even more difficult challenges as the wars in Afghanistan and Iraq have dragged on. Having fallen short of its recruiting targets in 2006, the Army Reserve paid out recruitment and retention bonuses in 2007 totaling more than $315 million, a 46 percent increase over the previous year. These increases proved instrumental in allowing the Reserves to exceed their goals in 2007, but experts wonder whether such costs can be sustained over the long term, and whether they will have the same effect.[82]

This chapter has considered the costs of our military power. I have discussed how the annual budget for the Department of Defense is allocated between pay and benefits for our service members, purchases of weapons systems and hard goods from defense contractors, and day-to-day operating expenses. I have also explained how the costs of waging wars are, and should be, considered as a crucial cost of our military power. These costs occasionally escape the same level of scrutiny applied to other forms of government spending, but they are a direct cost incurred by our government on our behalf.

Beyond the direct outlays by the federal government, our society pays other indirect costs. Money spent on military hardware cannot be spent at the same time on roads or bridges or schools. Individuals employed in the design and manufacture of such goods might otherwise be building automobiles or microchips. The engineers who design faster engines for aircraft might be improving the efficiency of the engines in our cars. The most gifted chemists and engineers who choose to develop new materials for blunting the impact of an AK-47 round or foiling an improvised explosive device have voluntarily opted out of an employment path that might have had them perfecting technologies to detect cancer, or discovering a potential cure for that cancer once found.

The costs mount. We must also consider how the growth of a large, permanent military that is, of necessity, controlled by the executive branch, has expanded the powers of the presidency at the expense of the Congress and the courts. Our Founders worried about precisely these costs when they designed the system of government that has sustained us for over 220 years, but their means for guarding against the accumulation of power in the hands of a single person have utterly failed.

Finally, we must take account of how our possession of great power invites resentment, scorn, and sometimes hatred. In its most extreme forms, this hatred is manifested in violence against Americans wherever they live, work, or travel. That, too, is an aspect of our power problem; and whereas it might be the hardest one to measure, in some respects it is the most important. These indirect and often intangible costs are explored in greater detail in the next chapter.

CHAPTER THREE

IT COSTS TOO MUCH

Many Americans believe that reductions in the military budget, and changes to our overall strategy, would result in less security for the American people. Those who argue that we must spend as much as we do on our military—or more—are generally aware of the costs documented in chapter 2, but they contend that such costs are necessary. To count only the costs of what we choose to spend for our military, defenders of the status quo often say, is to ignore the costs that would be forced on us by, for example, another terrorist attack. By some estimates, 9/11 cost the U.S. economy $250 billion.

Some have put forward plans for substantially increasing the defense budget. "There is no conceivable international scenario for the next generation," writes former U.S. senator Jim Talent, that would enable us to cut defense spending. Rather, Talent, now a senior fellow at the Heritage Foundation, calls on Congress and the White House to establish "a rule that the core defense budget should never sink below 4 percent of the nation's GDP."[1] In practical terms, that would dedicate an additional $131 billion for defense over the next five years, beyond the Bush administration's projections, and not including the costs of the wars in Iraq and Afghanistan.

Gary Schmitt, a resident scholar at the American Enterprise Institute, would see Talent's offer and raise it. "Dedicating 5 percent of the country's GDP—a nickel on the dollar—to defense is a wise investment," writes Schmitt, formerly the executive director of the Project for a New American Century. The benefits of "success in Iraq, the defeat of the global jihadists, and deterrence of other hostile states," he confidently predicts, "would be an immense return on money spent."[2]

Many Americans are skeptical. They know that the costs of maintaining and extending our military power are high, and growing steadily higher. Whereas most generally believe that this spending makes us safer, they are unlikely to support a dramatic boost in defense spending over and above the double-digit increases that the Pentagon has received since 9/11. A Gallup Poll taken in early 2007 found that 43 percent of Americans believed that the United States was spending too much on its military, the highest percentage in over fifteen years, and another 35 percent believing the defense budget to be "about right." Only 20 percent of poll respondents agreed with the statement that the United States was spending "too little" on its military.[3]

Despite such sentiments, politicians from both of the major political parties continue to call for increases in military spending, especially more spending on personnel. In the 2008 presidential campaign, Republican and Democratic candidates—John McCain, Hillary Clinton, Barack Obama—all favored increasing the number of active-duty personnel in the Army and Marine Corps, with McCain wanting to add another 150,000 on top of the increases approved by President Bush. Under a McCain administration, the Army and Marine Corps would have been more than 40 percent larger than they were prior to 9/11.[4]

The additional troops already programmed will be costly. When President Bush put forward his plan in early 2007, the Congressional Budget Office estimated that adding 92,000 men and women to the active-duty ranks would increase spending by $108 billion over the period from 2007 to 2013.[5] And the Army and Marine Corps will incur long-term obligations to these recruits that extend the costs far into the future. Still, as noted in the previous chapter, personnel costs account for only about a third of the Pentagon's base budget.

At a more basic level, proposals to dramatically increase military spending ignore some of the most important lessons of the past decade. They ignore the limited utility of conventional military forces against stateless enemies such as al-Qaeda. They imply that more troops on the ground in Iraq or Afghanistan would have delivered a swift, decisive victory. Proposals to add more troops are consistent, however, with the broader narrative favored by most Republicans, and a good number of Democrats, that we simply *must* spend more money to alleviate the burdens of our military.

But our power is a problem because it costs too much. We pay in dollars and cents, but the still greater costs are to our system of government and our culture. I explore all of those costs in this chapter.

More Than the Rest of the World

Critics of U.S. defense spending are quick to point out that the United States spends more on its military than all of the industrialized states of the world combined. Indeed, the factoid has become clichéd. The sheer magnitude of our defense budget has desensitized us to enormous expenditures that merely look small by comparison. What is the big deal about spending $6 billion for a Seawolf submarine? We spend that much in less than a month in Iraq. So what if the Joint Strike Fighter costs $120 million per plane? That's barely a third of the cost of a single F-22.

In a similar fashion, the scale of our dominance over any rival, or possible combination of rivals, has distorted our perspective. According to the International Institute for Strategic Studies' (IISS) annual survey *The Military Balance,* the United States in 2006 spent twice as much on its military as did all of our NATO allies combined. We spent seventy-four times as much as Iran, nearly twenty-four times more than India, and almost thirteen times as much as Japan.

Defenders of the status quo, those enamored of our position at the top—*way* at the top—of the global order like to argue that such comparisons are irrelevant, or at least seriously misleading. Because the United States is the wealthiest country on the planet, it costs us more to attract qualified soldiers, employ skilled shipbuilders, and attract the best scientists and engineers to work on military R&D. Economists and defense analysts attempt to take such considerations into account by estimating defense budgets according to purchasing power parity and market exchange rates. According to calculations that are widely accepted by most objective analysts, IISS concluded that our two closest rivals, China and Russia, spent a combined $191 billion in 2006, less than a third of what the United States spent on defense that year.[6]

Why do we spend so much, both in real terms, and relative to what others spend? Advocates of our current course contend that such expenditures are necessary, that they are driven by our global economic interests and that the functioning of the global economy depends on U.S. military power. Still others warn of impending catastrophe if U.S. military spending is cut. The United States must act as the lynchpin of the international order. Others stress the moral component, arguing that we have an obligation to spread the blessings of liberty to people denied basic human rights. Supporting this strategy will be expensive, and at a minimum requires a considerable expansion of our current military budget, but individuals who make such claims assert that whatever we require can be mobilized essentially at will.

But the essence of strategy is about setting priorities. Strategy helps us to separate the essential from the desirable and the desirable from the superfluous. Once we understand our priorities, this should guide us in allocating scarce resources. We may debate what should take precedence from time to time. And we should debate whether a particular proposal will help us to achieve our goals.

But we cannot avoid such discussions. Some writers and pundits dismiss talk of tradeoffs by pretending that we have an infinite reservoir of public will and public money just waiting to be tapped. They do this to absolve themselves from having to make hard choices about what we can do, as opposed to what we should do, or must do; in the process, however, they lose any reasonable claim to call themselves strategists. And they have no credibility when advising policymakers who must operate in a world of constraints.

The Four Percent Smokescreen (and Other Gimmicks)

The preferred tactic for mobilizing public support for defense spending is to portray that spending as a share of GDP. This has several advantages. First, it appears to be a small number—just 4 percent of GDP. Just four cents on every dollar. Is that too much to spend to make your children safe? The 4 percent of GDP figure also looks modest when compared with other countries. Whereas no one disputes that the United States spends far more on its military than any other country on the planet, there are a number of countries that *do* spend more as a percentage of their GDP. In their annual survey, IISS found that sixteen countries spent more than 4 percent of their GDP on defense in 2006. The CIA's *World Factbook,* which ranks expenditures of 173 countries worldwide, finds that 27 countries spent at least as much as the United States.[7]

A closer look at this list reveals just how irrelevant the statistic really is. There are a few very poor countries that spend a larger percentage of their meager GDP, but that translates to far less military capacity in real terms. Eritrea's 6.3 percent of GDP in 2005 bought them only $65 million for defense. Madagascar spent 5.4 percent of its GDP in 2006, but their $298 million budget could not pay for a single day of operations in Iraq. Burundi spent 5.1 percent of GDP, about $6 per person, to fund a $49 million defense budget. Other relatively wealthy countries at the top of the list are situated in a dangerous region, including Oman (9.0 percent of GDP, $3.2 billion), the United Arab Emirates (6.7 percent, $9.4 billion), and Qatar (4.5 percent, $2.3 billion), but still spent barely a fraction of what the United States commits to defense. Governments in poor countries that have the added misfortune of being surrounded by hostile neighbors would have to spend a far larger percentage of GDP in order to provide security for their people.

In general terms, then, what a country spends as a share of GDP doesn't tell us very much about how much it should spend.[8] My argument is that the considerable wealth of the United States, and our relatively advantageous geo-strategic position, should enable us to spend far less on defense as a percentage of GDP than do many other countries, and certainly less than we do today.

We have *chosen* to spend far more than others, both in real terms, and as a share of our output. We do so not because our own security is at stake, but rather because we fear that other countries might come under threat, or that entire regions may collapse into chaos, were it not for the U.S. military maintaining a constant presence in distant corners of the world.

By holding ourselves out as the indispensable nation, we have discouraged other countries from spending more on defense—in some cases deliberately. In the immediate aftermath of World War II, when a number of the most important trading partners of the United States were forced to rebuild their economies from a standing start, Washington worried that the diversion of precious financial resources to their militaries might impede their economic recovery. However, this argument loses its appeal with the passage of time. Given that military spending can have harmful long-term effects, why should Americans continue to pay the costs indefinitely into the future?

Washington has done so, in large part, on the assumption that the international system would be inherently less stable if a number of different countries were more capable of defending themselves. This was the logic of the 1992 Defense Planning Guidance, and it is consistent with the broader theory of hegemonic stability theory.[9] There is also the related fear that for other countries to take reasonable steps toward self-defense might be interpreted as hostile intent by neighbors. For example, one of the explicit rationales for the U.S. security guarantee to Japan, which spends less than 1 percent of GDP on defense, is that the United States does not want Japan to be strong militarily.[10] NATO operates in much the same fashion. No NATO country spends more than 3 percent of GDP on defense, and the average expenditure among NATO member countries—excluding the United States, of course—is a paltry 1.74 percent of GDP.

But just as the economic arguments lose their appeal as the international economy becomes more competitive, so too do the lingering fears of incipient turmoil and warnings of uncontrolled arms races begin to grate with the passage of time. European countries have been joined for decades in a political union; no one believes that France and Germany will lapse into a ruinous arms race if the United States were to withdraw its forces from Europe. In Asia, meanwhile, even bitter rivals—China, Japan, South Korea—have extensive trading relations and have cooperated to address common security challenges. It is unreasonable to believe that this cooperation would come to a halt if U.S. troops were withdrawn from South Korea and Japan. Americans have for too long carried the burdens and risks that should have been shifted to others. In the worst such cases, we are inadvertently encouraging our putative allies to engage in irresponsible behavior relative to the challenges and risks in their neighborhood.

Nowhere is that more evident than in the case of Taiwan. Policy experts can debate all day what Taiwan *should* be spending on its own defense; such decisions ultimately must be made by the people of Taiwan. In the meantime, however, it should rankle Americans that the Taiwanese currently spend a mere 2.6 percent of GDP on their military, about $416 per capita, at a time when U.S. military planners are dedicating tens of billions of dollars to design and deploy equipment to deter China from attacking Taiwan some time in the distant future. As the Cato Institute's Justin Logan and Ted Galen Carpenter note, "America is now in the unenviable position of having an implicit commitment to defend a fellow democracy that seems largely uninterested in defending itself."[11]

For some time now, the defenders of America as global cop have argued that because the United States is the wealthiest country on the planet, we should bear a greater share of the costs of sustaining the system that made us so wealthy. In making the case that we should—indeed that we must—spend as much if not more, the advocates of U.S. hegemony often stress that because we sit at the top of the global hierarchy, we have active obligations to sustain and extend this order. This "global public goods" rationale is explored in greater detail in later chapters.

For now, understand that when I say that we spend too much on our military, I mean that we spend too much relative to our own needs. We spend too much relative to alternative strategies that will keep us safe, but at far less cost. The primary obligation of government, *any* government, is to its own citizens, but much of the money that we spend on our military is actually intended to do for other governments what they should be doing for themselves. By dedicating resources to our military in order to defend others, our government is neglecting its responsibilities at home.

The Ubiquitous Enemy: Waste, Fraud, and Abuse

Could we purchase the same amount of military power—in terms of hardware, personnel, global presence, and the ability to wage war—at a far lower cost? Isn't much of the defense budget simply wasted on $500 toilet seats and

$50 hammers? A good amount, yes; but on balance, no. Our military generally spends money as the Congress intends—the problem is that politicians often *intend* the defense budget to be a conduit for patronage (aka pork).

As noted in chapter 2, government largesse insulates the military-industrial complex from market forces, and the Pentagon's weapons purchases are not always dictated by strategic necessity. Then Congress gets involved, doling out money and jobs, and keeping obsolete facilities open to suit their constituents' narrow interests. The net effect of this system greatly inflates the costs of our military for taxpayers while undermining efficiency, potentially to the detriment of national security.

Manufacturers of consumer goods specialize in understanding their customers, marketing their products to suit their needs, and generally striving to provide a quality product at a reasonable price. Manufacturers of military hardware spend their time and money on lobbyists. As investments go, lobbying is a pretty sound strategy when one considers the vast sums that these companies are trying to get from the government. For example, a list of the twenty "Big Lobbying Spenders of 2007" published in the *Washington Post* included three major defense contractors—Northrup Grumman, Boeing, and Lockheed Martin.[12] According to data compiled by the Center for Responsive Politics, Lockheed and its subsidiaries spent $10.6 million in 2007 on lobbying, but the company was the recipient of hundreds of millions of dollars in defense contracts during that year; the total cost of Lockheed's lobbying efforts were less than one-tenth what the government will pay for a single Joint Strike Fighter.[13]

Domestic political considerations corrupt the process still further. Is it any surprise that the Pentagon steers contracts and bases to certain congressional districts? For example, parts for the F-22 are made in forty-four states. Construction of the Virginia-class submarine is divided between Connecticut and Virginia, and the program spins off subcontracts to companies in a number of other states. The Tiltrotor Technology Coalition, formed in 1990 to save the V-22 from the chopping block, counted 140 members of Congress in its ranks.[14]

The potential for waste, fraud, and abuse is endemic to all forms of public spending. There is always a danger that contracts will be awarded to well-connected companies based on their political influence, and not because they offer the best product or service at the best price for the taxpayers. To guard against that, lawmakers and executive branch officials institute regulations. The most stringent regulations pertain to defense contracting. As the largest single recipient of the public's money, the Pentagon is a particularly attractive target for those seeking a quick fortune, by fraud or deception if necessary. As the bank robber Willie Sutton famously quipped, when asked why he robbed banks, "because that's where the money is."[15]

Federal regulators and law enforcement officials are well aware of this, which is why military procurement is an exceptionally complex undertaking. It takes a veritable army of attorneys and other experts to understand and comply with the government's Byzantine regulations governing how, when, and where to bid for and fulfill a government defense contract. Partly for this reason, few companies participate in the process.[16]

In recent years, the highest profile cases where individuals have been prosecuted for defrauding the government have all involved defense contracts and contractors.[17] That there continue to be prosecutions for such crimes would seem to justify the regulations, and the regulators to enforce them. But scrutinizing every single expenditure to ensure that the money is wisely spent, and investigating and prosecuting every possible case of fraud, also costs money. Indeed, a case could be made that government regulations cost the taxpayers more than they save.

Do they at least ensure that the taxpayers' money is well spent? Alas, no. As a recent Government Accountability Office (GAO) study showed, the regulations have been singularly ineffective in controlling costs and enforcing basic standards. Contractors have consistently failed to complete the most important weapon systems within their original budgets, and these systems are delivered, on average, two years behind schedule. The report found that ninety-five major systems had exceeded their original cost estimates by a total $295 billion over the period from 2001 through 2007.[18]

But the cost overruns and systemic mismanagement of public funds, egregious though they may be, are not the primary drivers of our power problem. A central argument of this book is that much of the money that is spent on defense might be better employed elsewhere. My argument is not predicated on the presumption that most of the monies allocated to national security are misspent. In other words, eradicating waste, fraud, and abuse would not translate into substantial cuts in the defense budget; indeed, they might not amount to much more than a rounding error.[19] Truly resolving the power problem will require much deeper cuts.

Conscription: A Cure Worse Than the Disease

Are there other means for dramatically reducing the costs of our military power? Absolutely. We could compel young people to serve in the military and dramatically reduce the pay and benefits that are essential inducements for the current all-volunteer force. Indeed, if we looked upon military service as an essential rite of passage for every citizen, if the choice for draftees was between jail or the Army, then we would need only to pay enough to keep them fed, clothed, and equipped. Salary would be all but irrelevant. And we wouldn't much worry about offering big bonuses to retain people if we were confident that a new cohort was always waiting in the wings.

But adopting conscription, or some other form of mandatory national service with a military component, as a way to reduce our manpower costs would be worse than doing nothing. Although a draft would succeed in getting bodies into uniforms, and at lower cost than the all-volunteer military, conscription is strategically unsound, morally reprehensible, and politically unthinkable.[20]

Our military is uniquely capable because it is comprised of individuals who serve of their own free will. Our outstanding soldiers, sailors, airmen, and Marines serve longer enlistments than soldiers in conscript armies. The troops work hard to succeed in their chosen profession, whereas draftees typically look for ways to escape or evade forced service. And notwithstanding our recent difficulties in retaining qualified personnel, today's volunteers still reenlist in far higher numbers than their predecessors in the conscripted force.

The military is willing to invest heavily in skills training and other professional development for volunteers; in contrast, the impulse with conscripts is to get them into the field as quickly as possible, on the assumption that they will only be available so long as they are required to serve. Shifting toward compulsory service would sacrifice quality for quantity, at a time when high-tech skills and in-depth training are in such high demand. A few highly skilled individuals—even relatively well-paid individuals—will do far more to keep us safe than a great number of poorly trained conscripts.[21]

Further, a conscript army is inconsistent with our national character, based as it is on the fundamental principle of the sanctity of the individual. The United States has resorted to conscription to man armies for major wars—including the Civil War, and both World Wars—but support for such measures declined precipitously in the latter half of the twentieth century. The underlying presumption that citizens are obligated to serve the state, at the discretion of political leaders, or simply by an accident of fate, continued to erode over time. Spurred on by a growing perception of unfairness during the Vietnam era as the affluent and the well-educated used deferments to avoid induction, and a complementary body of evidence showing that an all-volunteer military would be a more effective fighting force, the United States abolished the draft entirely in 1973.

Much of the rest of the world has moved in a similar direction. Today, very few countries rely on compulsion to fill the ranks of their militaries, and the number dwindles by the year. France, Spain, and Italy have all eliminated conscription in the last ten years. Russia is rapidly moving in that direction. Even China is pursuing a strategy for strengthening its military by focusing on a relatively small number of skilled recruits, as opposed to a vast number of disgruntled conscripts. Among the NATO allies of the United States, Canada, Britain, and Luxembourg have a long tradition of voluntary service, and several more have shed conscription since the end of the Cold War, including former Warsaw Pact states such as the Czech Republic and Romania.[22] Among the largest democratic states, only Germany still relies on compulsory national service. Critics note that the program mainly benefits hospitals and nursing homes that rely on the forced labor of young people to control their costs. Why pay nurses and medical professionals to change bedpans when the government can force a nineteen-year-old to do the work, and will pick up the tab?[23]

The advocates of a larger military typically shy away from talk of the draft, convinced that they can meet our manpower needs purely by voluntary means. Outspoken advocates of a draft, meanwhile, justify their calls not so much on the grounds of reducing the costs of our military, but rather out of a desire to distribute the burdens of citizenship more evenly between the well-to-do and the less-well-off.

After 9/11, such calls came from both ends of the ideological spectrum.[24] Senators John McCain (R-AZ) and Evan Bayh (D-IN) have introduced legislation to dramatically expand the Americorps program.[25] Although Americorps would remain voluntary under their bill, McCain adviser Marshall Whitman hinted that compulsory service might be right around the corner "depending on what the needs are in this war."[26]

But just as we rely on volunteers to fill the ranks of our firefighters and policemen, so must we pay for the other essential services of government. As Doug Bandow, a former special assistant to President Ronald Reagan who worked on the Military Manpower Task Force, explains, "Conscription only shifts the burden of paying to those who are drafted." "Instead of attempting to foist the cost off on the young," Bandow writes, "all Americans should share in the cost of protecting their society."[27]

When our young people make the fateful decision to don the uniform, we expect them to report for duty when called. But that obligation goes both ways. We as a society must keep faith with our troops; yellow ribbons on the back of our vehicles aren't enough. We must train our troops well. We must provide for their needs in both wartime and peacetime. We must do everything in our power to protect them from harm, recognizing all the while that it is their mission to go in harm's way. If our best efforts to protect them fail, we must treat them if they are wounded. We must care for them if they are disabled. And we must provide for their families if they are lost forever. This entails costs to our society as a whole, and we cannot obtain such services on the cheap.

Opportunity Costs

We pay to equip the members of the military with state-of-the-art equipment. We pay to recruit them. We pay them a salary while they are in uniform, and we pay them bonuses to encourage them to stay in uniform. We pay out even more when cold wars turn hot. These expenditures from the public treasury are relatively easy to measure. And they are enormous. But they are not unsustainable in strictly economic terms. Our ability to spend $600 billion every year on the military does not threaten to bankrupt us as a nation; after all, the United States has sustained higher spending in the past both in real terms, and as a percentage of output. It is true, however, that the diversion of resources from the private to the public sector risks undermining our economy on a more subtle level.[28]

How do we account for monies spent on national security that might have been spent on other things? Economists call these opportunity costs. The notion that public policy involves trade-offs was best expressed not by an academic, but by one of the most famous generals in U.S. history. Although he spent nearly his entire adult life in the U.S. Army, Dwight David Eisenhower believed that excessive military spending was inherently wasteful and unproductive. Indeed, Eisenhower reasoned that it was the economic strength of the United States that would ultimately enable it to defeat the Soviet Union, and he saw the escalating arms race as detrimental to the well-being of the United States.

Eisenhower harbored such sentiments for years. In 1947, he explained to his long-time friend and adviser Walter Bedell "Beetle" Smith that he worried about the harm that would be done to the domestic economy "through the annual expenditure of unconscionable sums on a [defense] program of indefinite duration, extending far into the future." Strategists, Eisenhower concluded, must recognize that "national security and national solvency are mutually dependent" otherwise the U.S. economy could crumble under the "crushing weight of military power."[29]

Eisenhower returned to this theme often. Testifying before Congress in 1951, he stressed that the United States would need to stay strong militarily in order to compete with the Soviet Union, but he emphasized that this must be done within the reasonable constraints of the domestic economy. "[O]ur system," Eisenhower said, "must remain solvent, as we attempt a solution of this great problem of security. Else we have lost the battle from within that we are trying to win from without."[30] Eisenhower reiterated this philosophy throughout his eight years as president. "To amass military power without regard to our economic capacity," he said in his 1954 State of the Union Address, "would be to defend ourselves against one kind of disaster by inviting another."[31]

When he assumed the presidency in January 1953, Eisenhower inherited from his predecessor, Harry S. Truman, a military budget for fiscal year 1953 that dedicated 14.2 percent of gross domestic product to defense, the highest share of the post–World War II era. Truman's final budget, submitted as he left office in January 1953, projected total defense spending of $45.5 billion for fiscal year 1954 at a time when nominal GDP was just over $377 billion.[32]

Eisenhower viewed that burden as intolerable, and even dangerous. He believed that if military spending rose too high it would ultimately undermine U.S. security, which he saw as a product of both military strength and economic strength. "Spiritual force, multiplied by economic force, multiplied by military force is roughly equal to security," he explained. For Eisenhower this was the "Great Equation." "If one of these factors falls to zero, or near zero, the resulting product does likewise."[33] He also worried that the high level of defense spending bequeathed to him by his predecessor might fundamentally alter the relationship between the citizen and his government, and would risk turning the United States into a so-called garrison state.[34]

Accordingly, Eisenhower sought to strike a new balance between military needs and the capabilities of the domestic economy. His first priority was to bring the Korean War to a close. That was a popular move. The war had dragged on inconclusively for over three years, and most Americans wanted to turn their attention, and dedicate their resources, to domestic needs.

Ike's second step was to alter public perceptions of the deepening Cold War. In a speech before the American Society of Newspaper Editors on April 16, 1953, just a few months after he took office, Eisenhower explained the tradeoffs inherent in the budding arms race with the Soviets and their presumptive allies in China, North Korea, and elsewhere:

Every gun that is made, every warship launched, every rocket fired signifies, in the final sense, a theft from those who hunger and are not fed, those who are cold and are not clothed. This world in arms is not spending money alone. It is spending the sweat of its laborers, the genius of its scientists, the hopes of its children.[35]

Eisenhower's remarks captured one element of the opportunity costs associated with an overgrown defense establishment, the diversion of people's talents and attention away from peaceful pursuits. But Eisenhower went to some lengths to illustrate an equally important—and more easily quantified—aspect of military spending's opportunity costs. He compared the costs of contemporary military hardware dollar for dollar to other things valued by society:

> The cost of one modern heavy bomber is this: a modern brick school in more than 30 cities.
>
>   It is two electric power plants, each serving a town of 60,000 population.
>
>   It is two fine, fully equipped hospitals.
>
>   It is some 50 miles of concrete highway.
>
>   We pay for a single fighter with a half million bushels of wheat.
>
>   We pay for a single destroyer with new homes that could have housed more than 8,000 people.[36]

The trade-offs today are even starker. The costs of military equipment and weapon systems have risen far faster than the costs of food, housing, schools, and roads. For example, whereas a bomber in 1953 cost the equivalent of a new school in thirty cities, we could today build 171 elementary schools for the cost of just one B-2.[37] Ike's bomber cost as much as fifty miles of highway; today's bomber could buy more than three times as much.[38] Our newest fighter plane, the F-22, costs about $356 million, or 66 million bushels of wheat.[39] A typical Arleigh Burke destroyer costs about $1 billion to build. With that same amount of money, we could buy more than 5,200 single-family homes at the median home price of $191,600, enough for nearly 21,000 people.[40]

Or, when speaking of opportunity costs, consider the infamous "bridges to nowhere." Quietly tucked into the 2006 transportation bill by Alaska Senator Ted Stevens, the bridges would have connected the town of Ketchikan to Gravina Island (home to about fifty people) and given Anchorage residents easier access to the northern wetlands. The costs to the federal government totaled about $225 million for each bridge, with further plans for expanding the wetlands bridge at a cost of $2 billion.[41]

Sen. John McCain turned these symbols of Washington's out-of-control spending into one of his most reliable applause lines on the campaign trail. His tale of what he did to stop them from being built fit neatly with his image as a fiscal hawk, a committed conservative who jealously guarded the public purse.

Granted, those were wasteful and silly expenditures. But while he loudly railed against bridges to nowhere and other pork-barrel projects, McCain also enthusiastically backed the Iraq War, which was costing at the time at least $10 billion a month. In other words, one month's time in Iraq cost the equivalent of at least forty-four $225 million bridges.

And that is just one mission, in just one country. As noted above, the entire defense budget for FY 2009, including DoD's baseline budget and the supplemental budgets for Iraq and Afghanistan, totals more than $600 billion, with some estimates placing that figure closer to $800 billion. In 2009, we will spend enough on national defense to build at least 2,600 bridges. That is six new bridges in every congressional district.

It is unlikely that we need that many new bridges, and, even if we did, no one is arguing that the nation should divert 100 percent of its defense spending to other things. Nor is it obvious that if we reduced defense spending by 10 or 20 or 30 percent that those monies formerly dedicated to national defense would necessarily be shifted to new government-sponsored infrastructure projects. But presumably *some* of what is currently spent on defense would be, and presumably some of these bridges would go to *somewhere*. This is not meant as a normative statement about the relative merits of bridges versus bombs and bullets. The point is merely to illustrate the opportunity costs inherent in all government spending.

Are Defense Costs Opportunities?

Some take a dim view of considerations of opportunity costs, particularly when comparing public and private expenditures. Big government advocates claim that public expenditures address the needs of all of society, while spending by individuals and businesses are aimed chiefly at satisfying the desires of a small group of people. Then there is the multiplier effect, the presumption that a dollar spent by the government on a public works project, for example, will have beneficial residual effects throughout the economy. By this logic, spending by the government is inherently more constructive than spending by individuals or businesses.

Indeed, this was precisely the charge leveled against Eisenhower by some of the leading Keynesian economists of his day, including John Kenneth Galbraith, James Tobin, and Paul Samuelson. In one particularly pointed critique, Tobin, who would go on to become the youngest member of John F. Kennedy's Council of Economic Advisers and ultimately to a Nobel Prize, castigated Eisenhower's economic philosophy, especially as it pertained to national security spending.

Fears of large federal government budget deficits and high inflation, and an aversion to higher taxes and more generous government spending, Tobin wrote, were forcing "Uncle Sam [to fight] with one hand tied behind his back." Whereas Eisenhower fretted over the diversion of too much private capital into federal coffers, generally, and the defense budget, specifically, Tobin viewed government itself as the key to growing the nation's productive power, and he implied that spending by individuals and businesses created a misallocation of resources throughout society into goods and services of dubious value.[42]

Such views about the supposed benefits of government spending have come under close scrutiny during the past few decades, and with good reason. Contrary to Tobin's claims, economists have demonstrated that government spending is often unproductive and inefficient, and certainly more so than spending in the private sector.[43] And yet, much of the debate surrounding spending for the war in Iraq, for example, is cast in terms consistent with Tobin's message from fifty years ago.

During her campaign for the presidency, for example, Sen. Hillary Clinton called on voters to consider the long-term costs of replacing equipment and providing medical care for troops and survivors benefits for their families. When these costs are included, the war in Iraq could cost well over $1 trillion. According to Clinton, "that is enough to provide health care for all 47 million uninsured Americans and quality pre-kindergarten for every American child, solve the housing crisis once and for all, make college affordable for every American student, and provide tax relief to tens of millions of middle class families."[44]

During his successful campaign for the presidency, Barack Obama had an even more expansive vision for how the money for the war in Iraq might have been spent, dedicating an entire speech to the subject during an appearance in Charleston, West Virginia, in March 2008. According to Obama, the share of Iraq War spending paid just by West Virginians would be enough to provide health care for 450,000 people, hire 30,000 new elementary school teachers, and provide tuition assistance for 300,000 college students. A project for rebuilding the nation's roads and bridges would employ 2 million construction workers and "would cost just six percent of what we spend each year in Iraq," Obama said. A program for developing alternative energy sources would employ as many as 5 million Americans for less than what the nation spent in an eighteen-month period in Iraq.[45]

Such arguments implicitly assume that money not being spent on a war, or the military more generally, would be spent by the *government* on other *government* programs. That is shortsighted and ultimately counterproductive. It is crucial to think about opportunity costs in a broader sense. Such costs apply not just to what the government is spending and where the government might be spending elsewhere, but also what average taxpayers are not able or willing to spend because they are on the hook for paying for an enormous and seemingly permanent military industry, and also for the occasional wars.

One final point on opportunity costs and trade-offs. Those who argue that monies spent on the military would, ipso facto, otherwise be spent by government on something else often believe that the federal government's role in, say, stimulating the economy, or educating children, or providing health care and housing, is equivalent to its obligations to provide for the common defense. A creative reading of the commerce and general welfare clauses of the Constitution has given rise to such interpretations of federal power, but they are not universally embraced. Many Americans believe that the government *should* provide a social safety net, but all Americans believe that government *must* act to protect their lives, liberty, and property.

The existence of competition in all other areas where the federal government occasionally becomes involved, and the absence of comparable competition with respect to national defense, proves the point. Although government schools act like monopolies, it is not illegal for parents to send children to private schools, or to educate them at home. By contrast, the government's monopoly over the use of force abroad is undisputed.

To the extent that our grand strategy influences the size and shape of our military, both are problems. But while a powerful and entrenched political constituency disproportionately benefits from, and therefore clamors loudest for, a very large defense budget, this domestic pressure could not sustain such massive expenditures without an overarching strategy to back it up. Our current strategy obligates us to defend others at the expense of our own physical and economic security. It requires us to build and maintain large quantities of ships, planes, and armored vehicles, plus to pay the people who operate this equipment. A different strategy, one focused on our needs, would require a very different, and much smaller, military.

The opportunity costs associated with our current grand strategy and its attendant military posture must be weighed against the trade-offs within and among the various agencies dedicated to the one undisputed obligation of government: national defense. In this context, it is perfectly legitimate to ask whether a dollar spent to recruit, train, equip, and feed an additional soldier in the active-duty Army will have the same impact on national security as a dollar spent on satellite surveillance of suspected terrorists, or on intelligence analysts tasked with interpreting information gleaned from electronic intercepts, or on diplomats responsible for interacting with people in foreign countries. It is precisely these types of trade-offs that advocates of more military spending prefer not to discuss.

The Cost to Our System of Government

There are other costs as well. The Founders of our great nation—men such as George Washington, Thomas Jefferson, and James Madison—worried that wars would give rise to an overgrown military establishment that would upset the delicate balance between the three branches of government, and between the government and the people. Their careful reading of history, as well as their own personal experiences, confirmed their worst fears. A government instituted to preserve liberties could swiftly come to subvert them. A gloomy Jefferson opined, "The natural progress of things is for liberty to yield and government to gain ground."[46]

Madison added another crucial caveat, seeing warfare as a kind of Petri dish for the expansion of state power at the expense of the individual. "Of all enemies of public liberty," he wrote in 1795, "war is perhaps the most to be dreaded, because it comprises and develops the germ of every other." "No nation," Madison continued, "could preserve its freedom in the midst of continual warfare."[47] As noted in chapter 1, Washington saw "those overgrown military establishments…as particularly hostile to republican liberty."[48]

The evidence to support such claims is irrefutable. Throughout human history, government has grown during wartime, or other periods of great anxiety, and it rarely surrenders these powers when the crisis abates. The government instituted federal income tax withholding during World War II, and it still remains in effect. It took over 108 years to roll back the federal excise tax on long-distance telephone calls, a tax ostensibly enacted to pay for a war that lasted less than six months: the Spanish-American War.

Or consider the question more holistically. As Bruce Porter notes in *War and the Rise of the State,* "the *nonmilitary* sectors of the federal government actually grew at a faster rate in World War II than under the impetus of the New Deal."[49] All aspects of state power expand during times of war, including those that have nothing to do with actually fighting and winning battles on land or sea.

Anticipating that dynamic and determined to prevent it, the Framers set out explicitly to impede the government's capacity for waging war. They focused their efforts on the one branch of government that they feared would be most warlike: the executive. With memories of George III's abuses fresh in their minds, and fearing that a U.S. king would be similarly inclined to infringe on individual liberties, the Founders took particular care to limit the president's war-making powers. Even so strong an advocate of executive authority as Alexander Hamilton conceded that the legislature alone possessed the power to initiate wars, whereas the president's powers were confined to "the direction of war when authorized or begun."[50] When anti-Federalists claimed that Hamilton and other advocates of the new federal Constitution were attempting to create an office of the executive with the powers of a king, Hamilton responded with emphasis:

> The President is to be commander-in-chief of the army and navy of the United States. In this respect his authority would be nominally the same with that of the king of Great Britain, but in substance much inferior to it. It would amount to nothing more than the supreme command and direction of the military and naval forces, as first General and admiral of the Confederacy; while that of the British king extends to the *declaring* of war and to the *raising* and *regulating* of fleets and armies—all which, by the Constitution under consideration, would appertain to the legislature.[51]

Several years later, Hamilton and Madison were locked in a bitter debate over a particular exercise of executive power: Washington's declaration of impartiality in the war between England and France. Madison (writing as Helvidius) forcefully reminded his interlocutor that "the power to declare war, including the power of judging of the causes of war, is *fully* and *exclusively* vested in the legislature; that the executive has no right, in any case, to decide the question, whether there is or is not cause for declaring war." The president's sole role, Madison explained, was to call Congress into session and inform them of the circumstances so that the legislature—not the president—could make a decision on the wisdom or imprudence of war.[52]

Notwithstanding Madison's intention that Congress control the power to declare war, one of Madison's successors recognized rather well Congress's relative powerlessness. In 1846, President James K. Polk sent U.S. troops into territory claimed jointly by Mexico and the United States. When Mexican forces attacked a contingent under Gen. Zachary Taylor's command, Congress declared war, handing Polk the conflict that he wanted all along. Two years later, Congress formally censured Polk for exceeding his constitutional authority but by then the damage had already been done. In a letter to his law partner in Illinois, Rep. Abraham Lincoln noted:

> Allow the President to invade a neighboring nation whenever he shall deem it necessary to repel an invasion, and you allow him to do so whenever he may choose to say he deems it necessary for such purpose, and you allow him to make war at pleasure.... The provision of the Constitution giving the war making power to Congress was dictated, as I understand it, by the following reasons: kings had always been involving and impoverishing their people in wars, pretending generally, if not always, that the good of the people was the object. This our convention understood to be the most oppressive of all kingly oppressions, and they resolved to so frame the Constitution that no one man should hold the power of bringing this oppression upon us.[53]

Thus, Madison's concerns have proved prescient, but his system for constraining executive power has failed to live up to his expectations. Although the Constitution grants Congress the authority to declare war, and the president the authority to direct it once declared, our responses to recurring crises—both real and imagined—have fundamentally altered the balance of power.[54]

The process has been challenged along the way. The Supreme Court has adjudicated between the two other branches when there were disputes. But the courts and the Congress are both less capable of checking presidential power precisely because of the existence of a large and permanent military establishment. With the power to launch military action—at any place, and at any time—already in hand, presidents have regularly done so. The vast majority of cases in which the U.S. military has been deployed abroad since the end of World War II have not come about by virtue of congressional action following months (or even weeks) of public debate.

In 1973, Congress attempted to recover some of its prerogatives, but the War Powers Act has failed to constrain the president's ability to wage war without the consent of Congress. The pattern is familiar: the president as commander-in-chief sends the military into a particular hot spot, the news cameras capture footage of the troops landing, and then the White House notifies Congress that action has been taken. Long before the provisions of the War Powers Act kick in, Congress has either endorsed the mission, or it has come to an end.[55]

In a few cases, Congress has passed wartime authorizations, ostensibly granting the president the right to wage war at his discretion, but this merely reveals the depths of congressional weakness. Members of Congress take an oath of office not so dissimilar to that of the president: both pledge to uphold the Constitution. Senators or representatives cannot in good conscience vote to unilaterally abrogate their duties and responsibilities to declare war as stipulated in the Constitution any more than they can hand over to the president any of the other powers listed in Article I, Section 8, including the right to levy taxes, establish rules for the U.S. armed forces, and regulate interstate commerce and trade with foreign nations.

On rare occasions, Congress has passed resolutions objecting to the introduction of U.S. troops into a particular conflict only to be summarily ignored. In November 1995, the Republican-controlled Congress voted by a margin of 243–171 to prevent President Clinton from sending U.S. forces to Bosnia-Herzegovina as part of the Dayton Peace Agreement. Clinton sent them anyway. The Congress mounted no serious campaign to bring the troops home, and it is difficult to see how they would have succeeded even had they tried. Efforts in recent years by the Democratic-controlled Congress to bring an end to the war in Iraq repeatedly failed.

This subtle shift in the character of our system of government is one of the costs of our military power. It is a cost that is harder to measure than what we spend every year on our military, or on our wars, but is far more significant over the long term.

Many Americans who favor a large military engaged in numerous missions around the world concede that executive power grows during periods of crisis and threat, but they argue that times have changed so dramatically since the time of the founding of the Republic that Americans need no longer be concerned with the Founders' warnings. The Constitution is not a suicide pact.[56] The world is a dangerous place. There are people out there who wish to do us harm, and we must kill them before they kill us. If we feel insecure, despite having spent trillions of dollars on defense over the course of several decades, still more military spending will solve the problem.

Others dispute that these costs are worth worrying about, or even that they are costs at all; indeed, a few modern constitutional theorists contend that the accumulation of power into the hands of a single person, and more specifically the president's ability to wage war unencumbered by the Congress, is a positive good. John Yoo, a law professor at the University of California, Berkeley, who previously served in the Justice Department's Office of Legal Counsel, has consistently argued that the president's inherent powers to wage war are essentially unlimited. As Yoo sees it, the Founders "understood 'the executive power' in light of the British constitutional tradition, and in that tradition, taking the country into war was a royal prerogative." Writes Gene Healy in his book *The Cult of the Presidency*, "Though Article I, Section 8, of the Constitution gives Congress the power 'to declare War,' that power, Yoo argued, was far narrower than most modern scholars understood it to be, and it did not limit the president's ability to wage war at the time of his choosing."[57]

As noted above, Madison, Hamilton, Jefferson, and others realized that war was a vehicle whereby governments infringed upon individual liberty; it was appropriate, therefore, that they sought ways to limit their new government's propensity to wage war. Although he does not necessarily concede that point, to the extent that there are constitutional limits on the president's war powers, Yoo wishes to remove such restrictions. The confluence of "rogue states," terrorist organizations and weapons of mass destruction, he explains, requires a very different conception of warfare and war powers than the one the Founders envisioned. Given the threats of the twenty-first century, Yoo writes, "we should not...adopt a warmaking process that contains a built-in presumption *against* using force abroad."[58]

Actually, we should. Although there may be occasions when military force is required to eliminate an urgent threat to national security, and we must therefore maintain a strong military to deal with such threats, our capacity for waging war far exceeds that which is required for such contingencies. Our conventional military power is usually irrelevant when dealing with non-state actors such as al-Qaeda. In many cases, it is actually worse than irrelevant—it is counterproductive. Our vast military power too often robs us of our ability to discriminate between vital interests, and peripheral ones. We have the capacity to intervene in dozens of places around the world, and we often do so, divorced from any regard as to whether such interventions advance U.S. security. Our recent experience has shown that they often have the opposite effect.

Stirring Up Resentment Abroad

Our ability to wage war—and our propensity to do so—engenders resentment and hostility abroad. This hostility in its most extreme form is manifested in acts of terrorism against Americans. The Defense Science Board in 2004 put the matter succinctly: "American direct intervention in the Muslim World has paradoxically elevated the stature of and support for radical Islamists, while diminishing support for the United States to single-digits in some Arab societies....Muslims do not 'hate our freedom,' but rather, they hate our policies."[59]

As the 9/11 commission report explained, "America's policy choices have consequences. Right or wrong, it is simply a fact that American policy regarding the Israeli-Palestinian conflict and American actions in Iraq are dominant staples of popular commentary across the Arab and Muslim world." The commissioners hastened to add, "That does not mean U.S. choices have been wrong. It means those choices must be integrated with America's message of opportunity to the Arab and Muslim world." Or, put another way, even our well-intended policies carry costs, and these costs must be counted against our other important objectives.[60]

That is hardly a novel concept. Foreign policy experts have recognized that our power, and our propensity to use that power, invites anger and resentment. In extreme cases, that anger and resentment turns to violence. Robert Kagan, among the leading advocates of our current grand strategy—and, as noted in chapter 1 the man who, with William Kristol, coined the term "benevolent global hegemony"—freely admits that it makes us a target of terrorism. "It is precisely America's great power and its willingness to assume the responsibility for protecting other nations," Kagan writes in *Of Paradise and Power*, "that make it the primary target, and often the only target."[61]

In *The Case for Goliath*, Michael Mandelbaum characterizes U.S. policies that redound to the benefit of others as "gifts" because they "neither request nor pay for them." Curiously, he then contends that the United States "does not exactly suffer punishment," for providing these gifts, "although there are people around the world seeking to kill Americans out of hatred of its global role as well as the values it embodies."[62]

Such statements imply that we have no choice; that the costs of U.S. power are real, but they are also necessary. But at a more fundamental level, they reflect an inability to accurately assess all of the costs that we incur on account of our current grand strategy. The advocates of U.S. global hegemony employ gimmicks in an attempt to dismiss or diminish the costs, either by misrepresenting the scale of our superiority over prospective rivals, concealing tens or sometimes hundreds of billions of dollars within "emergency" appropriations, or simply by expressing spending as a share of national output.

But our current strategy costs us much more. Global hegemony has changed our government in profound and lasting ways. It extends beyond the Founders' concerns that an executive that had the power to wage war at will would be equally unconstrained in its exercise of extra-constitutional authority at home. What the Founders might not have appreciated was the extent to which the logic of warfare has extended to every nook and cranny of our life. The Bush administration declared that every place on earth is part of the battlefield in the "war on terrorism." The government has the right, said Bush administration lawyers, to scrutinize all manner of communication—telephone conversations, e-mail exchanges, text chats—to cull for patterns, for signs of criminal behavior, even when the objects of their surveillance are not suspected of having committed a crime. White House lawyers further implied that the war will have no definitive end point, that it will go on forever, meaning that the post-9/11 powers that they have claimed are essentially permanent.

To the extent that some of what they assert is true—indeed there are people who would like very much to get their hands on a nuclear device and detonate it in Manhattan or in Los Angeles—that, too, is a cost that many in Washington, DC, would prefer to ignore or dismiss entirely. Those who do not dismiss it—who admit that our great power and our willingness to use it make us a target for terrorism—have failed to accurately assess realistic alternatives. The advocates of global hegemony claim that the benefits that we derive as a nation from our military power are far greater than the costs; so much greater, in fact, that it makes no sense to even consider any alternatives.

This book now turns to scrutinizing such claims. It is not merely the costs of our power, but also our propensity to use it, that makes us less safe. Accordingly, solving our problem begins with reexamining common assumptions about the supposed benefits of U.S. power, and then considering new criteria for how and when we should use it.

CHAPTER FOUR

WE USE IT TOO MUCH

Our power is a problem because it costs too much, and it costs too much because we have too much. The United States has far more power than we need to defend ourselves and our vital interests, but we incorrectly believe that our security rests on a stable world order, and that we alone are capable of imposing that order. If we focused most of our attention on our own security, we would need less power, and we would use it less.

Consider how we have used our power in recent years. We use it to advance our security interests, the most important of which is to protect the territorial integrity of the United States. That object has not changed throughout U.S. history, and is consistent with how virtually all other countries employ their militaries: for self-defense. But we also take responsibility for defending others by binding ourselves to treaties negotiated during the Cold War, a conflict that ended nearly two decades ago. We fulfill these lingering obligations by deploying U.S. military equipment and personnel abroad, but also by extending to other countries the protection of our massive nuclear deterrent. In addition, we use our conventional military power to protect loosely defined global economic interests, which in practical terms means affording protections to sellers so that they can sell, and buyers so that they can buy. Our military provides such services, even when U.S. citizens are not a party to the transactions, on the specious grounds that the proper functioning of the international economic system is contingent upon our global military presence. This rationale is particularly prevalent with respect to one product that flows on the global market—oil—and the region from which much of that product originates—the Persian Gulf.

We also use our power, or we threaten to use it, in ways that have not even a hypothetical connection to defending the United States, or protecting Americans from physical or financial harm. We occasionally attempt to protect others from harm (including, in some cases, from their own governments), out of a sense of duty, as though we have a moral obligation—and the ability—to spread the blessings of liberty to people denied basic human rights. And when natural disasters or other tragedies strike, the U.S. military is often the first on the scene.

It is often said that the United States can only be secure if the entire world is secure, but the defenders of the status quo overstate the disorder that would ensue if the U.S. military was focused more specifically on our security, as opposed to the security of others. In a related vein, they grossly overstate the degree to which the United States is even capable of maintaining such an order. I have already documented the many ways in which the hegemonists understate the costs of our current grand strategy. This chapter explores the many exaggerated claims of the benefits that we supposedly enjoy as the world's policeman. In the next chapter, I examine the other aspect of our power problem: the use of U.S. military power to serve purely humanitarian ends, missions that have nothing to do with defending vital U.S. interests, but which we undertake purely out of a presumed moral obligation to help those in distress.

The World's Sheriff

It has become commonplace for people to refer to our military as a global constabulary force; some go so far as to say that the government of the United States acts as the government for the entire world.[1] The United States lacks any formal authority to do these things. There has been no global plebiscite conferring such powers upon us. Likewise, the U.S. Constitution doesn't explicitly stipulate that our government must perform this role—it speaks only of the common defense of "We the People of the United States"—nor have Americans been asked if they want it to. Indeed, polls show that a majority of Americans aren't interested in playing this role. And this shouldn't come as much of a surprise. As a leading advocate of our current strategy admits, "to make sacrifices largely for the benefit of others counts as charity, and for Americans, as for other people, charity begins at home."[2]

Uncle Sam has not been granted formal powers of global governance. Washington is unable to force its will on others in the way that past hegemons did. But the advocates of our current grand strategy contend that the absence of overt resistance to U.S. power implies a tacit acceptance of our global role, affording the United States a legitimacy that previous empires lacked.[3] Although many snipe at our power, some fret that we will not always use our power in useful or constructive ways, and a few fear that our great power will be used against them, the defenders of the status quo tell us that they would all be even more anxious if we were to use our great power less often.[4]

These notions, that most of the world welcomes our global military presence, and our power, and that chaos would ensue if the United States were to step back from its self-appointed role as global sheriff, are not new. As discussed in chapter 1, since the earliest days of the post–Cold War era, many foreign policy experts have warned of impending global catastrophe if the United States were to focus its attention on self-defense. Such fears became even more widespread in the wake of 9/11, and ultimately served as one of the justifications for the invasion of Iraq. For example, Michael Ignatieff, at the time a professor at Harvard and currently a member of the Canadian Parliament, endorsed the Iraq War as necessary for advancing world order and intimated that only the United States was capable of undertaking such a mission. Quoting Herman Melville, Ignatieff explained that it fell to Americans to "bear the ark of the liberties of the world."[5] A few months later, British prime minister Tony Blair spoke before a joint session of Congress in which he addressed those Americans asking, "Why me? And why us? And why America?" Blair had a simple answer: "Because Destiny puts you in this place in history, in this moment in time, and the task is yours to do."[6]

One wonders how these men know so well what destiny intends for Americans. In fairness, however, many Americans—including most famously George W. Bush—routinely invoke God's will as sufficient to justify our actions abroad. It is well beyond the scope of this work to inveigh on the theological merit of such pronouncements, but it should be obvious that such beliefs are an insufficient guide for the conduct of U.S. foreign policy. Although Bush and others might genuinely believe to be doing God's work on Earth, the United States is not nearly that powerful. The costs and risks associated with bearing the weight of the world on our shoulders are not so inconsequential that we can ignore the essential responsibilities that should be at the core of *any* nation's foreign policies; first and foremost of which are concerns over physical security.

These core obligations should be at the forefront of their—and our—minds when weighing what to do, and where to do it, and should constrain policymakers' inclinations to intervene militarily. Imminent threats take precedence over urgent ones; urgent displaces important; important overshadows annoying, or marginal. Chaos on one's borders is of greater concern than unrest on the other side of the planet, and threats to one's own citizens must take priority over threats to others. A government that properly prioritizes all that it must do will necessarily be focused on ongoing crises in the here and now, even as it prepares for hypothetical ones in the future.

Putting aside the supposed commands of "destiny," and focusing on our own security, it should be obvious that our challenges are manageable, and certainly far less serious than that of many other countries around the world. We are protected by two vast oceans, have no fear of a war with Canada or Mexico—the only two countries that could invade us by land—and we possess an array of diplomatic assets and military capabilities that enable us to deploy forces on short notice virtually anywhere in the world. Indeed, the sheer size and scale of the U.S. military, in terms of number of ships, aircraft, and personnel, so dominates any discussion of world affairs that policymakers often simply assume that any foreign policy initiative will include a substantial military component—even when non-military solutions are usually more appropriate. As the familiar expression goes, when all you have is a hammer, every problem starts to look like a nail.

As discussed in chapter 1, we held onto our hammer after the collapse of the Soviet Union, and we pounded a number of nails, intervening militarily in more places in the fifteen years after the fall of the Berlin Wall than we had in the nearly forty-five years of the Cold War. Despite making some cuts in the military, policymakers retained a still-sizable force out of fear that the world might descend into chaos were it not for the presence of hundreds of thousands of U.S. troops around the world. Indeed, defenders of the status quo now, nearly two decades after the end of the Cold War, often argue not that we spend too much on our military, but rather that we spend too little. And in a certain sense that is correct. *If* the United States maintains its current foreign policies, predicated on the erroneous assumption that all of the problems of the world are our problems, and that other countries are congenitally incapable of dealing with urgent challenges on their borders, or in their immediate neighborhood, then we most certainly will have to increase military spending.

Conversely, if we were to focus on all of the instruments of our power— including our military and economic strength, our relatively favorable geostrategic position, our reservoir of soft power (still considerable despite the erosion that occurred during George W. Bush's tenure as president), and, perhaps most important, our model of constitutional governance based on a separation of power between contending branches—we should see a very different grand strategy emerge, one that capitalizes on, rather than diminishes, those great strengths. As it is today, our current grand strategy ignores—or, worse, undermines and erodes—that which makes us strong. We have no hostile neighbors, but our current grand strategy assumes responsibility for countries that do. Our Founders limited our likelihood of being involved in foreign wars by investing the war powers in the Congress, but our current grand strategy hands these decisions over to the executive branch, or, worse, to our allies who might engage in reckless behavior and draw us into wars without the consent of the American people. The advocates of benevolent hegemony contend that the international economic order might come crashing down without the omnipresent U.S. military threatening random pirates or fraudulent operators. A different grand strategy would build on the more plausible assumption that the international economic order is far too complex, and the scale of transactions far too great, to be policed by a single superpower, no matter how large and intrusive that superpower's military might be. A new grand strategy, built around these very different assumptions about our interests and the way the world works, would require U.S. policymakers to separate and prioritize urgent concerns from less urgent or irrelevant ones, and focus on devolving many of our current military obligations to other countries.

The conceptions of national interest foisted on the American people by leaders in both major political parties, and the rationales and justifications put forward for military action to safeguard our supposedly tenuous security, are based on the simple proposition that the world is sitting atop a combustible log pile, that every incipient conflict can become the spark that engulfs the planet, and that the United States is the only country with a bucket of water to extinguish the spark before it ignites a flame.[7] Madeleine Albright's confident assertion that "We stand tall and we see further than other countries into the future, and we see the danger here to all of us," nicely encapsulates the dominant worldview among policymakers in Washington. Believing that every simmering ethnic and sectarian conflict is likely to bloom into full-scale war, Washington contemplates sending the U.S. military into the middle of these squabbles. Believing that demographic trends will precipitate a pell-mell scramble for scarce resources, and that these scrambles are likely to turn violent, U.S. policymakers offer to preserve a peaceful global economic order. Seeing every tin-pot tyrant with a megaphone as the next Adolf Hitler, someone in Washington makes plans to whack them before they realize their wicked ambitions. As Senator John McCain proclaimed in his defense of the first Gulf War, if America failed to act to reverse Hussein's aggression against Kuwait, "there will be inevitably a succession of dictators" that would present "a threat to the stability of this entire globe."[8]

In 1994, the *Atlantic Monthly*'s Robert Kaplan warned of an equally alarming prospect: "the coming anarchy." In Kaplan's view, Western strategists needed to start concerning themselves with "what is occurring...throughout West Africa and much of the underdeveloped world: the withering away of central governments, the rise of tribal and regional domains, the unchecked spread of disease, and the growing pervasiveness of war."[9] Less than two years later, William Kristol and Robert Kagan wrote, "American hegemony is the only reliable defense against a breakdown of peace and international order."[10]

That was not true in 1994, or 1996, and it is not true today. Although the stated rationales have changed since 9/11, with various advocacy groups using the fear of future terrorist attacks as a vehicle for pushing their pet projects—from nuclear disarmament, to removing Saddam Hussein, to averting global climate change, to ending the so-called U.S. addiction to oil—the underlying reality has not. Most of the time, our government has no business sending U.S. troops into the middle of foreign tangles, because most military interventions have only the slightest connection to the problems they purport to solve, and, to the extent that there is a connection, the use of the military is likely to exacerbate the problem. We are left, then, with the same flawed rationales as before 9/11: the erroneous belief that the United States is the only country on the planet with the wisdom, foresight, and capacity to propel the planet toward the future, and the related notion that we alone are capable of preventing the world from descending into total, bloody chaos.

People who favor the United States performing the role of global sheriff envision the world as both more threatening and simpler than it actually is.[11] Indeed, to read much of what passes for serious discussion in foreign policy circles today, one might conclude that the United States isn't simply the world's indispensable nation, but rather that it is the world's *only* nation, or at least the only nation with the sense and the foresight to even have a foreign policy in the first place. But our fear of instability is largely overblown: failed states and civil wars rarely represent security threats to the United States. Such conditions, however, often represent security threats to *other* states, usually nearby states, that should be expected to deal with most such crises long before they engulf a particular region, let alone consume the planet.

At the same time, the world is vastly more complex than the interventionists would have it: overthrowing undemocratic regimes, fixing failed states, or stopping civil wars or ethnic and sectarian violence, are all exceptionally difficult tasks. It could be reasonably argued that in an era of transnational threats and weapons of mass destruction we can't afford to be absolutely certain that a threat will materialize, and that in such circumstances the costs of inaction are outweighed by the costs of action. President Bush made that argument explicitly with respect to Iraq.[12] But Bush's logic was intended to apply not merely to one case, but to all cases. Speaking to West Point Cadets in June 2002, he declared: "In the world we have entered, the only path to safety is the path of action. And this nation will act."[13]

Get Your Retaliation in First

Although presidential rhetoric often gets ahead of what presidential administrations are actually willing to do, in March 2003 President Bush demonstrated his willingness to make good on his pledge to use U.S. military power to eliminate a potential threat *before* the threat from that regime manifested itself when he launched the war against Iraq—a classic case of preventive war.[14]

Historically, preventive wars have rarely passed the cost-benefit test. Bismarck put the point vividly when he characterized preventive war as akin to "committing suicide from fear of death."[15] Taking account of the great strength of the United States relative to the countries that we might wage war against, contemporary advocates of preventive war presume that what comes after war will be an improvement over that which came before—both in terms of U.S. security, and often to the welfare of the people in the country we plan to attack.[16]

The most recent instance of preventive war, the invasion of Iraq, has proved far more costly than originally estimated. Meanwhile, the potential benefits still seem very uncertain. Carnegie Endowment Senior Fellow Robert Kagan contends that "A stable, pro-American Iraq would shift the strategic balance [in the Middle East] in a decidedly pro-American direction,"[17] but it is also true that post-Saddam Iraq could become even more dangerous than it was before we invaded. If a civil war, for example, precipitates a wider regional conflict, or if future generations of Iraqis focus their enmity on Americans for having unleashed chaos in their country, then we'll have paid a high price for less, rather than more, security.

The most fervent advocates of the Iraq War argued that the United States should attack Iraq first because it would be relatively easy.[18] Proving that the United States had the power to eliminate odious regimes, they argued, would allegedly increase the likelihood that Kim Jong Il and the mullahs in Iran would capitulate to U.S. demands. But if they did not, an emboldened United States would be in an even stronger position to turn on them.[19]

In retrospect, the war hawks were probably correct in at least one respect: regime change *was* relatively easy in Iraq, easier certainly than it would be in many of the other countries on the list of failed or failing states, and easier than in either North Korea or Iran, the other two countries named in Bush's "Axis of Evil." But this fact refutes rather than confirms the theory of prevention. To the extent that Iraq was to have been relatively easy, the enormous costs and still uncertain benefits of our intervention there suggest that preventive regime change followed by long-term nation building will be even harder elsewhere.

The Iraq War is merely the latest of many missions that we have undertaken in our self-appointed role as global cop. If the world truly needed just one order-imposing hegemon, and if the United States were the only country willing and able to play this role, then the difficulties that we have encountered—such as the vast disparity between the predicted and actual costs of one operation in one medium-size country—would spell big trouble for several billion people. But we should not be so pessimistic.

To be sure, if it were to materialize, there is a point at which Robert Kaplan's "coming anarchy" would threaten U.S.—and not just U.S.—interests. Niall Ferguson supposes that, if America were to step back from its role as a global policeman, the world would be characterized by "Waning empires. Religious revivals. Incipient anarchy. A coming retreat into fortified cities. These are the Dark Age experiences that a world without a hyperpower might quickly find itself reliving."[20]

But it is instructive that Ferguson had to reach back to the ninth century to find a historical precedent on which to base his argument. In fact, there is little reason to believe that the world will descend down this path if the United States hews to a restrained foreign policy focused on preserving its national security and advancing its vital interests. That is because there are other governments in other countries, pursuing similar policies aimed at preserving their security, and regional—much less global—chaos is hardly in their interests. On the contrary, the primary obligation of government is to defend the citizens from threats, both foreign and domestic. Curiously, our conduct in recent years suggests that U.S. policymakers doubt that other governments see their responsibilities in this way.

On Free Riding

Why do other countries not do more now? Why do other governments underprovide for their own defense, on the hope or expectation that the U.S. military will ride to the rescue if they get in trouble? In large part because that is how

Washington likes it, and the leaders of other countries therefore have little reason to change.

By spending hundreds of billions of dollars on our military, by holding out this so-called public good as a boon to all mankind, and by actually using this enormous military in defense of others on occasion, we have discouraged our allies from spending more and doing more. The Europeans, the Japanese, the South Koreans, and others have the economic wherewithal to substantially increase their own defense spending, and take greater responsibility for regional security, but they have not done so. Indeed, at present, it is not in their interest to do so.[21]

"The most consequential problem in European-American relations," writes Michael Mandelbaum, is "the failure of those governments to muster the resources to make major contributions to global governance. Their failure means that when the United States acts unilaterally, it does so as much by default as by design."[22] But while Mandelbaum recognizes this crucial problem, he can conceive of no realistic alternative. "For better or for worse," he concludes, "the world has, in the first decade of the twenty-first century, no substitute for the United States as the provider of governmental defense services to the international system. The American government and the American public...will *not have the option* that, all other things being equal, they might well prefer: sharing that burden with others."[23] If Mandelbaum is right, and if we do not change course, or create new options, then we will remain locked in a vicious cycle in which our allies grow weaker, the gap between our commitments to them and the means available to us to meet those commitments will grow wider, and the resources that will be required to close the gap will be provided almost exclusively by U.S. taxpayers. But to the extent that this is a problem largely of our own making, then it is equally in our power to fix it by ceasing to underwrite the security of others, therefore pushing them toward self-reliance.

The free riding of our allies is more than simply opportunistic; it also reflects differing conceptions of threat, which are a function of our imagined responsibilities at the center of a unipolar world. Advocates of benevolent global hegemony contend that Americans are more inclined to assume global responsibilities, a function of American exceptionalism combined with a pervasive culture of weakness among our allies. Although they concede that it would be nice if our allies would do more, they counter that it would be irresponsible to base our strategy on the assumption that they will. On the contrary, the hegemonists assume that the allies would not because they have not done so since at least the end of the Cold War.[24]

This ignores the extent to which our grand strategy has discouraged them from doing so. Many countries do not see a need for power of their own. Our possession of great power has contributed to a steady expansion of our concepts of security, and a commensurate erosion of their responsibilities.

The problem has been exacerbated by the perception held by many U.S. foreign policy scholars that our power confers upon us the ability to fundamentally shape the global order at relatively low cost. Through our faith in our ability to solve problems in a proactive way, we expand our definitions of what constitutes our national interest, and other countries' security challenges become our own. We are not content to tolerate threats that seem tolerable to weaker states. We wish to solve problems, and we believe that we have the power to do so. This confidence has been battered, but not broken, by what has occurred in Iraq. Still, one of Iraq's many lessons is that the ability to act does not automatically translate into the ability to succeed.

Even more important, power—the ability to act—does not confer wisdom; it does not tell us when we *should* act. On the contrary, as Machiavelli noted in his discourses: "Men always commit the error of not knowing where to limit their hopes, and by trusting to these rather than to a just measure of their resources, they are generally ruined."[25]

As Machiavelli would have predicted, the notion of what Americans must do to preserve and advance our own security has steadily expanded over the years to encompass the defense of others. Seemingly unconstrained by the resources at our disposal, we are driven by our dreams of fashioning a new global order. But we are also driven by false fears. We believe that we can only be secure if others are secure, that insecurity anywhere poses a threat to Americans everywhere. If someone on the other side of the planet sneezes, the United States is supposedly in danger of catching pneumonia. The putative cure is preventive war. Such geostrategic "hypochondria" has gotten us all into much trouble over the years.[26] We would be wise to take measure of our relative health and vitality, and not confuse a head cold with cancer.

The Problem with Global Public Goods

Beyond the erroneous view that U.S. security is so fragile that we must act to prevent instability anywhere in the world is the related, but equally false, belief that U.S. participation in the global economy is contingent upon our vast military power. The advocates of U.S. global hegemony often argue that because the United States is the leading beneficiary of the international economic system, we have both a special obligation and a unique interest in maintaining that order.[27]

Such sentiments formed in the wake of World War II, and hardened over the course of the Cold War. In Western Europe, and in parts of East Asia, the people were devastated by war, and fearful that a third world war was in the offing. For several decades, the United States played the role of protector. The role was largely self-appointed, but it was also generally accepted. For starters, there was no attractive alternative. The countries of Eastern Europe were not given a choice after the end of World War II; the Red Army was there when Hitler's Third Reich collapsed, and there the Red Army stayed—for nearly forty-five years. By way of comparison, some historians refer to the U.S. military presence in Western Europe as an "empire by invitation."[28]

In the post–Cold War era, we have maintained our global military presence. Individuals enamored of the role of the United States as the world's sheriff point to the domestic analogy of fighting crime. We'd much prefer if everyone behaved themselves, and respected the rights of others, but the world doesn't work that way. And because others will not act, we must.

"The United States does act as an international sheriff, self-appointed perhaps but widely welcomed nevertheless, trying to enforce some peace and justice in what Americans see as a lawless world where outlaws need to be deterred or destroyed, often through the muzzle of a gun," writes Robert Kagan. "Europe, by this Wild West analogy, is more like the saloonkeeper. Outlaws shoot sheriffs, not saloonkeepers."[29]

It is a deeply flawed analogy, based on the mythical Wild West portrayed in Hollywood movies. The picture of sniveling, cowardly townspeople hiding behind the heroic sheriff, standing alone against the outlaws—Gary Cooper in *High Noon* is the enduring archetype—makes for good drama, but is no more grounded in reality than the Wild West portrayed in Mel Brooks's *Blazing Saddles.* The people living in the Western territories in the late nineteenth century were independent and autonomous individuals. They were highly capable of defending themselves, and inclined to take matters into their own hands when the long arm of the law couldn't quite reach their corner of the world, which was most of the time. The members of the notorious James-Younger Gang learned that lesson the hard way. When they attempted to rob the First National Bank in Northfield, Minnesota, in September 1876, the townspeople cut them to pieces, killing gang members Clell Miller and William Stiles, and wounding a number of the other would-be bank robbers who took flight. The gang split up, but a massive posse comprised chiefly of private citizens carrying their own guns chased down and eventually captured the three Younger brothers: Cole, Bob, and Jim.[30]

Kagan's analogy is not merely flawed; it is also curious, particularly if it is intended to increase public support in the United States for our continuing to play the role of embattled sheriff. Americans spend hundreds of billions of dollars every year providing security so that others do not have to. We sometimes take risks, including the chance of being shot by outlaws, but we supposedly expect nothing in return. Indeed, when we do act, we measure the success or failure of such efforts not by how well we are doing, but rather by how others are doing. Why, one might ask, have we borne such costs, and incurred such risks, so that others may benefit from our largesse?

We have done so, ostensibly, because the costs of doing so are small, and are largely incidental to actions that we take mostly for our own benefit. Our situation is analogous to that of an "owner of a large, expensive, lavishly-furnished mansion surrounded by more modest homes," explains Mandelbaum. If that owner chooses to pay for security guards to patrol the street, "their presence will serve to protect the neighboring houses as well, even though their owners contribute nothing to the cost of the guards."[31]

But where Mandelbaum sees merit in a situation in which the average American "pays and the rest of the world...benefits without having to pay,"[32] there are ample grounds for questioning his conclusions. By definition, public goods have two characteristics.[33] First, once provided, their benefits cannot be denied to those for whom the original provision was not intended. Economists refer to this as nonexcludability. The other crucial feature of public goods, nonrivalrous consumption, holds that the value of the good is not diminished as additional consumers partake of it.

In *The Logic of Collective Action,* economist Mancur Olson uses the example of a parade down a busy city street to show that public or collective goods must be defined by the particular group that they serve. On the one hand, some spectators will pay to sit in the bleachers along the parade route, and the parade for them is a private good, not so different from other forms of entertainment such as sporting events or plays. For people living or working in tall buildings that overlook the street, on the other hand, the parade is a free good. Because it would be impractical to compel all witnesses to the parade to pay for this particular form of entertainment, and likewise and conversely infeasible to exclude nonpayers from viewing the spectacle, the organizers of the parade expect some degree of free riding.[34] They should also expect some complaints. Some neighbors might object to the noise, the traffic, the litter from the crowds, and might suffer other inconveniences associated with the event. Such harmful effects are the other side of the public goods coin; call them public bads.

Olson uses a number of other analogies to detail the problem of free riding and the related "collective action problem" in his seminal text. The discussion, however, is grounded almost exclusively in the context of domestic policy. Specifically, Olson notes the difficulty that interest groups have in obtaining and sustaining support from those who benefit from their activities. "Though all of the members of the group ... have a common interest in obtaining the collective benefit, they have no common interest in paying the cost of providing that collective good."[35] It is precisely for this reason why governments and labor unions rely on coercive taxation and compulsory membership, respectively, to guarantee payments from prospective beneficiaries.

Economists and political scientists have applied public goods theory to the study of international relations and alliance behavior over the past forty years, and the resulting economic theory of alliances has some important differences from our understanding of public goods in a domestic context.[36] Olson began the discussion in 1966, and, with co-author Richard Zeckhauser, observed two pervasive features of alliance behavior. The first is the free-rider problem endemic in all public goods, alternatively described as the exploitation thesis, whereby smaller members in an alliance free ride on the security guarantees provided by larger members. The second condition is suboptimality, the tendency of individual member states within an alliance to provide a less than optimal amount of security. What individual members commit to defense, Olson and Zeckhauser showed, is affected by what their alliance partners spent.[37]

A number of writers disputed elements of the Olson-Zeckhauser thesis, some going so far as to question the premise that alliances are collective goods in the first place. The realization that defense on an international level is not a pure public good should factor into considerations of when—and even whether—to offer protection to others, particularly to those who are unlikely to provide comparable benefits in return.[38] When individual alliance members develop additional military capacity, such capacity is intended chiefly to fulfill a private need—namely their own defense—but these expenditures often also serve particular domestic economic interests.[39] In the process, these member states move away from being free riders, as the exploitation thesis predicts, but paradoxically the alliance assets become less public, per se. That alliances constitute imperfect mixed goods, at best, becomes even clearer when disaggregating the goals that alliances seek to achieve.

For example, during the Cold War, NATO's mission included both deterrence and defense functions. It might be technically true that extended deterrence—the pledge to respond to an attack on one as the equivalent of an attack on all—is neither rivalrous nor excludable and therefore would qualify as a public good. For instance, threatening retaliation for an attack on Berlin would have the same effect as a threat to respond to an attack on Bologna, *provided the threats succeeded in deterring an attack.*[40] However, because strategic deterrence offered through the threat of nuclear retaliation could not be relied upon 100 percent of the time, the proposed public good being offered—more generally, security—is dependent on the alliance's ability to defend member states in the event that deterrence fails. In that context, there is a finite quantity of resources allocated to defense, not all areas of the alliance can be defended equally well, and policy-makers must choose where military assets are deployed. The allocation of assets to one ally necessarily diminishes the amount that can be used by another ally, and is likely to be affected by a host of considerations that on the whole would make that benefit excludable, and therefore not a pure public good.[41]

Meanwhile, consider the other aspect of public goods. A public good provided to one member of a group, by definition, can be provided to others at little or no marginal cost. If that were true of alliances, then new members could be added without diminishing the security of existing members. Is that actually the case?

Adding new alliance members might not, strictly speaking, undermine the value of the alliance writ large—assuming, again, that the threat of retaliation by all in response to an attack on one succeeds in deterring an attack. But given that deterrence *can* fail—Britain and France's alliance with Poland in 1939, after all, did not deter the Nazis and the Soviets from negotiating the Molotov-Ribbentrop Pact and then jointly attacking the Poles—then the addition of new members increases the likelihood that all alliance members will be drawn into a war.[42] As such, to the extent that the ultimate benefit sought from the alliance—greater security for all members, which may be defined as the assurance that they will not become involved in a war—is diminished by the addition of new consumers and therefore the supposed public good is *not* nonrivalrous. On the contrary, small, weak countries on the periphery of a given alliance's zone of influence will be more vulnerable to attacks than are the more capable core members located far from hostile neighbors. Therefore, as new members have been added to NATO over the past ten years, all previous members of the alliance have suffered a diminution of the benefits that they receive from the alliance so long as deterrence remains contingent (and how can it not?).

The risk for NATO members was dramatically revealed in August 2008 by the dispute between Russia and Georgia over the separatist territories of South

Ossetia and Abkhazia. Advocates of Georgian membership in NATO contended that NATO's refusal to grant a Membership Action Plan for Georgia and Ukraine at the NATO summit in Bucharest in April 2008 served as a green light to Russian aggression, and were equally convinced that a strong show of support for Georgia before the August crisis would have deterred the Russians from intervening. *Washington Post* columnist George Will put the matter succinctly: "If Georgia were in NATO, would NATO now be at war with Russia? More likely, Russia would not be in Georgia." It seems at least equally likely that Georgian leader Mikheil Saakashvili's confidence that the alliance members, and especially the United States, would come to his assistance, encouraged him to launch an ill-considered attack on South Ossetia and therefore that a stronger signal of support from alliance members would have only increased the Georgian leader's appetite for confrontation with Russia. This alternative point of view takes account of the moral hazard problem endemic to alliances in general, but also appreciates NATO's eroding credibility in particular. If the "Georgia in NATO" advocates had had their way, the skeptics warn, the United States might have found itself in a shooting war with Russia. There is simply no way of knowing which side is correct.[43]

At its more basic level, however, to the extent that one accepts the public goods rationale at all, one must also accept the exploitation thesis that smaller, weaker countries will free ride on the backs of larger, stronger countries. In practical terms, this means that essentially *all* countries free ride on the United States.

Those who celebrate the role of the United States as the world's policeman do not dispute the free rider problem, but they dismiss it far too lightly. Free riding thrives where authority is weak or ambiguous. In the United States, many people benefit from government services, but they pay for these services, indirectly at least, through taxation.[44] Few taxpayers enjoy paying taxes, but most recognize that some government is necessary, and that it must be paid for. For those who disagree, and who would wish to opt out, the IRS will find them. You cannot legally refuse to pay for public safety programs initiated by the government, even if you do not directly partake of the programs, or if the government that creates and maintains them is populated by people you didn't vote for.[45]

Thus the United States as world government analogy falls apart; whereas there are no legal free rides at home, the international system is full of free-riding behavior because there is no widely accepted normative standard of global governance. There are no accepted criteria for adjudicating questions of who should pay for what and how much. There are no provisions for forcing people to pay even if we could reach agreement on a formula for calculating such things. In effect, in an increasingly interconnected global system, every act that a government takes on behalf of its citizens—and for which its citizens pay—*might* redound to the benefit of non-payers in other countries. But it is difficult, if not impossible, to develop a framework for compelling compliance, or for efficiently allocating responsibilities among the many different players.

This is not to suggest that the activities of individual players do not benefit others within the international system; they do. Economists call these positive externalities. There are in fact many such instances that occur independent of any formal treaty obligating members to assist one another. To use a hypothetical example, when Canadian police capture, Canadian prosecutors try, and Canadian judges sentence, a Moroccan-born citizen of the Netherlands on charges of providing material support to a terrorist organization, all of these law enforcement functions are paid for solely by Canadian taxpayers—but many non-Canadians benefit. Still, because an individual working in government does not have an infinite capacity to apprehend all suspects, try all cases, and incarcerate all criminals, he or she must prioritize, and can and should be expected to give priority to his or her country's needs over those of others. It is not simply a case of patriotism; it is basic common sense.

In a similar vein, because the U.S. government's central responsibility under the Constitution is to protect the people of the United States, every person who draws a federal paycheck is and must be focused above all else on their duties and obligations to their employer—the government of the United States, and, indirectly at least, the American people. Although their work activities might, from time to time, benefit people in other countries, it would be unreasonable for people elsewhere to expect that they will. And, paradoxically, to the extent that they do have such expectations, this will discourage these individuals from demanding (and paying for) their governments to fulfill these same duties.

Recall the case of the wealthy landowner whose purchase of security services for his home ostensibly benefits his neighbors. The analogy to the United States creating a global public good as a side-effect of its providing for its own security is less advantageous for the United States than the advocates of benevolent global hegemony posit. After all, no one in the neighborhood benefits if the occupants of smaller houses discontinue their home monitoring services, leave their homes and cars unlocked, and advertise the fact that their property is unlocked and unguarded. This tendency of the weak to free ride on the strong, and to grow still weaker in the process, is a recurrent condition predicted by the economic theory of alliances.

If free riding and suboptimality were the only problems associated with alliances as collective goods, then our many security commitments might still be preferable to realistic alternatives. There are other costs and risks, however. First, as already noted, interests are not fixed. Americans' conceptions of what we need to be safe are shaped by our power. We are less willing to simply tolerate insecurity in far corners of the globe so long as we perceive, incorrectly in many cases, that our power gives us the ability to fix this insecurity. But we persist in believing such things. We continue to act, even if we do not always succeed, while other countries underprovide for their defense. Sensing that still more instability will result as a function of others doing too little, we are caught in a vicious cycle in which we feel compelled to acquire still more power to fill the void.

Meanwhile, just as a person's actions might inadvertently benefit others, the opposite is also true; when a person's actions have a detrimental effect on the well-being of others, economists call these negative externalities. The negative externalities that occur by virtue of our providing global public goods should not be taken lightly. Americans tend to see our actions as transparently good, our intentions beyond reproach. We prefer to focus on the good that comes from U.S. military interventions, and dismiss the unintended "bads" as the unfortunate but necessary side-effect of our well-intended actions.[46]

In Robert Kagan's Wild West analogy, the Europeans (in the role of saloonkeeper) look upon the U.S. sheriff as more dangerous than the international miscreants that Uncle Sam is trying to bring to justice. "From the saloonkeeper's point of view," Kagan explains, "the sheriff trying to impose order by force can sometimes be more threatening than the outlaws, who, at least for the time being, may just want a drink."[47]

Kagan reminds us, perhaps unintentionally, that when we provide a service for which, by definition, we are not paid and that we have not been asked to provide, others might reasonably object, and they might even take steps to stop us from acting, even if they ultimately fail to prevent it. In this context, consider the discussion of public bads at the beginning of this section, where some neighbors were harmed by the staging of a parade, but were not compensated for their losses. Analogous situations arise when the United States intervenes militarily on behalf of a particular government, or on behalf of a people who are oppressed by their government, and the harmful effects of the intervention are felt by others who just happen to be living in the vicinity.

That is certainly what happened in the case of Iraq. In the months before the invasion, the Bush administration attempted to convince Iraq's neighbors to support the mission, but not all were willing to do so. NATO ally Turkey feared that the collapse of Saddam Hussein's regime would pave the way for Kurdish independence. Tiny Jordan, already straining under the burdens imposed by as many as 1.7 million Palestinian refugees, feared an influx of new refugees from Iraq. Saudi Arabia worried that the toppling of Sunni rule in Iraq would strengthen Shiite Iran—a long-time nemesis—and would also embolden the sizable Shiite minority in the kingdom to rise up against the Sunni House of Saud. Although some people in all of these countries may have been generally content to see Saddam's tyrannical rule come to an end, they opposed the manner in which the United States brought it about because they worried (correctly, as it turned out) that the effects of regime change in Iraq would be harmful to them.

Just as the sheriff and the bandit might shoot up a saloon, or, in the modern context, as a police officer called to the scene of a domestic disturbance might inadvertently kill an innocent bystander, there is always a risk that the U.S. military, in its putative role as provider of global public goods, will cause harm. The extent to which our role as global sheriff is seen as legitimate determines whether such well-intentioned accidents will be deemed acceptable or intolerable. For a growing number of people around the world, the answer is clearly the latter.[48]

Nuclear Non-Proliferation and Extended Deterrence

As mentioned above, deterrence can be considered a public good within an alliance if it succeeds, but constitutes a public bad if it fails, by increasing the likelihood that all members will be drawn into wars that might otherwise have concerned only a few states. The advocates of American hegemony tend to dismiss such risks. They also tend to assume that if the United States were to focus its efforts toward its own defense, adopting a more restrained and less costly military posture, that other countries would be more likely to try to defend themselves. Although most Americans would welcome such a move, the hegemonists fear it.[49] For example, Michael Mandelbaum warns that if the U.S. military presence in Europe and East Asia were withdrawn, "the countries in both regions would feel less confident that no threat to their security would appear. They would, in all likelihood, take steps to compensate for the absence of these forces." And one of the steps that these countries might take, Mandelbaum darkly warns, is the fateful decision to acquire nuclear weapons.[50] Mandelbaum and other advocates of American hegemony celebrate the extent to which our possession of a large nuclear arsenal, and our professed willingness to use this arsenal to defend others, advances a collective interest—namely, the slowing of the spread of nuclear weapons.[51]

U.S. counter-proliferation policy actually proceeds on several tracks. We devote some resources to converting nuclear weapons into nuclear material for peaceful use, and we have also paid to dismantle thousands of nuclear warheads since the end of the Cold War. The Bush administration experimented with using military action, or the threat of action, to discourage states from moving down a nuclear weapons path, but these efforts largely failed. Iraq had no nuclear weapons program, and the other two targets of the Bush administration, Iran and North Korea, accelerated their nuclear programs following the U.S. invasion of Iraq.[52]

Extended deterrence constitutes the third aspect of U.S. nuclear non-proliferation policy. Beginning during the early years of the Cold War, Washington offered to afford the citizens of London, Paris, and Tokyo the same protections granted to Americans living in Louisville, Portland, and Topeka. By extending such security guarantees, U.S. policymakers sought to stiffen the allies' resolve to stand fast against Soviet and Chinese pressure, and they also hoped to discourage these allies from developing their own nuclear arsenals.

This effort was not entirely successful. Over the years, the United Kingdom and then France chose to develop their own nuclear weapons. The UK detonated its first device in 1952; France joined the nuclear weapons club in 1960. But some U.S. allies resisted the temptation. Japan has remained a non-nuclear weapon state, even though it many years ago acquired the technical capacity to go nuclear.

That the British, French, and Japanese each responded in slightly different ways to the U.S. pledge of extended nuclear deterrence should not surprise, because extended deterrence is far less reliable than traditional deterrence. There is no doubting Washington's commitment and capacity for responding to an attack on any square inch of U.S. territory, from Bellingham, Washington to Bangor, Maine. But "extended deterrence cannot work unless both potential challengers and the defender's allies are convinced that the defender's commitment is credible," notes Christopher Layne, and maintaining the credibility of that commitment is a potentially risky proposition.[53]

Eisenhower was the first U.S. president to confront this problem. "It is cold comfort," he once said, "for any citizen of Western Europe to be assured that—after his country is overrun and he is pushing up daisies—someone still alive will drop a bomb on the Kremlin."[54]

Eisenhower was hardly alone. Henry Kissinger, an outspoken critic of Eisenhower's foreign and defense policies, implicitly questioned the efficacy of extended deterrence because he too doubted the credibility of our pledge to use such weapons on behalf of others. "Because the consequences of our weapons technology are so fearsome," Kissinger wrote in 1957, "we have not found it easy to define a *casus belli* which would leave no doubt concerning our moral justification to use force."[55] Thomas Schelling, a leading strategist of the Cold War, shared Kissinger's concerns. "To *fight* abroad is a military act, but to *persuade* enemies or allies that one would fight abroad, under circumstances of great cost and risk, requires more than a military capability," Schelling wrote in his seminal work, *Arms and Influence,* published in 1966. Extended deterrence "requires projecting intentions. It requires *having* those intentions, even deliberately acquiring them, and communicating them persuasively to make other countries behave."[56]

Whereas U.S. policymakers wrestled with the challenges posed by extended deterrence throughout the course of the Cold War, especially as it related to the credibility to actually use force that makes deterrence work, this problem has grown only more acute as the superpower confrontation fades deeper and deeper into the past. Perhaps the most important change, explains Robert Jervis, is that "few imaginable disputes will engage vital U.S. interests."[57]

Much as during the Cold War, the credibility of our commitment hinges on a future president's willingness to risk our cities for someone else's. Washington has volunteered to become entangled in wars that do not engage vital U.S. interests in the hope that the mere offer of such protection will deter aggression against our allies, and also to discourage our allies from wanting to defend themselves.[58]

It is beyond dispute that a number of countries that have the technical capacity to develop nuclear weapons have chosen not to do so; Japan and South Korea, who both have formal security treaties with the United States, would certainly fall within this category, as would a few NATO countries. Others speculate that Taiwan might choose to develop nuclear weapons if the Taiwanese come to doubt U.S. willingness to risk war on their behalf. These doubts have even greater merit than those of formal allies in NATO and East Asia, as the United States has no mutual defense treaty with Taiwan.[59] Iran's decision to move forward with its nuclear enrichment program, a possible precursor to weapons development, has stirred talk among other Gulf states of the need for a deterrent of their own.[60]

There are many different reasons why a prospective nuclear weapons state, even a country that already possesses the technical capacity to become one, might ultimately choose not to go down that path. Cost is an important factor.[61] There is also the international community's likely reaction. It is reasonable to conclude that the U.S. security guarantee has factored into some countries' calculations of whether or not they should proceed down the nuclear weapons path, but it is hardly the only factor. After all, South Africa gave up its nuclear weapons, but it did not do so on the assumption that the U.S. deterrent would take the place of the one that they dismantled. Ukraine and Belarus both divested themselves of the nuclear arsenals that they inherited following the collapse of the Soviet Union, and neither has been afforded protection by the U.S. arsenal. Finally, with respect to Japan, there are many reasons why it is unlikely to develop nuclear weapons, even though they are certainly capable of doing so. As the only country in history to have been the victim of a nuclear attack, the Japanese political culture has shown a particular aversion to nuclear weapons.[62]

Given the tenuous nature of extended deterrence, and given the costs and risks associated with our adopting such a posture, U.S. security guarantees to non-nuclear states that are contingent upon the United States having preponderant military power deserve closer scrutiny. At a minimum, we should not take at face value the claims that U.S. extended deterrence is crucial to preventing the proliferation of nuclear weapons, nor should we assume that the removal of such security guarantees over time would precipitate a rush to acquire nuclear weapons.

The Mother of All Public Goods Fallacies: Oil

Of all the public goods rationales offered in defense of the U.S. military's global posture, none is more important than the presumption that the U.S. military must ensure access to the world's energy resources—especially that most important resource, oil, from that most volatile region, the Persian Gulf. Even those who are willing to concede that the patterns of international trade, which seemed tenuous in the years immediately following World War II, or during the tense years of the Cold War, might no longer depend on the active protections of the U.S. military, make exceptions in the case of oil.[63]

It is obvious—painfully so for U.S. consumers who in early 2008 saw the inflation-adjusted price of a gallon of gasoline nearly double over a five-year period[64]—that the flow of oil is essential to the functioning of the U.S. economy. But the claim that Americans and the rest of the world benefit from, indeed is dependent on, a U.S. military presence in the Middle East to guarantee the flow of oil and natural gas from the region does not withstand close scrutiny. In this section, I explain why many of the fears of disruptions in the flow of oil are grounded in fundamental misconceptions about the way that global energy markets operate.

The U.S. military presence in the Persian Gulf is largely irrelevant—and may well be counterproductive—to ensuring reliable access to energy. Further, to the extent that U.S. policies are useful—in other words, to the extent that the U.S. military posture in the region constitutes a public good—they run afoul of the same problems associated with public goods as discussed in this chapter, especially free riding. The free riders include energy consumers in Europe and Asia, but especially the regimes sitting atop the vast oil reserves in the region whose very survival depends on their ability to get their product to market. If the public goods argument that is associated with ensuring the flow of oil can be shown to be critically flawed, then we must also question other policies ostensibly geared toward keeping the international economy open for business.

Unpacking all of the faulty justifications that have given rise to a permanent U.S. military presence in the Middle East would be a long and arduous process and is well beyond the scope of this work. The problem begins with a basic misunderstanding of energy markets. For starters, for all the talk of U.S. "dependence" on foreign oil, the United States is less dependent on foreign sources of oil than are many other countries.[65] Not that that means anything. Oil is traded globally, therefore the point of origin—be it foreign or domestic, Nigerian or Norwegian—is essentially irrelevant. Our cars don't care where the oil comes from any more than they care what port it was received in or where it was refined into gasoline.

It is a grave error, therefore, to exaggerate the strategic and economic significance of Persian Gulf oil for U.S. consumers.[66] Although Saudi Arabia is the world's largest oil exporter, and possesses the world's largest known reserves, Canada is the leading source of crude oil imported into the United States. In addition to domestic production, which provides for more than 35 percent of our energy needs, another 25 percent comes from Canada, Mexico, and Venezuela. If one includes both crude and refined petroleum, the share is slightly larger. The Persian Gulf region as a whole accounts for less than 20 percent of U.S. oil needs.[67]

If the point of origination really mattered in oil markets, it might be said that our strategic posture in the Persian Gulf more closely approximates a public good to the extent that the supposed benefits that our military presence provides are enjoyed chiefly by nonpayers, and our provision of security for one or a few does not diminish the benefits enjoyed by many. Because the majority of oil used by U.S. consumers originates in the Western Hemisphere, our presence in the Middle East is actually aimed at protecting the flow of oil for others, including relatively wealthy people in Europe and Japan, and hundreds of millions of new consumers in India and China.

Beyond the fact that point of origination is irrelevant, the public goods rationale for using the U.S. military as security guards for Persian Gulf oil—or oil from anywhere else, or any other given product or resource, for that matter—is badly flawed in other ways as well.[68] The U.S. military presence is not essential to ensuring that the rest of the world has access to Persian Gulf oil, and yet it is costly, a massive wealth transfer from U.S. taxpayers to oil producers and oil companies, and also to energy consumers outside of the United States.

A better approach from the U.S. perspective would distribute the costs and risks of safeguarding the flow of all natural resources and finished goods—not just oil—among the principle beneficiaries of this trade. The United States is one of the beneficiaries of such exchanges, but it is hardly the only one. Indeed, the United States is no more dependent on trade with foreign nations, and therefore no more vulnerable to potential trade disruptions, than are many other countries around the world.

That is not what many Americans believe. They still shudder at the memories of the Arab oil embargoes of the 1970s, and tend to think that our military presence in the Persian Gulf reduces the risks of a repeat of those unhappy times.[69] But Americans incorrectly attribute the long lines at gas stations as a direct consequence of OPEC's withholding oil from certain countries, when in fact the shortages were largely the result of misguided U.S. government policies. The economic effects of the oil embargoes were extremely limited.[70] Embargoes increase transaction and transportation costs—adding one or more middlemen willing to sell to the embargoed end user and forcing embargoed products to take a roundabout route to their final destination—but short of a naval blockade of an enemy's ports, governments cannot prevent products from eventually making their way into countries willing to pay for them.[71]

The whole notion of energy dependence or independence is flawed at its core, and to the extent to which such concerns have motivated the U.S. government's actions for at least three decades, it need not have been that way. It might have been possible to make a case, on strictly strategic grounds, for Cold War–era policies that sought to deny the Soviets control over the resources in the Middle East. Those policies, however, need not have involved propping up autocratic rulers, such as the Shah of Iran. A formal military presence in the region was even less necessary.[72]

Leaving aside a debate over U.S.-Middle East policies during the Cold War, it is much harder to make the case for a continuation of these policies after the collapse of the Soviet Union. It is particularly misleading to argue that the presence of U.S. military forces in the primary oil-producing region of the world drives down the cost of gasoline and other petroleum products for U.S. consumers.

Americans consume many natural resources, and we don't regularly employ military means to secure access to them. Granted, of all natural resources petroleum is the most important, and a major disruption in the flow of oil would have serious short-term consequences on the U.S. economy. But these short-term hardships would be offset by a number of other factors, including the substitution of energy from other sources, or by changing work habits and commuting patterns. Indeed, many of these substitution effects are already well under way, as the price of oil and gasoline has fluctuated sharply over the last ten years.[73] Adaptation might include a shift to "alternative fuels," but might also include oil from other regions of the world. Brazil recently discovered a deep-water field that could contain as much as 33 billion gallons of crude oil.[74] Closer to home, some recommend new exploration in various offshore locations, exploration that up to this point has been heavily restricted due to concerns over the potentially harmful environmental effects.

Much of the discussion about possible new sources of oil misses an essential point. There are enormous deposits of unconventional crude oil—for example, locked in shale rock in the Rocky Mountains, or in the hard to exploit strata of the "Bakken formation" in Montana, North Dakota, Saskatchewan, and Manitoba—but such deposits cannot be economically extracted given current technology.[75] Meanwhile, it might be economical to convert millions of tons of coal into liquid petroleum if current prices for oil remain high, and if environmental considerations were not factored in. For now, however, despite the significant increase in crude oil prices that occurred over the past five years, it makes more sense to continue pumping more easily accessible and refinable petroleum from well-known sources. Some of these deposits happen to exist in the ground under politically unstable regions in West Africa, or under the control of autocratic regimes such as Saudi Arabia and Venezuela. But the gasoline in the world's cars today is just as likely to have originated from beneath stable, democratic, nation states (or their territorial waters), including Canada, the United Kingdom, and Norway.

I have shown that the fears of economic calamity arising from oil price shocks are largely overblown because consumers and producers adapt to market disruptions relatively quickly. Still, although the effects of an oil-price shock—from, say, civil unrest in Saudi Arabia, or from the closing of the Strait of Hormuz—on

U.S. economic security would be mitigated over time, the short-term effects would be painful. Many critics of U.S. policy in the Middle East claim that shifting the United States away from a "dependence" on foreign sources of oil would insulate us from even these short-term disruptions.[76] But, as noted above, oil prices are set on a global market; therefore, short of the complete elimination of petroleum as an energy source—which no sensible person advocates—no combination of inducements, penalties, or sanctions on individual behavior could completely insulate the U.S. economy from oil price shocks.

U.S. policy in the Persian Gulf should not be based on the assumption that the region's energy resources will not make it to market absent the presence of U.S. troops. The movement of goods and services is driven by the iron laws of supply and demand. Oil is essential in the global economy, but we should not fear that there will be another oil embargo, or, if there is one, that it will be particularly successful. As oil is the principal source of revenue for the Persian Gulf countries, an explicit attempt to withhold this source of their wealth from world markets would certainly be more painful for the perpetrators of such a policy than for their intended victims.

On a slightly broader level, others contend that the presence of the U.S. military in all corners of the globe ensures "stability" in various regions, and that this stability is a precondition for the proper functioning of economic markets.[77] To be sure, governments assume responsibility for enforcing the rule of law in order to protect citizens from harm. From a strictly economic standpoint these same enforcement mechanisms provide security for market actors—consumers willing to travel to their local store to buy products, and merchants willing to open their doors, freed from the fear that their goods will be stolen rather than sold.

Here again, the stated rationales for our military posture and broader strategy with respect to Middle Eastern oil fail a simple cost-benefit test. Whereas the analogy of providing security for commerce makes sense on the local and national level—federal, state, and local governments obviously do have a responsibility for protecting their citizens—these same governments have no responsibility to protect merchants and consumers of other countries. That obligation falls to their respective governments, and to the merchants and consumers themselves. Collectively, all of the states in the Persian Gulf have an incentive to guard against regional instability; and if conflict does erupt, they have a vested interest in ensuring that it does not threaten the flow of oil. And it doesn't much matter whether these countries are governed by kings or emirs, petty despots or enlightened democrats. It is in the interest of all governments, even governments not necessarily committed to principles of Western-style democracy, to guard their sources of wealth and power. In this respect, the Persian Gulf states can be expected to continue to sell oil because it is in their economic interest to do so. And if this same source of their economic livelihood—and in some cases regime survival—is threatened, they should be expected to pay the costs to protect it.

What about the danger that a single country might gain control of most or all of the Middle East's oil? That may have been a legitimate concern during the Cold War, when Western strategists worried that the Soviet Union might be able to attain hegemony over the region, but there is no comparable threat today. Iran, for example, would have little hope of overrunning Saudi Arabia, displacing its government, and maintaining control over the flow of Saudi oil. Outside powers, including the United States, could intervene with over-the-horizon assets and obliterate any mobilized Iranian military assets without breaking a sweat, if they so decided. Most important, the costs of any strategy geared toward preventing this serious but highly unlikely event must be compared against the costs of alternative strategies.

The last time when another country attempted to gain control over a significant share of the region's oil—Saddam Hussein's invasion of Kuwait in August 1990—presented just such a challenge. At that time, economist David Henderson of the Naval Postgraduate School examined the potential power of Iraq's "oil weapon" and proclaimed it a "dud." The cost to the U.S. economy of Iraq withholding its oil from global markets would have been minuscule, Henderson predicted, and would total not more than one half of one percent of gross national product.[78]

Compare the cost savings purportedly gained by denying Saddam's bid for regional hegemony against the actual costs of our military presence in the region. In 1997, Graham Fuller and Ian Lesser of the RAND Corporation estimated that the U.S. military presence in the Persian Gulf region cost taxpayers between $30 and $60 billion annually.[79] From 1992 to 1999, the total value of all oil imports from the region averaged $10.25 billion each year.[80] A more recent analysis of military expenditures in the Persian Gulf, taking account of both peacetime expenditures, as well as expected wartime costs, estimated total annual defense costs between $47 and $98 billion.[81] The total value of crude oil imports from the Persian Gulf totaled $40.0 billion in 2005 and $46.5 for 2006.[82]

If the disparity between what we get and what we pay is not enough to prove the utter inanity of our policies in the Persian Gulf, consider just the dollar costs of the current mission in Iraq. The war, merely one aspect (albeit a very important one) of the broader strategy of maintaining U.S. hegemony in the region, has cost the U.S. government, on average, nearly $120 billion each year.[83] In other words, the mission in Iraq is costing every person in the United States approximately $400 per year. During the five-year period from 2003 to 2008, the average inflation-adjusted price of a gallon of gasoline increased by nearly $2, which translates into an additional $945 in fuel costs per person, per year.[84]

It is possible to argue that the price of gasoline might have increased at a far faster rate had the United States not invaded Iraq in March 2003, but one need not rely on that hypothesis to prove the deeper point. The costs and purported benefits of our current strategy—of which the mission in Iraq is only one part—are dramatically out of balance, and though the benefits (such as they are) will be felt by many, the costs have been and are borne almost exclusively by Americans. After all, the rising cost of fuel has affected every consumer in the world, yet only U.S. consumers pay the higher prices *and* the costs of the U.S. military presence in the Persian Gulf and elsewhere.

Finally, it is not even clear that the U.S. military presence is having the net positive effect that its advocates contend: providing security for the region and thereby holding down the price of oil. Although U.S. troops afford a level of security greater than that which regional actors might choose to provide, they have also been a notably *destabilizing* influence. After all, the U.S. military posture in the region—for example, those troops left in place after the Gulf War—has been a rallying point around which our enemies have whipped up anti-U.S. and anti-Western sentiment. Former deputy defense secretary Paul Wolfowitz admitted that the presence of U.S. troops in Saudi Arabia had "been Osama bin Laden's principal recruiting device" and he intimated during congressional testimony before the Iraq War that the removal of Saddam Hussein from power would enable the United States to draw down forces in the region.[85] That we have still not done so more than six years after the invasion of Iraq suggests that we don't fully appreciate the need for a dramatic change of course.[86]

A related concern is that terrorists might seize control of crucial oil fields and use this control either to starve their enemies of an essential resource, or else use the profits from the sale of oil to finance their nefarious operations. This problem is not unique to Middle Eastern oil; related worries arise from al-Qaeda's increased activity in sub-Saharan Africa, central Asia, or oil-rich Indonesia.

The presence of U.S. military forces is not essential to preventing such groups from consolidating control over oil-producing countries or regions. For starters, these worst-case scenarios are unlikely to transpire, irrespective of whether or not the U.S. military remains permanently stationed in any given region, and besides, we are not the only country with an interest in stopping them. In the highly unlikely event that al-Qaeda were able to seize control of the instruments of power in a given state, however, terrorist leaders like Osama bin Laden and Ayman al-Zawahiri would immediately be subject to all manner of direct attack; to survive, terrorists must remain in the shadows. And so long as they remain concealed, there are a variety of ways to choke off their access to funds and otherwise disrupt their operational planning.

In the end, none of the stated public goods rationales for having the U.S. military act as the regional police force for the Persian Gulf withstand scrutiny. Ensuring that oil flows on the global marketplace is in the interest of all parties who participate in that marketplace, and the United States is just one of many. Because we and other net consumers can adapt or shift to alternative suppliers, the costs and risks of maintaining order in the region should primarily be borne by the people who would be most harmed by a major disruption: the oil producers. Precisely the same logic could be applied to any product or resource; it makes no sense for Americans to bear a disproportionate share of the costs and risks of policing the planet while the rest of the world free rides on our largesse.

Following the end of the Persian Gulf War in 1991, President George H. W. Bush crowed "By God, we've kicked the Vietnam syndrome once and for all!"[87] The syndrome might have been welcome six years ago when fond memories of easy victories in Kuwait in 1991 and the appearance of seeming successes in Kosovo in 1999 and Afghanistan in 2001 encouraged U.S. policymakers to believe that U.S. military power was uniquely effective and should be used more often.

The debacle in Iraq has shattered many of these illusions. Much as there was a Vietnam syndrome during the 1970s and early 1980s, there will likely be an Iraq syndrome in the years ahead. This means that the American public and their representatives in Congress will ask far more questions about the next proposed military intervention than they did in late 2002 and early 2003. Ohio State University Professor John Mueller predicted in November 2005, several months before the violence in Iraq took a pronounced turn for the worse, and when the costs of the conflict were still relatively low, that the Iraq syndrome would have far-reaching effects on U.S. grand strategy.[88]

But there are a number of factors driving U.S. interventionism, and the Iraq syndrome will not be sufficient to turn around the ship of state. This chapter has examined the many flawed assumptions driving our current grand strategy, including the false notion that our physical security and economic prosperity requires us to adopt a hyperactive military posture abroad. The next chapter details how our possession of an enormous military—a military ostensibly shaped by that grand strategy—imposes additional obligations on us to intervene. We might ultimately prove able to change our grand strategy. We might come to appreciate that there is a stable middle ground between American hegemony and total chaos, and U.S. policymakers might strive toward finding that balance according to a rational assessment of the costs and benefits. If we don't change the structure of our military, and its forward posture around the world, we will likely not reduce our propensity to intervene, and we will not, therefore, have truly solved our power problem.

CHAPTER FIVE

THE HEGEMON'S DILEMMA

Our power is a problem not merely because we spend hundreds of billions of dollars on our military, and thereby divert resources away from the private economy and from other domestic spending. The problem goes much deeper than that. Our vast power, and our propensity to use it, is also a problem because it discourages others from defending themselves. Our government's willingness to use U.S. military power to defend others—for example, by pledging to treat an attack on them as the same as an attack on us—increases the risks that Americans will be drawn into foreign wars. Deploying military assets to safeguard the flow of goods and services is broadly consistent with our government's responsibilities under the Constitution, but becomes less defensible when we end up picking up all of the costs, even though we are only one of many beneficiaries of global trade. Finally, our power and our use of that power contribute to the mistaken notion that any misfortune, anywhere, ought to be a primary concern for the United States, and that we, and we alone, are capable of averting such tragedies.

This represents a curious paradox. On the one hand, the defenders of benevolent global hegemony contend that our interests align with those of most other countries, and hence the lack of balancing behavior in the international system constitutes an implicit endorsement of our authority. In his 1992 State of the Union Address, President George H. W. Bush declared that "the world trusts us with power—and the world is right. They trust us to be fair and restrained; they trust us to be on the side of decency. They trust us to do what's right."[1] Over a decade later, National Security Adviser Condoleezza Rice echoed these sentiments. "Why would anyone who shares the values of freedom seek to put a check on those values?" she wondered aloud during a speech to the International Institute for Strategic Studies. "Power in the service of freedom is to be welcomed," Rice explained, "and powers that share a commitment to freedom can—and must—make common cause against freedom's enemies."[2]

On the other hand, our policies appear to be based on the presumption that other countries do *not* share our interests and values. We act as though we cannot count on them to defend themselves from external threats, and to address problems in far distant regions long before they threaten us. We see ourselves as something more than a normal nation—concerned with more than our own security—and we see other countries as something less than normal, insufficiently interested in their own security to be trusted with such matters.

As previously noted, it is not unreasonable to assume that our bitter experience in Iraq will temper our enthusiasm for taking on still more challenges. The American public, chastened by the fact that the "cakewalk" war has turned out to be anything but, is already exhibiting a greater skepticism toward similar missions. But even if the politicians and policymakers respond to these shifting winds of public opinion, and come to the belated realization that a country blessed with relatively few urgent security threats need not become involved in most foreign conflicts in order to be prosperous and secure, we are still likely to be drawn into foreign entanglements so long as we retain the power to intervene.

In the previous chapter, I showed that Washington's irrational fears of impending global chaos, combined with a misplaced confidence that we alone are capable of preserving global peace and security, was counterproductive and outdated. I also demonstrated how our attempt to police the globe in order to safeguard the flow of goods and services, and especially the flow of oil from the Middle East, unfairly burdens U.S. taxpayers while affording other beneficiaries a free ride. In this chapter, I explain why it is not enough to simply constrain, by force of will, our interventionist tendencies. We must also, by consciously reducing our military power, limit our ability to become entangled in the affairs of others. So long as the United States retains its role as the global hegemon, the self-described indispensable nation, we will be expected to intervene whenever and wherever we have the capability to do so, which, in practical terms, means nearly always and anywhere; and if we choose not to, we invite anger and resentment. And in both cases—when we do intervene and when we don't—we risk undermining our own security.[3]

The Responsibility to Protect

The geostrategic context that seems to compel the United States to be drawn into peripheral conflicts is such a dramatic departure from an earlier time in our history that it is worthwhile to explore the dominant mind-set at the end of World War II. When representatives from the United States, Great Britain,

France, the Soviet Union, and China first met in San Francisco in April 1945, they agreed that the primary threat to world peace was great power conflict, and they constructed the United Nations to attempt to prevent that scenario above all others.[4] The five powers feared that small disputes would spark big wars, as they had in the recent past; they reasoned that they might be dragged into these conflicts, and then into wars with one another. The great powers were so worried that even conflicts far outside of their traditional spheres of influence would ultimately have adverse consequences for them that they set out to prohibit *any* member of the United Nations from using force except in self-defense. The clearest expression of this was Article 2, Section 4 of the UN Charter, which stipulates, in part, that "all Members shall refrain in their international relations from the threat or use of force against the territorial integrity or political independence of any state."

The respect for national sovereignty expressed within Article 2, Section 4, was not sacrosanct, however; small countries could not simply hide behind national borders because there was always a danger that the five permanent members of the United Nations Security Council (UNSC P5) would authorize the use of force against them. During the course of the Cold War, it rarely came to that. But as the memories of great power conflict fade, policymakers and scholars of international relations have in recent years advanced new justifications for the use of force by one state against another, and some have sought to circumvent the Security Council entirely. They argue that the protection of human rights is a moral duty for all, and that foreign intervention—including military intervention—is warranted to avert human suffering and to halt genocide. Convinced that one or more member of the UNSC should not be able to block other states from enforcing this norm, they seek out different institutions to confer legitimacy on intervention. While such sentiments are noble on their face, by circumventing the Security Council, the pro-interventionists risk provoking the very great power wars that the founders of the UN strove so mightily to prevent.

It may never come to that, and if small wars spark great wars, the process might take years to develop. But the more permissive attitude toward the use of force evolved rapidly in the late 1990s.[5] The United States inadvertently provided the impetus when the Clinton administration went around the Security Council twice in the span of six months in 1998–99. During Operation Desert Fox in December 1998 the United States and the United Kingdom rained down a shower of cruise missiles on Iraq. Less than six months later, the United States launched a war against Serbia over Kosovo. UN leaders correctly feared that the

United States was on its way toward establishing a new precedent for the use of force that might cut the international body out of the loop entirely.

In response, UN Secretary-General Kofi Annan challenged the UN General Assembly in 2000 to decide when and how humanitarian interventions should take place.[6] In December 2001, the International Commission on Intervention and State Sovereignty, established under the supervision of Canadian Prime Minister Jean Chrétien, issued its response. In a report titled "The Responsibility to Protect," the commission proposed a conception of state sovereignty based on "a dual responsibility: externally, to respect the sovereignty of other states, and internally, to respect the dignity and basic rights of all the people within the state."[7] The commission further recommended that the principle of non-intervention should yield to the "international responsibility to protect [if] a population [of a state] is suffering serious harm, as a result of internal war, insurgency, repression or state failure, and the state in question is unwilling or unable to halt or avert it."[8]

That idea gained traction over the next few years, but was overshadowed by the 9/11 attacks, the ensuing U.S. intervention in Afghanistan, and the bitter international debate over the U.S. invasion of Iraq. Then, in March 2005, Secretary-General Annan presented a package of proposals for reforming the United Nations, building on the specific recommendations of a High-Level Panel he had appointed the previous year. Although UN members summarily dismissed a number of these reforms, the attendees at the UN World Summit, held on the sixtieth anniversary of the founding of the institution, unanimously accepted the doctrine of the responsibility to protect (R2P), and within the next year the UN Security Council had affirmed the principle in at least two subsequent UNSC resolutions, 1674 and 1705.[9]

Notably, the new UN rules stipulated that collective action, including military action, could only be taken with the expressed approval of the UNSC. Still, although there appears to be broad agreement on the principle of a responsibility to protect, there remain very serious differences on how that responsibility should be fulfilled. If a state intervenes militarily without strong international support as expressed through the UNSC, even if such actions are justified by the R2P principle, that state's actions might encourage others to act in ways that are contrary to the international norms expressed in the UN Charter.[10] The fundamental contradiction at the heart of the new international order pits the sovereign rights of nation-states against the rights of outsiders to use force against these same states when they are suspected of engaging in brutal crimes against their own people.

This contradiction is plainly apparent in the differing international responses to the U.S. military interventions of the past two decades, none of which were specifically directed toward the defense of U.S. territorial integrity or the preservation of the rights and liberties of U.S. citizens.[11] For all the criticisms of U.S. unilateralism, many in the international community have at least tacitly welcomed some U.S. interventions, whereas others have complained mightily on other occasions when the United States chose not to become involved; the U.N.'s sixty-plus year prohibition against unilateral military action has been selectively ignored.

For example, the most recent war in Iraq might be seen as consistent with the international community's "responsibility to protect,"[12] but Annan called the Iraq War (and he stressed the *second* Iraq War) "illegal" because the U.S. invasion was not formally sanctioned by the UN Security Council.[13] But neither was the Kosovo campaign, which Annan referred to as illegal but legitimate, and which other R2P advocates have since invoked as a model for future interventions.[14]

In short, there is no objective standard governing the use of force, and what standards there are have become more permissive over the course of the past decade. The criteria for military intervention are obvious when there is a threat to a particular country or countries, and they act in self-defense. But that is the *easy* standard. The other standard, governing the use of the military to protect human rights, remains unclear. Brent Scowcroft, a member of the High Level Panel that produced the *A More Secure World* report, candidly admitted as much while speaking alongside Annan at a Council of Foreign Relations event in December 2004.

Noting that the UN was built on principles of sovereignty and independence of its member states, Scowcroft also maintained that "under certain circumstances, when a country is so negligent in providing for the security of its citizens, then the international community must act." "Preemption," Scowcroft explained "is accepted as part of self defense. But when it is a putative threat rather than one that is overwhelmingly imminent, then there is time...to mobilize the international community to help."

But then he went on to admit that much depends on what the individual states actually do. "[I]f one of the permanent members of the Security Council or a major state considers something to be in its vital interest, the U.N. is not going to be able to do anything about it. And that is [the] imperfect nature of the body that we have."[15]

For advocates of a more aggressive application of the R2P doctrine—more aggressive even than was envisioned by the authors of that doctrine—the United

Nations is too imperfect. Using the U.S.-led air war over Kosovo and Serbia as their preferred template, several scholars have attempted to lower the bar even further, to facilitate the use of preventive war to serve a range of desirable ends—from the preservation of human rights to preventing the proliferation of mass-casualty weapons. In short, a principle explicitly advanced under the guise of multilateralism has become a vehicle for legitimating, in some cases after the fact, unilateral military actions.[16]

Those unilateral actions have so far been undertaken by just one state. And the reason is simple: among the 192 member states of the United Nations, the United States alone possesses both the military capacity and—as demonstrated in both Iraq and Kosovo—the political will to take action anywhere in the world, and although it would prefer to have allies, it is prepared to go it alone.[17]

To be sure, many of the new interventionists would prefer to rely on multilateral institutions as a mechanism for conferring legitimacy on military actions that are, on the surface at least, clearly inconsistent with international legal norms.[18] Such institutions might provide a de facto stamp of approval, but many have become mere appendages of U.S. power. In practical terms, some within the international community have simply come to expect that the one country that is both convinced of its inherent legitimacy, and that possesses the capacity to act alone—irrespective of whether *any* multilateral institution declares it acceptable—will act.[19]

In fact, it is not an oversimplification to say that many of the liberal interventionists have grown impatient with multilateralism. As Michael Ignatieff put it in January 2003, "Multilateral solutions to the world's problems are all very well, but they have no teeth unless America bares its fangs."[20]

Anne-Marie Slaughter, Dean of the Woodrow Wilson School of Public and International Affairs at Princeton, and the Council on Foreign Relations' Lee Feinstein surveyed the Bush administration's interventions, and concluded that the United States needed to bare its fangs more often. "The biggest problem with the Bush preemption strategy," they wrote in *Foreign Affairs* in early 2004, "may be that it does not go far enough." Pointing to the urgent danger posed by weapons of mass destruction (WMD) in the hands of unstable regimes, and in a dramatic expansion of the original doctrine to "protect" the victims of genocide and other crimes, Slaughter and Feinstein invoked a "collective 'duty to *prevent*' nations run by rulers without internal checks on their power from acquiring or using WMD." The ultimate object, they explained, should be to "shift the burden of proof from suspicious nations to suspected nations" and thus pave the way for an even more permissive attitude toward the use of force.[21]

This erosion of the concept of state sovereignty has important implications for U.S. foreign policy; not because we have reason to fear that it will be used against us, but rather because of the burdens it imposes on us. As there is no internationally accepted standard concerning the legitimacy of humanitarian intervention, most policymakers around the globe are left to decide whether or not their particular state will employ force to serve humanitarian ends. But policymakers in Washington have fed unrealistic expectations that the United States would not discriminate on the basis of our national interests but would instead advance policies for the betterment of all humankind. President Bush declared in his second inaugural address that it was "the policy of the United States to seek and support the growth of democratic movements and institutions *in every nation and culture,* with the ultimate goal of ending tyranny in our world."[22]

In principle, this would have applied to a number of autocratic states that pose no direct threat to the United States; indeed, some are among our staunchest allies in the so-called war on terror. But Bush elided the contradiction. In the same speech, he averred that "America's vital interests and our deepest beliefs are now one," again implying that his administration would give no quarter to regimes or states that did not treat their people humanely.[23] But two recent cases—the genocide in Darfur and the suffering in Myanmar (Burma) following the devastating Cyclone Nargis—reveal the ambiguity of the concept of the responsibility to protect, and point to serious problems for Bush's successors if that ambiguity is not clarified.

The Cases of Darfur and Myanmar

For the past five years, the world has been horrified by the violence taking place in the Darfur region of western Sudan. With some estimates placing the death toll in excess of 400,000, and with hundreds of thousands more who have been raped, tortured, and driven from their homes and villages, members of Congress, former government officials, and media celebrities have castigated the Bush administration and the United Nations for failing to stop the killings. The urgency of these cries for action intensified in 2005 after the U.S. State Department determined that the events in Darfur constituted genocide.[24]

On August 31, 2006, the UN Security Council adopted Resolution 1706, which invited the Sudanese government to consent to the deployment of a UN force to stop the violence and protect the security and freedom of movement of UN personnel. But this approach struck Brookings Institution scholar William

O'Neill as wholly inadequate. O'Neill wondered what would happen if Khartoum did not consent. "If it says no, the Security Council has a choice," O'Neill explained, "It can find troops from countries willing to send their young men and women into a hostile environment, or it can do nothing. As difficult as the first option might be, if the UN does not act, the 'responsibility to protect' will become an empty phrase, as meaningless in the 21st century as 'never again' was in the 20th."[25]

As it happened, the Sudanese government did not agree to accept a UN force and the crisis dragged on for another year. The international body returned to the issue in March 2007, when a UN force and UN High Level Mission to Darfur criticized the Sudanese government for its role in the conflict. Within two months, the UN Security Council unanimously passed Resolution 1755, which explicitly invoked the responsibility to protect as its rationale for becoming involved in the crisis, and a few months later adopted Resolution 1769, authorizing the deployment of a 26,000-strong joint UN-African Union force. Once again, however, the Sudanese government resisted. In July 2008, the prosecutor at the International Criminal Court (ICC) formally requested an arrest warrant for Sudanese president Omar Hassan Al-Bashir on charges of genocide, war crimes, and crimes against humanity over the past five years in Darfur. Although some saw this as a positive step, others worried that the prosecutor's pursuit of Bashir would create greater instability in the Darfur region and possibly undermine peace negotiation efforts.[26]

Whether UN troops ever arrive in Darfur in large number may ultimately be beside the point. Knowledgeable observers contend that "expectations of what UN troops would do were wildly inflated." "The International Crisis Group, one of the most vocal and influential participants in the debate on Darfur," notes Alex de Waal, "simply assumed that the implementation of the responsibility to protect was achievable."[27] But that is consistent with other possible interventions contemplated under R2P. In a study for the Henry L. Stimson Center, Victoria Holt and Tobias Berkman note that although there has been considerable emphasis on when and whether intervention under a responsibility to protect might be warranted, too little attention has been paid to "*how* third-party intervention forces can best protect civilians caught in conflict."[28]

Even the best-intended military interventions, those specifically aimed at advancing the cause of peace and justice, can have horrific side-effects, most important of these being the real possibility that innocent bystanders and those the operation seeks to protect may be inadvertently killed or injured.[29] Military intervention, after all, is merely a euphemism for war, aka organized violence. War, even when practiced with the precision and skill that the U.S. military exercises in battle, involves killing. Such killing can never be limited solely to the perpetrators of the particular crime. This is particularly true when our stated goal is the overthrow of an undemocratic regime that is complicit in these crimes, because it is extremely difficult to separate the true believers from the unwilling accomplices given that such regimes routinely force people to serve the state against their will. Those killed leave behind a legacy of bitterness: parents, spouses, children, friends, few of whom may have actively supported the former regime, but all of whom may forget the noble intentions of the invading force and later direct their wrath at those responsible for their misfortune. In many cases, they will not blame the regime that invited the assault, but rather the party that dropped the bomb or fired the bullet.

Meanwhile, an intervening party's true intentions are never so obvious—and obviously altruistic—that others might not question its motives. Even before the ICC indictment, Khartoum was suspicious of the outsiders' goals, particularly Western nations and the United States, given the previous interventions in Bosnia, Kosovo, and Iraq. These incipient suspicions were further heightened "by the parallels made by some U.S. politicians between 'saving' Kosovo and 'saving' Darfur." "It was not lost on Sudan's leaders," notes one commentator, "that NATO's humanitarian intervention in Kosovo" led to independence for the province. Khartoum could reasonably infer that an ulterior motive among some in the "save Darfur" movement was the dismantling of Sudan.[30]

Advocates of intervention in Darfur have consistently invoked the responsibility to protect, but as of September 2008, the people of the region seem no closer to peace and security than when the violence began, over five years ago.

Another recent case reveals the further difficulties associated with R2P as a principle governing when and whether states are entitled or obligated—or both—to intervene militarily. Although R2P advocates generally agree that the principle should apply in Darfur, and although the UN Security Council has explicitly invoked the principle in authorizing action there, views diverge sharply with respect to Myanmar. When a massive cyclone struck the Burmese coast in May 2008, it left at least 22,000 people dead and hundreds of thousands more in dire circumstances. The humanitarian crisis deepened when the ruling government denied visas to aid workers and took other measures that impeded humanitarian assistance from reaching victims of the disaster.[31] Within a few days after the cyclone struck, some outside observers, including most notably French foreign minister Bernard Kouchner, began to speak of using the international community's "responsibility to protect" in order to pry open the

Burmese government.[32] A few weeks later, former U.S. secretary of state Madeleine Albright echoed these calls, but worried that the "invasion of Iraq [had] generated a negative reaction that has weakened support for cross-border interventions even for worthy purposes."[33]

Some of the most outspoken supporters of the war in Iraq exhibited no such worries, however. Matthew Continetti of the *Weekly Standard* characterized arguments against Kouchner's call to apply the responsibility to protect doctrine to Myanmar as merely "rationales for ambivalence." In addition to airdrops of aid, Continetti argued for a more assertive approach that ultimately would end in the collapse of the ruling junta. As he put it, "conscience and justice demand" that we "help the Burmese people overthrow the tyrants who allowed this tragedy to unfold."[34] But even some of the most committed advocates of R2P, including Gareth Evans of the International Crisis Group, were reluctant to invoke the doctrine with respect to the tragedy in Myanmar. The co-author of the original R2P report wrote:

> If it comes to be thought that "R2P," and in particular the sharp military end of the doctrine, is capable of being invoked in anything other than a context of mass atrocity crimes, then such consensus as there is in favour of the new norm will simply evaporate in the global South. And that means that when the next case of genocide or ethnic cleansing comes along we will be back to the same old depressing arguments about the primacy of sovereignty that led us into the horrors of inaction in Rwanda and Srebrenica in the 1990s.[35]

Back to the same old depressing arguments indeed. The international system is still based on the sovereign rights of independent states, but this norm has eroded over the past two decades. In practice, power trumps these norms. All five of the permanent members of the UNSC have the ability to exert great influence in their respective regions. Russia, China, and the United States possess large conventional armies, and though the British and the French armies are far smaller, both of these Western allies possess technologically advanced militaries, and are certainly quite capable of projecting force.

The P5 are not the only countries that possess both the capacity and the will to act militarily. Other regional powers have invoked humanitarian concerns in recent years to justify military intervention, and oftentimes these claims have merit. For example, Australia and New Zealand led a multinational force into the Solomon Islands in July 2003, and Australian troops have deployed to troubled East Timor on more than one occasion. Over the course of a few months in 1997, roughly 7,000 troops (mostly Italian) restored stability to a violent, anarchic region of Albania as part of Operation Alba. In addition, European and African forces have historically played leading roles in operations in Africa, including a Nigerian-led intervention in Sierra Leone in 1998, and an EU-led multinational force sent to Bunia, in the Ituri district of the Democratic Republic of Congo in June 2003.

Despite this pattern of regional involvement in humanitarian crises, U.S. policymakers' stated desire to act as the guarantor of the New World Order (as George H. W. Bush put it), as the indispensable nation (as Bill Clinton and Madeleine Albright envisioned it), and as the principal defender of freedom in the world (according to George W. Bush), has created unrealistic expectations that U.S. troops will continue to be deployed on missions that have no plausible connection to U.S. national security interests.

Those Who Can, Should

That such expectations exist, and that we actually do incur obligations merely by virtue of our vast military power, derives from a simple aphorism: when it comes to humanitarian intervention, those who can, should.[36]

Among policymakers and global opinion leaders, Tony Blair has been one of the most eloquent and persistent advocates of a broad application of a nation's responsibilities to advance human rights. But even Blair understood that the interventionist impulse was constrained by the capacity of individual member states. When challenged during the run-up to the Iraq War on why he supported a war to remove Saddam Hussein from power, but was not pushing for the removal of other equally odious dictators, Blair responded forcefully on the point. "They ask why we don't get rid of Mugabe, why not the Burmese lot. Yes, let's get rid of them all. I don't because I can't, but when you can you should."[37]

Blair was more convinced of the rectitude of military intervention in Iraq than were many of his European counterparts. And to the extent that British citizens have been more supportive of humanitarian intervention than other Europeans, this might be a legacy from the British colonial tradition.[38] The British military remains active around the world. The United Kingdom maintains bases in many far-flung places, and British troops have also deployed in harm's way on numerous occasions over the past two decades. In addition to their sizable military contingents in Iraq and Afghanistan, the United Kingdom has deployed its troops to Bosnia-Herzegovina, Croatia, Kosovo, Georgia, and Cyprus as part of peacekeeping missions. British troops took the lead in restoring order after civil conflict wracked Sierra Leone in 1999 and Liberia in 2003.

But while other countries can, and often do, justify their decision to intervene based on special circumstances, such as their obligations to the people living in their former colonies—for example, the Dutch in Indonesia, the Portuguese in Angola, or France in the Ivory Coast—these same countries can reasonably point to their limited capacity for intervening everywhere to justify a selective approach to intervention. It is much harder, however, for the United States to invoke the "limited capacity" justification because our power *seems* so vast, and because we have embarked—rhetorically at least—on a grand mission to reshape the global order, and to treat any threat to that order as our primary concern. Thus, though we are constrained by our available military resources, and though these resources have been in recent years heavily invested in Iraq and Afghanistan, this has not stopped various organizations from appealing to the United States to intervene militarily in still more places.[39]

Just because the U.S. government is pressed to intervene does not mean that we always send troops when called. Some of the places where U.S. troops did *not* go—for example, Rwanda, Congo, and Burma—are as well-known as those where they did. But this selective pattern of intervention reveals that each and every decision to send troops abroad reflects a choice based not on a calculation of U.S. national interest, but rather on a far more subjective standard that immediately opens us up to charges of hypocrisy, double standards, or, worse, racism.

Advocates of military intervention explicitly invoke this form of argument to shame U.S. policymakers into action. "We saved Europeans. Why not Africans?" asked Susan Rice, Anthony Lake, and Donald Payne, in making the case that the Bush administration should launch air strikes and take other military action—including a blockade of Sudanese ports—to force the government in Khartoum to end the depredations occurring in Darfur. Prior UN approval of such a mission was unlikely, but ultimately unnecessary, they argued, because after all, "the United States [had] acted without U.N. blessing in 1999 in Kosovo to confront a lesser humanitarian crisis (perhaps 10,000 killed) and a more formidable adversary." The responsibility to protect, Rice, Lake, and Payne averred, provided sufficient justification for U.S. action. Finally, they dismissed claims that the U.S. military lacked the capacity to execute such an operation because of its commitments in Iraq, Afghanistan, and elsewhere. Although they conceded that "our ground forces are stretched thin," they argued that "a bombing campaign would tax the Air Force and Navy, which have relatively more capacity" and therefore would not pose an undue burden on the U.S. military as a whole.[40]

These same sorts of arguments could be made, and sometimes are, with respect to many humanitarian crises. A U.S. Navy ship is almost always within twenty-four hours of any distressed mariner, and is equally able to come to the assistance of people victimized by disasters on land. If the problem is bad guys with guns, and the call is for someone, anyone, to take them out, U.S. military aircraft possess the ability to drop a bomb on any square inch of the planet. Our planes can take off from one of dozens of airstrips here in the United States, or from the archipelago of bases scattered around the world. They can also launch from aircraft carriers at sea. Such missions can often be carried out with little or no prior planning. And if we don't want to risk the lives of our pilots on such missions, we could use the unmanned aerial vehicles that can remain in the air for twenty-four hours or longer, and can be controlled by operators seated in air-conditioned rooms many thousands of miles away.

Though the aphorism that "those who can, should" is simple, the application of it is not. For starters, the ability to act militarily does not convey the ability to succeed, as has been shown in both Iraq and Afghanistan. Many of the world's problems cannot be solved by even the precise application of military force—blunt force is even less useful. Military forces are particularly ill-suited to fostering the spread of liberal democracy and economic development. Meanwhile, even if an intervention succeeds in the narrow military sense of the term, and we kill or otherwise disable the bad guys without killing or injuring innocent bystanders, our decision to intervene usually causes us to get involved in complicated disputes which we don't completely understand, and from which it is difficult to extract ourselves.

Conversely, we are damned if we don't, too. Because we have the physical ability to apply military force anywhere and at any time—or even that we *appear* to have such capabilities—does not mean that we always will, or should. The danger is that by our refusal to act we will invite still more resentment, and occasionally hatred.

The Parable of the Drowning Man

By way of illustration, imagine our situation as analogous to that of a man standing on the end of a pier, holding a life ring. He sees a man in the water, crying for help. What obligation does the man on the pier have to the man in the water?

What responsibilities inhere in the simple fact that the man happens to be stand-ing at the end of the pier at that particular moment in time, and that he holds in his hands an instrument that might save the drowning man's life?[41]

In terms of legal obligations, it would appear that the answer is quite simple: none. In most cases, the man on the pier is not required to throw the ring to the man in the water. But just because there may be no formal legal requirement to come to the aid of distressed persons does not imply that individuals will not act. Human beings have a strong desire to help others in need when it is within our capacity to do so. In the case of the drowning man, it doesn't cost the man on the pier anything to throw the ring, nor does he put his life at risk. And the benefits for the man in the water are enormous.

Such simple analogies cannot begin to guide our conduct in the real world of international politics, however. First and foremost, governments have an obligation to their citizens. If our government deploys the military to save the drowning man, or to rescue people caught in the cross fire of a civil war, or who have been victimized by some natural disaster, it can reasonably be accused of betraying its obligations to U.S. citizens if those same resources that are lost or destroyed in the humanitarian operation are later needed for self-defense. Such cases are rare. As noted throughout this book, our physical security is not so tenuous that the future of the Republic would be threatened by the loss of a few Humvees or a helicopter.

These sorts of cold, mathematical calculations must be multiplied a thou-sandfold when the "resources" in question are our soldiers, sailors, airmen, and Marines. In many recent cases, a president or secretary of state might have been able to justify in his or her own mind, or explain squarely to a parent, spouse, or child, why they chose to risk the lives of our servicemen and women on mis-sions that are not directly related to the defense of this country. What's more, given the nature of many post–Cold War military operations, many of those left behind may well understand that their departed loved ones volunteered to serve in a military that has rarely been employed for defending their homeland, and that they gave their lives for a noble cause.

Even if it were true that the use of the U.S. military did not detract from its ability to fulfill its core obligations, and even if such uses were consistent with a broader understanding of our military's purpose, that still would not be suf-ficient to overcome all of the objections to humanitarian intervention because it is often difficult to limit a mission to "purely" humanitarian relief. Sending the U.S. military to rescue people in distress will rarely result in the elimination of the source of their distress. If the true object of military intervention is to achieve the latter, as opposed to merely mitigating the former, then "sending in the military" doesn't begin to convey the magnitude of the mission.

If there is a presumed moral obligation to come to the aid of another human being in mortal distress—in other words if the individual man on the pier was subject to a responsibility to protect—it would constitute a betrayal of that obligation to *merely* throw the ring, and to not also jump into the water if the drowning man was unable to grasp the ring. Few, however, who believe that those who can, should, would go that far. Just as there are obvious limits to what is expected of the person standing on the pier, few advocates of humanitarian intervention argue that a country should incur great costs, expose its military personnel to grave risks, or otherwise undermine its security to satisfy the norm of a responsibility to protect.

Still, the interventionists tend to exaggerate the utility of military force and to grossly understate the costs. These costs and risks of intervention are borne not simply by one man standing on one pier, and not solely by the men and women who have volunteered to serve in our military and have thus pledged to follow the lawful orders from their chain of command, but by all Americans whenever the U.S. government chooses to act. For if the man in the water is *being* drowned by others, then throwing the ring will not remedy his situation, but by merely attempting to save him, the man on the pier invites the wrath of the drowning man's assailants.

Some people might say that such considerations should not prevent us from intervening. We can see that a great wrong is being perpetrated, and we possess the power to right that wrong, even if our intervention might fail, and even if there are risks associated with doing so. But most cases are not so clear cut, because we often do not know or we choose to ignore all of the relevant details. When we intervene in the internal affairs of a foreign country, we are often taking sides in a civil conflict. How confident can we be that we are on the side of right?

Sometimes the answer seems obvious enough, for example in the case of the military junta ruling Myanmar in the spring of 2008. When foreign governments and independent NGOs offered to provide assistance to the hundreds of thousands of Burmese citizens displaced by the cyclone, the government resisted, fearing that the presence of numerous foreigners on Burmese soil might weaken their tenuous hold on power. In the process they effectively condemned many thousands of people to suffer needlessly, and a few thousand, perhaps more, to die.[42] But in Burma as elsewhere, merely sending troops and supplies will not actually solve the deeper problems that gave rise to the suffering in the first place. And particularly in the more complicated cases, the advocates for military intervention must explain how and why our government should send U.S. forces to foreign lands, and what it expects to accomplish by doing so.

The Constitution clearly stipulates the object of the U.S. government is to protect "We the People of the United States." Our government is supposed to act in our common defense, not the defense of others. It does not have the explicit authority to embark on missions to serve the needs of people in other lands. When such missions are clearly intended to serve a national security purpose, the power to intervene militarily inheres in the government's responsibility to defend this country, our people, and our way of life, from threats. But this same rationale does not apply to interventions that have no such connection.

To the extent that advocates of U.S. military intervention make their case on the grounds that we have a "responsibility to protect" they imply that the U.S. government has an obligation to come to the assistance of others, even when our own interests are not at stake, and even when doing so is dangerous for our troops. Some might be willing to admit that these interventions impose risks on all Americans, even those not serving in the military, because our government's decision to jump into the middle of an internal dispute may invite retaliation.[43] But solving our power problem requires a fundamentally different conception of what does or does not constitute a legitimate intervention, beginning with the basic precept that government should strive to advance, rather than undermine, the security of its citizens.

Escorting Kids to Kindergarten

When we deploy our military on missions that have no connection to advancing U.S. national security, we risk undermining our ability to use them in places, and on missions, that might. That is what Condoleezza Rice was getting at when, as the leading foreign policy adviser to the then Texas governor George W. Bush, she castigated the Clinton administration's foreign policy as a dangerous distraction from the urgent security challenges facing the United States. "Carrying out civil administration and police functions is simply going to degrade the American capability to do the things America has to do," Rice warned. "We don't need to have the 82nd Airborne escorting kids to kindergarten."[44]

The foreign policy intelligentsia's response to such sentiments then and since has been almost universally negative, and in June 2008, Rice wholly recanted her earlier stance.[45] Her new rationale—that such missions are essential, that America's physical capacity for such missions is boundless, and that the only possible constraint is the "imagination" of the American people—boils down to a presumption that the United States is uniquely capable of achieving success. It assumes that the United States is so dominant, our military so powerful, our technological superiority so unassailable, that we can handle multiple missions simultaneously. It also assumes that the use of the military in Country A does not in any way limit our ability to deploy to Country B, C, and/or D.[46] This is a dangerous delusion, no more grounded in reality than King Canute's abortive mission to stop the tides. But so long as most of the world looks upon the United States as always capable of intervening, there will always be demands that we do so. To return briefly to the man on the pier analogy: although a number of countries are standing on the end of metaphorical piers, and capable at least of throwing rings to a few drowning men, the United States is the only country that stands on the end of every pier, apparently capable—if only we choose to do so—of saving every drowning man.

Appearances are deceiving. The U.S. military's capabilities are limited. The perception that our military power is somehow magical, a powder to be sprinkled on all manner of foreign social ills, is problematic because it creates expectations that we cannot possibly meet.

Could we consciously choose not to intervene in places where our vital interests are not directly engaged? Could we reapply a more stringent standard to military intervention while retaining our massive military power as a hedge against uncertainty? We could, but to do so would run afoul of the evolving norm of a responsibility to protect, which holds that those who can, must. Only by constraining our ability to intervene can we avoid involvement in messy and dangerous interventions that do not advance and often undermine U.S. security.

Goliath or Sisyphus?

The norm of a responsibility to protect holds that all states with the ability to intervene to avert humanitarian crises resulting from intrastate sectarian violence and civil war must do so. They must do so, even though such interventions are likely to fail, and even though—by becoming involved in such internal disputes—the intervening parties risk engendering the ire of all those involved in the dispute. As discussed in chapter 4, we are further expected, by virtue of our pledge to come to the assistance of at least sixty different countries with whom we have formal treaty obligations to extend the protection of our nuclear arsenal over their cities, to commit the lives and livelihood of our soldiers for their defense, and to incur the considerable costs of maintaining such forces so that they do not have to. Likewise, we maintain a global military presence to facilitate the public good of global trade, even though we are only one of many beneficiaries of this trade.[47]

Some might think hegemony a noble calling, perhaps even a divine obligation, but most people disdain thankless tasks. Recall the story of Sisyphus, the man condemned by the gods to roll an enormous rock up a mountain. When the rock came to the summit, it would roll back down into the valley, and Sisyphus would begin the process anew—for eternity.

Even though they might not recall why the gods imposed this sentence on Sisyphus, many people know the story, hence the adjective "Sisyphean," meaning "endlessly laborious or futile." Sisyphus was a crafty man, too smart for his own good, as it turned out. After his death, he tricked Persephone, the Queen of the Underworld, into allowing him to return to the world of the living. But when the gods discovered his treachery, they retrieved him to Hades. Always jealous of mortals who challenged their authority, the gods reasoned that the most horrible form of punishment was being condemned to perform an impossible task.

The story of punishment for excessive confidence, bordering on arrogance, is a constant in ancient mythology, and it appears in other traditions as well.[48] But no god has condemned the United States to pursue a futile task for eternity. Our great nation was not the victim of some accident of fate or science. Unlike Peter Parker, who is always haunted by the admonition that with great power comes great responsibility, Uncle Sam was not bitten by a radioactive spider at the end of the Cold War. Unlike Goliath, whose great size and strength was as much a curse as a blessing—he did, after all, fall victim to David's stone—Americans have *chosen* to take on these burdens. Or, more accurately, our political class has chosen these burdens for the rest of us.

If the American people were given the choice, they would almost surely choose a different course. Tufts University Professor Daniel Drezner observes, "Most Americans, on most issues, articulate what George W. Bush characterized as a 'humble' foreign policy during the 2000 campaign. They want a prudent foreign policy based on security against attacks and threats to domestic well-being."[49] In polls, Americans consistently reject hegemony in favor of burden sharing. In a survey conducted by the Chicago Council on Global Affairs in July 2006, 75 percent of respondents believed that the United States "should do its share to solve world problems together with other countries" and only

10 percent wanted the United States to "remain the preeminent world leader ... in solving international problems." By a similar margin, respondents agreed with the proposition that "The U.S. is playing the role of world policeman more than it should be."[50] Bruce Stokes and Andrew Kohut of the Pew Research Center point out in their book *America against the World* that since the end of the Cold War, "no more than 13 percent of Americans have said the United States should be the single most important leader in the world."[51]

Advocates of U.S. hegemony are aware of this gap between the public and the policymakers, and hope that the voters are never afforded a genuine choice between global hegemony and global self-reliance.[52] If Americans were allowed to decide, they would shed the burdens of being the world's policeman, reframe our foreign policies in ways that advance U.S. security, and redirect our nation's resources commensurate with this new strategy. In the next chapter, I explain why and how we should.

CHAPTER SIX

CURING THE POWER PROBLEM

As discussed in chapter 1, the basic outlines of our current grand strategy trace to 1992, when aides to the then defense secretary Richard Cheney sketched out the Pentagon's plans for the first decade of the post–Cold War era. The primary objective of U.S. foreign policy, the Defense Planning Guidance (DPG) document explained, was to "prevent the re-emergence of a new rival" capable of challenging U.S. power in any vital area, including Western Europe, Asia, or the territory of the Soviet Union.[1] To accomplish this task, the United States would retain preponderant military power not merely to deter attacks against the United States, but would also employ this power in a proactive way to "preclude threats" before they materialized, and to destroy or impede the spread of nuclear weapons to countries that might resist U.S. predominance.[2]

U.S. power, according to the DPG, was crucial to the very functioning of the global order. The United States would be the global hegemon, the undisputed power in every region of the globe, and would stand prepared to act—preventively, if necessary—to halt the rise of potential challengers. Any power, held by any other country, be they friendly, economically advanced democracies, or hostile and impoverished autocracies, would be viewed with suspicion.[3]

President George W. Bush's 2002 National Security Strategy picked up where the 1992 DPG left off. "Our forces will be strong enough," the National Security Strategy declared, "to dissuade potential adversaries from pursuing a military build-up in hopes of surpassing, or equaling, the power of the United States."[4]

What has actually happened? Following a few years of post–Cold War cuts, U.S. military spending began to rise again in 1998. Over the ten years from 1998 to 2007, and holding constant for inflation, U.S. military spending increased by 66 percent. During that same period, inflation-adjusted world military expenditures, excluding that of the United States, grew just 33 percent.

Only two countries drove most of these increases: Russia and China. Based on figures compiled by the Stockholm International Peace Research Institute, Russia spent just $13.5 billion on its military in 1998; today it spends more than two and a half times that much, $35.3 billion. China has increased its spending at an even faster rate. In 1998, China's military expenditures totaled $19.2 billion; in 2007, it spent more than three times that much, $58.2 billion.[5]

And what of the rest of the world? Leading U.S. allies have not kept pace. Japanese military expenditures have remained essentially flat over the past ten years, and have actually declined slightly since 2001. Germany's defense budget stood at $40 billion in 1998, but today totals just under $37 billion, an 8.5 percent decrease. France has increased its defense expenditures only modestly, about 6.4 percent over the past ten years. The United Kingdom has grown its military by 22 percent since 2001; Israel by the same amount.[6]

To reiterate: the aim of our policies over at least the past six years, as stated in the 2002 National Security Strategy, was "to dissuade potential adversaries from pursuing a military build-up in hopes of surpassing, or equaling, the power of the United States." This is consistent with the objectives set forth in 1992, namely that we would retain preponderant military power not merely to deter attacks against the United States, but also to deter "potential competitors from even aspiring to a larger regional or global role."[7]

It hasn't worked out that way, at least not in a way that advances U.S. security. On the one hand, our overwhelming power has not dissuaded potential adversaries such as China and Russia from buying more weapons, investing in new technologies, courting potential allies, and seeking other ways to challenge our power. On the other hand, to the extent that our preponderant military power and our security guarantees to wealthy client states have had any effect, they have made these other countries more dependent on the U.S. military, and less willing to provide for their own defense. And, contrary to the assumptions inherent within the DPG, our allies' relative weakness imposes additional risks and burdens on us, diminishing U.S. security by increasing the likelihood that we will be drawn into peripheral conflicts. It is clear that the experiment in U.S. foreign policy over the last sixteen years has not achieved what it set out to do.

A truly different strategy is needed.

Aligning Power and Interests

My alternative approach proceeds from a particular view of U.S. power that is the polar opposite of that held by the advocates of our current policies. Whereas they see U.S. power as an unadulterated good, beneficial for Americans and for the other six billion plus residents of our planet, I see instead a host of problems. For starters, the United States need not engage in risky, and often counterproductive, missions abroad in order to be secure at home. Most missions to impose order in a civil conflict or to relieve extraordinary suffering, can and should be addressed by other states whose security interests are more likely to be affected by the spillover effects.

Likewise, the international economy is far more resilient than the advocates of benevolent global hegemony imagine. The United States is only one of many parties that have an interest in seeing the relatively free and open trading system remain so. Although it is appropriate that Americans should continue to push this loose order in a more free and open direction, we should also strive to distribute the burdens of policing the planet among all of the beneficiaries of global trade.

Our power is also costly, and maintaining our hegemony is likely to grow costlier still. The advocates of our current approach recognize that primacy carries a price, but they see those costs not as something to be avoided, but rather something to be overcome. If the American people don't like to intervene in other people's disputes, the object is to get them to like doing so. If others increase their spending in order to resist our hegemonic role, we have to increase spending still more.

Military power should properly be seen as a means to an end. It is neither intrinsically good nor evil. If our military power, and our use of that power, advances our security interests, that is good. If it does not, that is bad. And, as it happens, we have seen the power problem of the United States played out in various ways over the last two decades. Although our power is ostensibly intended to keep Americans safe, the fact that we have more power than we need actually makes us all less safe. Given this paradox, we must reduce our military power and we must adopt a new, more circumspect attitude toward the use of force.

We should shrink our military because the costs do not match the benefits we derive from it, and are particularly unappealing when contrasted with the realistic alternatives. The best of these from the U.S. perspective is a new global order in which other countries assume a greater responsibility for defending themselves and for dealing with regional security challenges before they become global challenges. Reducing our military power, therefore, will advance broader U.S. interests by precipitating a more equitable distribution of risks and responsibilities across the international system.

It will be difficult to transition from our current unipolar order to a new multipolar one. Other countries will be expected to bear additional costs, and many will resist. Resistance will also come from within the United States, especially from that cadre of Americans who are enamored of the idea that we can dominate the global order, and that it is in our interest to do so. But the risks that U.S. security will be undermined during this transitional period can be mitigated if we establish clear and stringent standards concerning when and whether to use force.

Reducing our power and thereby constraining our *ability* to intervene militarily around the globe will limit our *propensity* to intervene. After all, if the president woke up one day to discover that the U.S. military had been cut in half, it should affect his decisions on when and where this suddenly smaller military would be used.

But that is not what I am advocating. I don't wish the U.S. military to be cut in half overnight. I *do* wish for the United States to adopt a far more cautious approach to military intervention and to resize the military to conform to that new grand strategy.

That is not easy to do. As this book has shown, our capabilities often dictate our strategies. And given that there are domestic constituencies that favor various forms of military spending, these interest groups have often exerted an important influence over not merely how much military power we have but also how it should be used.

But it should operate the other way around. To build and sustain a massive military, and to then consider where to use it, puts the military cart before the strategic horse. I favor the opposite approach. Policymaking entails making choices, a willingness to explicitly consider trade-offs between the irrelevant and the urgent, between the nice to do and the must do. These choices also apply to our force structure, both the total size of our military, and the mix of planes and personnel, ships and submarines, within that military.

In an ideal world, government provides security for individuals while simultaneously affording them considerable freedom to pursue their own ends, provided of course that those pursuits do not infringe on the security and liberty of others. In the real world, preserving such liberties must exist in constant tension with the government's obligation to preserve and protect the Republic.

As noted throughout this book, the Founders, fearing the costs of military power, costs measured both in blood and treasure, but also in the character of the fledgling Republic—recall Madison's warning that war was the greatest enemy of liberty—defined national interests in ways that constrained the nation's propensity to wage war.

We should adopt a similar approach today. Our national interest begins certainly with U.S. physical security, defense of the homeland, protecting the nation from direct attack, and deterring would-be invaders and occupiers. It also includes preserving our way of life, particularly our individual liberty and economic prosperity. Because both of these things depend on the participation of the United States in the international system, we must remain engaged in the world, but it is wrong to assume that we can only do so from a position of global military dominance. The international system exists in spite of, not because of, the power of any one state, and it is the height of arrogance and folly to presume that the world will descend into chaos if the United States shapes its military to advance its vital national interests and adopts a more discriminating approach toward the use of force.

The Founders were also deeply skeptical of warfare's capacity for effecting good ends. Benjamin Franklin declared that "there never was a good war, or a bad peace."[8] They held such views despite the fact that they had all lived through a war that gave them what they most desired: the freedom to construct a new political order apart from the British monarchy. These patriots, to a person, would have much preferred that the same ends would have been achieved by other means.

Even George Washington, the taciturn general who led U.S. forces to victory and in the process forever established himself as the father of the new nation, wished for the United States to be a nation at peace. He especially hoped that we would remain aloof from other people's wars. Historian Joseph Ellis describes Washington's approach to foreign policy as grounded in a skeptical, some might even say pessimistic, view of an essentially immutable human nature that tended inexorably toward conflict. Ellis points to Washington's warning from his Farewell Address: "There can be no greater error to expect, or calculate upon real favours from Nation to Nation. 'Tis an illusion which experience must cure, which a just pride ought to discard." Washington, Ellis explains, perceived that nations—unlike human beings—would always "behave solely on the basis of interests." This conception of international relations, consistent with that of twentieth-century realists such as Hans Morgenthau and George Kennan, Ellis continues, "was formed from experience rather than reading, confirmed by early encounters with hardship and imminent death, [and] rooted in a relentlessly realistic view of human nature."[9]

This attitude toward entanglements with other nations combined with the Founders' inherent skepticism about the utility and efficacy of state action. They feared that government power, mobilized for foreign policy aims, can just as easily be directed to stifling liberty at home. These doubts and fears led them to cast a skeptical eye on war, and to adopt a very stringent standard for when and whether to go to war.

A similarly high standard would serve us well today. The Founders' concerns that wars—and an enormous and permanent military to prosecute these wars—would impose huge costs to our system of government, shift the balance between the branches, and expand the government's authority over the citizenry, have proved prescient. Likewise, we have learned—or at least we should have—that the costs of waging wars are rarely offset by the benefits that we derive from them. We need new rules governing the use of force.

New Rules: Four Criteria for Military Intervention

A smaller U.S. military focused on defending our core national interests cannot be in the business of defending other countries that should defend themselves. The same principle applies to interventions seen as serving a higher humanitarian purpose. Therefore, the United States should not commit to a particular military mission overseas unless there is a *compelling U.S. national security interest* at stake. This would seem at first glance to be a rather broad mandate, but U.S. national security has rarely been threatened over the past two decades. It should be noted that this criteria is more stringent than that set forth by the Weinberger-Powell Doctrine, which held that U.S. combat forces should not be sent overseas "unless the particular engagement or occasion is deemed vital to our national interest *or that of our allies.*"[10]

Whereas the Weinberger-Powell Doctrine presumed that allied interests were essentially synonymous with our own, we should be extremely wary of equating the two. We should revisit our obligations to each and every ally, and establish clear criteria for why, under what circumstances—and, crucially, by whose authority—these obligations might translate into the commitment of U.S. military personnel.

We should be particularly on guard against those situations that separate our own public from decisions of when and whether to go to war. The reason why is quite simple, and relates directly to the second criterion governing the use of force. The U.S. military should not be engaged in combat operations unless there is *a clear national consensus* behind the mission.

Popular support must be built around reasonable expectations of costs, as opposed to best-case scenarios. This consensus must be durable enough to survive temporary setbacks, and history shows that it is impossible to sustain domestic support when the mission does not advance vital national interests. The American people offered lukewarm support for the humanitarian mission in Somalia in 1993; they demanded a change of course when they saw the costs played out in the streets of Mogadishu. The same can be seen with respect to the Iraq War. It was not just that Americans thought, indeed were told, that the war would be cheap and easy; they also believed that even low-cost, low-risk wars should advance compelling U.S. national interests. The Bush administration marketed the war as a mission to overthrow a dictator with a functioning nuclear weapons program and hinted of ties to al-Qaeda. Support for the Iraq venture evaporated when the public learned the truth.[11]

We don't have to create new mechanisms for ascertaining public attitudes on such crucial questions; we need only use the tools provided for us by the Founders, namely by reasserting Congress's constitutional authority over the war powers.

The Founders did not create a democracy. They did not anticipate, nor did they desire, that important decisions would be settled by plebiscite. They did, however, intend that the public would communicate their wishes through their elected representatives. They expected that it would be difficult to build a consensus around any particular policy, and they deliberately constructed a system that constitutional scholar Edward S. Corwin aptly described as an "invitation to struggle" over important decisions between the executive and legislative branches.[12] The most important of these was the decision to take the country to war.

That is certainly what James Madison believed. Recall his assertion that the most important passage of the Constitution was the assignment of the war power to the legislature, as opposed to the executive branch. This crucial provision, however, runs counter to the impulse—promulgated after World War II, and expanded upon during successive rounds of NATO expansion in the post-Cold War period—to obligate the United States to become involved in foreign military conflicts, and therefore not with the explicit authorization of Congress. Indeed, a key objection to the League of Nations charter, one that ultimately contributed to the Senate's refusal to ratify that treaty, was precisely this constitutional concern—that a collective security organization would supplant Congress's authority as stipulated by the Founders.[13]

That such constitutional concerns are "now typically derided as 'isolationist,'" notes the Cato Institute's Stanley Kober, "merely indicates how far we have come from the founding vision of the United States." In short, Kober explains, "the pursuit of alliances has the effect of undermining what Madison regarded as the single most important characteristic of American democracy."[14]

Restoring Congress's proper role in determining whether and when to go to war will not be enough.[15] Renegotiating security treaties with key allies and terminating our trip-wire missions around the world that are designed to draw us into other people's conflicts will not by itself prevent a future president or Congress from choosing to send our troops into such conflicts. Cutting the military will not, by itself, constrain our government's propensity to wage war. We must also temper the public's occasional enthusiasm for war by ensuring that they understand the costs.

This idea also found favor among some of the Founders. Whereas some people today speak blithely of a "democratic peace" whereby democratic states are supposedly less warlike than undemocratic ones,[16] Madison was not so naive. He recognized that democracy was no panacea for curing man's propensity to wage war. He worried that wars of passion—wars precipitated by the public's desire for revenge, honor, or national pride—were every bit as dangerous to liberty as wars initiated by princes and kings. Madison also sought, therefore, ways to restrain the popular impulses that might drive the new government toward war.

The best mechanism, Madison surmised, would be to subject "the will of the society to the reason of the society." People must be made aware that their actions have consequences; they must be cognizant of the trade-offs inherent in pursuing a military versus non-military course.

The federal government tends to avoid such hard choices. Deficit spending enables politicians in Washington to write checks today that will be paid for far into the future. Though such expenditures may be justifiable in periods of great emergency, Congress has so perverted the definition of "emergency" that we now need a total reset. For starters, we should go back to Madison's preferred solution that "each generation should be made to bear the burden of its own wars, instead of carrying them on at the expense of other generations."[17] In other words, no more wars on the credit card. Forcing the advocates for war to consider the costs of war ahead of time, including an explicit accounting of how it will be paid for and what other expenditures will be cut or taxes raised, will help to frame the decision to go to war as a choice against competing priorities.

We cannot establish the likely costs of military intervention against the alternatives if we do not know what our troops will actually do. Therefore, the third criterion that should constrain our interventionist impulses is closely related to the second. When choosing to go to war, the government should not involve the U.S. military in foreign operations without *clear and obtainable military objectives.* Further, every plan for getting into a war must have an equally detailed plan for getting out.

Such questions are practically irrelevant when a country's very survival is at stake; the British and the Soviets didn't ask for an exit strategy when the Nazis were bearing down on them. For Americans after Pearl Harbor, only Japan's unconditional surrender would have sufficed.[18]

But the criteria discussed here pertain to wars of choice, wars that we launch on others, that we choose to initiate because we believe it will advance our security. Once the advocates for war have shown how the nation's interests will be served by military intervention, and once the public has signaled its willingness to support the cause, including agreeing to pay for it, the military's role should be limited to achieving military objectives. Other unrelated tasks, including attempting to fashion a new political order that will bring contending factions together, or engaging in post-conflict reconstruction projects to repair physical infrastructure damaged not by the war but by years of neglect by previous governments, should be left to others, including the other countries in the region who will be most directly affected by the chaos and disorder that would ensue if such projects do not go forth.

Colin Powell was speaking to the problem of post-conflict reconstruction in his famous Pottery Barn principle: "You break it, you buy it." What Powell actually said to President Bush in August 2002, according to Bob Woodward's account of the exchange, was even more perceptive: "You are going to be the proud owner of twenty-five million people." Powell warned the president, "You will own all their hopes, aspirations, problems.... It's going to suck the oxygen out of everything."[19]

Another prominent military leader had similar concerns about the tendency of wars to drag on for years. As he prepared to lead the 101st Airborne Division across the border separating Kuwait from Iraq in March 2003, Maj. Gen. David Petraeus could have been forgiven a bit of triumphalism. And yet, despite the fact that Saddam Hussein's days in power were clearly numbered, Petraeus was haunted by a nagging question: "Tell me how this ends?"[20]

Petraeus and Powell understood that it is rather easy to start wars, but it is awfully difficult to end them. Policymakers must explicitly account for this when choosing to send American troops to war.

The first three criteria are not enough to establish the wisdom and legitimacy of military intervention. The American people will support the use of force when national security interests are at stake, but that doesn't by itself make intervention acceptable. After all, we can incinerate any place on earth in a matter of minutes. That obviously does not imply a *right* to do so. This leads to the fourth and final rule governing foreign military intervention: *force should only be used as a last resort*, and only after other measures for dealing with the particular national security threat have been exhausted.

Civilized societies abhor warfare. Even wars initiated for the right reasons, and waged with due respect for international norms, are, in a real sense, a failure: a failure to resolve matters by peaceful means.

These four criteria are hardly revolutionary. As already noted, they mirror the precepts of the Weinberger-Powell Doctrine from the Reagan era, as well as aspects of just war theory that have been around for centuries. But we have lost sight of them in recent years. Our capacity for waging war has enabled us to avoid discussions of whether a particular intervention was truly necessary. As we solve our power problem, reducing and reshaping our military to focus on U.S. vital national security interests, we cannot afford to be distracted by challenges that can and should be handled by others. Accordingly our default position should be one of non-intervention and the burden of proof should shift to the advocates of military intervention.

Shifting the Burden of Proof

The governing presumption should be strongly against military intervention, because even well-intentioned wars unleash a host of unintended ends, most of them bad, and because the costs and risks for the intervener are far higher than the advocates of intervention are normally willing to admit. But even those interventions that are explicitly predicated on the grounds that they are necessary to advance U.S. national security must meet very strict standards. In particular, the pro-intervention faction must not only explain exactly how the particular intervention will make us safer, but they must also account for the possibility that this same intervention might have the opposite effect.

It was the latter aspect that was most neglected in the run-up to the war in Iraq. The focus in late 2002 was too much on the nature of Saddam's regime, and speculation into his WMD program, and too little on how overthrowing his government would, for example, reduce the threat of terrorism, improve the image of the United States or make a wider war in the Middle East less likely.

One CIA official recalled conducting a review of a biological weapons program at an Iraqi university. "We were trying to find something," the anonymous official explained to veteran reporters David Corn and Michael Isikoff. "We were motivated. We knew this was important." But he ultimately blamed himself for succumbing to the impulse to "find something." "It was our job to be skeptical," he said.[21]

That is certainly correct, and the Congress, the media, and the American people have rightly faulted the intelligence community for its inaccurate assessments of Iraq's weapons programs. But, in fairness, and given the litany of disastrous interventions of the past twenty years, *all* Americans have a duty to be skeptical. Policymakers asked to cast a difficult vote, journalists covering a story from an uncomfortable angle, citizens choosing to support a particular candidate, or a particular mission, need to ask the difficult and penetrating questions *before* we go to war.

Dwight David Eisenhower, in his famous farewell address, believed that a similar level of citizen engagement—and a healthy dose of skepticism—was needed to block the military-industrial complex from gaining "unwarranted influence" that would "endanger our liberties and our democratic processes." In particular, he hoped that "an alert and knowledgeable citizenry" would ensure that all of the elements of national power would be applied "so that security and liberty may prosper together."[22]

There were skeptics before the Iraq War. There were those who warned that the invasion of Iraq was likely to set in train a host of unintended consequences, many of which would threaten U.S. interests in the region, and undermine U.S. security more generally.[23] These sorts of pessimistic but ultimately *accurate* assessments that the Bush administration, hawks in Congress, and the too-credulous media deemed at the time unduly negative, deserve greater attention from Ike's elusive "alert and knowledgeable citizenry." Our bitter experience in Iraq could still help elicit such critical scrutiny in the future.

Yet incredibly, events in Iraq seem not to have shaken the faith of the most fervent advocates of intervention. On the contrary, and in anticipation of a rising tide of skepticism engendered by the high costs and dubious benefits of the Iraq War, the advocates for war have chosen to create their own lessons of Iraq—lessons that reinforce their preconceived notions and that imply that the next intervention will go well. The problem, they say, was not that George W. Bush chose to overthrow Saddam Hussein's government, but rather that the Bush administration made some critical errors at crucial times in the course of the post-war reconstruction, errors that had the effect of snatching defeat from the jaws of a certain, unmitigated victory.[24]

The arguments are by now painfully familiar: The Bush administration didn't use enough troops. They didn't secure the borders. They disbanded the Iraqi army. They failed to provide water, power, and sanitation. They didn't provide security. They didn't hand out enough money. They didn't hand out enough money quickly enough.

The premise behind these and other explanations for what went wrong in Iraq is that success in future wars is not just possible, but likely, so long as the United States is prepared to devote the resources, and the political will, to make it happen. "America has frequently used force on behalf of principles and tangible interests," wrote Ivo Daalder of the Brookings Institution and the Carnegie Endowment's Robert Kagan in August 2007, "and that is not likely to change."[25]

But as David Hendrickson and Robert Tucker wisely concluded in a paper published by the Strategic Studies Institute at the Army War College, "though the record of Iraq war planning [deserves scrutiny], critics also have neglected the larger lesson that there are certain limits to what military power can accomplish." "For certain purposes, like the creation of a liberal democratic society that will be a model for others, military power is a blunt instrument, destined by its very nature to give rise to unintended and unwelcome consequences. Rather than 'do it better next time,' a better lesson is 'don't do it at all.' "[26] We may reluctantly choose to initiate wars in the future, but we should do so with a very clear sense of the risks, and with a sober sense of the likelihood of failure.

When Georgetown University Professor David Edelstein surveyed the historical record of post-war occupations from the time of Napoleon to the present day, he found that two-thirds of all occupations fail, and there are strong reasons to suspect that Americans will not easily improve on this dismal track record in the twenty-first century.[27] For one thing, our deep-seated cultural attitudes toward military power affect the strategies that our troops employ. To the extent that the U.S. military has traditionally been poorly suited to occupy and rebuild other nations, its problems stem from American citizens' ambivalence, even skepticism, about whether such missions are worth our while.[28] Indeed, they rarely are. Our aversion to long-term military occupations, counterinsurgency, and nation building reflect an instinctive understanding that the costs of such undertakings are rarely offset by the benefits.

The advocates of intervention often address this challenge by exaggerating the likelihood of success, and inflating the benefits that will flow from that success. Equally important, however, they misrepresent the costs by pretending that the combat phase of operations is all that matters. The pro-war faction rallies the requisite public support, and cheers when the bullets fly and the bombs fall. Within a short period of time—a matter of weeks in the case of the first and second Iraq wars, and in Afghanistan—the governing elites of the targeted country are either removed from power, or at least thoroughly defeated, and the opposing army, such as it is, is destroyed, and major combat operations are declared to be over.

If and when we encounter an insurgency, the initial response is to deny that one exists. For starters, to admit that we are confronting an insurgency runs counter to some of the most cherished notions of American exceptionalism, including the conceit that the United States is always a liberator, and never an occupier. Liberators are greeted with flowers and kisses, as we witnessed in France in 1944, or in Kuwait in 1991. By contrast, occupiers must deal with those individuals who oppose, and resist, the presence of foreign troops in their country.

The advocates for war claimed that there would be no serious opposition in Iraq. Our troops, they predicted, would be seen as liberators. And in some parts of the country, those expectations proved accurate. But on the whole, certain core assumptions about the way the U.S. military would be received in Iraq have had a detrimental effect, particularly in the crucial early stages of the war.[29] When finally forced to admit that we were in fact facing an insurgency the Bush administration and other defenders of the war presented it as an *unanticipated* cost.[30]

We as a nation should never again fall victim to such systematic distortions of the likely costs of war. When we go to war, we must appreciate that there will be winners and losers in the target country, and we must expect that the losers will fight hard to regain their lost status.[31]

We must further expect, given our military's technological advantages and sheer destructive power, that the fight is likely to be conducted by unconventional means, involving acts of terrorism and other tactics favored by insurgents. Such a fight will be difficult. Counterinsurgency operations are protracted, time-consuming, and risky; it is difficult to measure progress, and setbacks are to be expected; it is almost impossible to bring our advantages—especially our technological edge—to bear. When we attempt to do so, the use of such means often proves counterproductive. Insurgents attempt to goad attackers into inadvertently killing or injuring innocent bystanders. Each victim of this collateral damage leaves behind a legacy of anger, or even hatred, among parents, spouses, children, and friends. The risk that insurgents will capitalize on this bitterness to grow their ranks requires our troops to use particular care in the use of force.

Consider an example from another military campaign that still enjoys strong support from the public at large: the war in Afghanistan. The use of air power to attack suspected insurgent strongholds has enraged Afghan leaders and the local population causing them to question our intentions. Afghan President

Hamid Karzai's "first demand" of Barack Obama was for the President-elect "to put an end to civilian casualties."[32]

To the extent that success in counterinsurgency requires a greater tolerance for risk by the counterinsurgent forces, it is incumbent upon political leaders to make the case that these additional risks are worthwhile.[33] Thus did some of the most fervent advocates of the war in Iraq bemoan the supposed lack of leadership exhibited by President Bush in rallying the public to the cause of winning that war. But such cries for leadership have been heard before. In the waning days of the Clinton administration, Andrew Erdmann called on the country's leaders "to recast the public's conception of its national interests and stoke its will to preserve them." Erdmann, who went on to serve on George W. Bush's National Security Council as Director for Iran, Iraq, and Strategic Planning, called for a program of "strategic candor" to "foster a realistic public understanding of the challenges, opportunities, and potential costs of leadership in international affairs."[34]

Erdmann dramatically misconstrued the public's appetite for such interventions and therefore grossly exaggerated the impact that skillful politicians can have on changing public attitudes. To the extent that politicians do understand that the public has no stomach for long-term projects aimed at rebuilding shattered societies, this explains why we had so little "strategic candor" in the run-up to the war in Iraq. And Bush was hardly alone: strategic candor was also in short supply during the debate surrounding Bill Clinton's interventions in the Balkans in the 1990s.

A prudent approach to intervention lies not in attempting to recast perceptions of national interest, but in recognizing instead that such interests are largely immutable, that preserving or advancing such interests is rarely served by launching wars of choice, and that successful military operations require strong public support that can only be sustained when these interests are genuinely engaged.

This does not mean that intervention is never a wise choice. It does mean that the burden of proof lies with those making the case for war; not those advising against. The key is to understand, at the outset of a war, that it is likely to be extraordinarily costly in lives and money. We must anticipate that some form of resistance or insurgency is likely, and that success is uncertain even if we play our cards right, and even get lucky. It only makes sense, therefore, to engage in such operations when truly vital national interests are at stake, when the object is clear and attainable, and only after we have exhausted all other options.

A New Profile of Power: Right Sizing the Force

Applying stringent criteria to the use of force will not by itself eliminate our impulse to become involved in other people's wars. The lessons of Iraq, which teach us that war is an imprecise instrument that unleashes a host of unintended consequences, many of which are harmful to our national security, will not by themselves constrain our propensity to intervene. This is particularly true given that there are so many people trying to spin the Iraq story to suit their ends. We also need a new grand strategy, predicated on self-reliance, which dissolves the burdens of global hegemony and demands more from regional powers. >

There are faint signs that a strategic transition is already underway. The 2006 National Security Strategy backed away somewhat from the startling unilateralism that had characterized the first four years of the Bush administration. Despite the fact that the Bush administration showed some faint rhetorical interest in sharing the burdens of policing the world with others, however, its unwillingness to reduce our massive military signaled its expectation that the United States would remain the world's indispensable nation. Taking their cue, our allies have proved understandably disinterested in spending more on their militaries. In order to make burden sharing a reality, the United States must combine a new grand strategy and a greater skepticism toward military intervention with a new profile of power: namely, a smaller military that is explicitly oriented toward defending U.S. security.

We should not reduce our military without at the same time rethinking how the remaining forces shall be used. If a finite number of assets are stretched to the limit to cover excessive global commitments, there is a serious risk that we will damage morale and readiness and ultimately create a "hollow force"—a military with inadequate equipment, insufficient funding, and too many missions for too few personnel. Former Army chief of staff Gen. Eric Shinseki expressed these sentiments rather well upon his retirement in June 2003: "Beware the 12-division strategy for the 10-division army."[35]

The scope of our military missions should be sharply restricted. We must work diligently over the next few years to renegotiate or abrogate security treaties to transform our various overseas commitments into more equitable alliances, and we should completely divest ourselves of any open-ended obligation to come to the aid of others. Though it is true that few countries currently have military forces capable of influencing events far outside their spheres of influence, all countries have forces for self-defense. In the absence of the threat posed by a would-be global hegemon such as the Soviet Union, other countries should be expected to act as first responders against all manner of threats in their respective regions.

Some of our military leaders are already moving in a new direction. Before becoming Chairman of the Joint Chiefs of Staff, the then chief of naval operations Adm. Mike Mullen presented a new maritime strategy that formally recognized the U.S. Navy as only one of many players in an increasingly interconnected international system. In an op-ed titled "We Can't Do It Alone," Mullen cast his proposal for a "1,000 ship navy" as "a global maritime partnership that unites maritime forces, port operators, commercial shippers, and international, governmental and nongovernmental agencies to address mutual concerns." Mullen did not propose to create a new global alliance complete with headquarters and staffs. Rather, "membership in this 'navy' is purely voluntary and would have no legal or encumbering ties," he explained. "It would be a free-form, self-organizing network of maritime partners—good neighbors interested in using the power of the sea to unite, rather than to divide," and in which all participants contribute as their capabilities and interests allow.[36]

Mullen noted that the U.S. Navy might not participate in certain maritime operations, but that would not preclude cooperation among interested parties. "National sovereignty comes first. Nations which can provide assistance should always be prepared to do so. But nations which need that help must first be willing to ask for it. Not everyone will welcome U.S. participation . . . but they may welcome that of their neighbors and allies."[37]

Secretary of Defense Robert M. Gates praised Mullen's approach. "We should not forget that in this age no single nation is capable of addressing the myriad threats we face." "The 1,000-ship Navy initiative," Gates said at a meeting of Navy flag officers, was "in line with the President's and the Quadrennial Defense Review's call for partner-building," but more important it was "the only way we can meet threats that [were] not limited to any single nation or region."[38]

The same principle should apply to force planning across the board. A military geared to defending U.S. security should include a strong navy to defend our shores and a highly capable air force to defend our airspace. We should retain a small nuclear arsenal for deterrence. We need a small, professional Army available on a moment's notice, bolstered by a relatively large reserve component that can be quickly mobilized if the security of the United States is ever directly threatened. The Marine Corps should continue as an expeditionary force, geared toward projecting conventional power when required.

That might sound like a tall order; in fact, a right-sized military would be far smaller than today's force. Most of the cuts would involve the Army and Marine Corps, but the Navy and Air Force can be scaled back as well.

A Focused Navy

The U.S. Navy has been cut in half since the end of the Cold War, but it remains focused more on the defense of others than on the defense of the United States. The Navy's long-range shipbuilding plans envision a fleet of 313 ships by 2019 even as most objective observers believe this goal to be completely unrealistic.[39] A right-sized U.S. Navy might have not more than 200 ships, but the number is less important than the mix of vessels in the fleet. A navy concentrated in the Western Hemisphere would require roughly half as many aircraft carriers as we have today (six versus eleven). It would still possess a large number of smaller surface vessels, especially frigates and destroyers, but perhaps not more than 100 such vessels in total. The submarine fleet—which today numbers fifty fast-attack subs, plus another fourteen ballistic missile submarines—could also be cut.

Such proposals are sure to elicit howls of protest from the tens of thousands of people employed in the shipbuilding industry, and their representatives in Congress, but the interests of the many (all taxpayers) must take precedence over those of the few. For example, the defenders of the Virginia-class subs must justify their costly platform against reasonable alternatives. This is not an easy case to make; refueling the Los Angeles-class submarines would substantially extend their service lives, and at a fraction of the cost of the new Virginia-class vessels. More to the point, the U.S. Navy's capacity to wage undersea warfare is beyond challenge, and it could sustain this posture well into the future. Although some countries have a handful of diesel-powered submarines capable of operating in or near their territorial waters, these vessels pose little if any threat to U.S. national security. Our submarine force should be geared toward ensuring that that remains the case going forward.[40]

The smaller surface combatants in our fleet—cruisers, destroyers, and frigates—should be subjected to the same level of scrutiny that we apply to aircraft carriers and submarines. So far, the littoral combat ship (LCS) has been a high-priced disappointment, and the DD(X)/DDG-1000 Zumwalt-class destroyer has fared even worse.

This is simply unacceptable. As we shift to a networked force of smaller, highly adaptable vessels we must ensure that the shipbuilders deliver their goods on time and on budget. Policymakers can aid this process by carefully defining requirements. The ships that we ask the shipyards to build must satisfy the core mission of guarding the ocean approaches to our vast nation, and in support of counterterrorism operations on rare occasions, but we should not expect that the U.S. Navy will be regularly engaged in offensive operations on the other side of the planet.

Take, for example, what are likely to be the most important maritime missions of the twenty-first century: keeping open vital sea lanes of communications (SLOCs). Safeguarding the flow of essential commodities and finished goods is, and will be, a vital mission for the U.S. military, but other nations have as much, if not greater, interests in seeing that certain crucial waterways remain open. Any country with a coastline maintains maritime defense forces that could work in conjunction with other navies should hostilities threaten a shared strategic interest. Those regional powers that have the requisite blue-water naval assets (for example, Britain, France, India, and Japan) would have no incentive to disrupt international commerce; on the contrary, they would be at the front of the line to guard the vulnerable choke points that are most crucial for their interests.

The closure of one or more key waterways is not an idle concern. The Suez Canal was shut down during the Suez Crisis of 1956, then again in 1967 during the Six Day War, and remained inoperable until 1975. Major disruptions in the Strait of Malacca, the narrow waterway between Malaysia and Indonesia, would have a similar impact, but would fall hardest on those countries in East Asia that are most dependent on the flow of goods through these waters.[41] China, Japan, and other Asian nations share a concern that the passage remains unencumbered, given that 50,000 vessels transit the strait annually, and an estimated 15 million barrels of oil pass through it every day.[42]

In general, Japan and Australia should be expected to assume a larger role in the Western Pacific; India seeks—and should be afforded—greater responsibilities over its trade routes to both the Middle East and Asia; and the United Kingdom, France, Italy, and all other EU states with navies, should be expected to do the same in the Eastern Atlantic, the North Sea, the Baltic Sea, and the Mediterranean.

Controlling vital SLOCs—a central mission for the U.S. Navy during the Cold War—may still be relevant in the coming decades, but the mission has changed, and the ships that will be needed to support the mission should change with it. Whereas sea-lane control was once intended as an offensive measure, to deny adversaries the use of certain geographic "choke points," sea-lane control in the modern era aims to ensure the free flow of goods and is therefore primarily defensive in nature. What's more, given that the sea-control mission will be shared with other countries, most of whom will be operating in close proximity to their home waters, our force planning should focus on our core obligations, principally in the Western Hemisphere. That mission could be supported by the "small boys" of the fleet—cruisers, destroyers, and frigates. In the unlikely event that a regional conflict threatened to close a strategic choke point, naval and air forces from many different countries would be able to respond.[43]

Aircraft carriers are particularly ill-suited to operating in restricted waterways or close to shore. For one thing, carrier-based aircraft are at a distinct disadvantage against land-based aircraft. The vessel itself, meanwhile, is vulnerable to small units employing a host of asymmetric means, including potential suicide attacks by determined foes desperate to disable the single greatest symbol of U.S. power. There is no peer competitor today or in the medium-term future who could even begin to challenge the U.S. Navy's dominance on the high seas. Thus, a new emphasis on defending the waters closer to home would facilitate a transition to smaller ships, including smaller carriers that may someday be focused on the launch and recovery of unmanned aerial vehicles.[44]

A Leaner Air Force

The U.S. Air Force is seen as responsible for control of the air space over much of the planet, including all of North America, most of Europe, and parts of East Asia, not to mention Iraq and Afghanistan. An Air Force focused on controlling the skies over the United States, and the airborne approaches to same, would be quite large—certainly larger than any other air force on earth. A right-sized Air Force could easily accomplish the essential missions of maintaining control of the airspace in and around the United States with half as many fighters as currently planned.

The question then becomes which planes to buy. Under the necessary constraints imposed by a much smaller procurement budget for fighter aircraft, cost containment becomes paramount. The Air Force wants to purchase additional F-22s, but the Raptor's whopping price tag—$216 million per plane if one counts only costs going forward (the Air Force calls these "flyaway" costs); $356 million per aircraft counting costs over the life of the program—and its poor air-to-ground capabilities make it a prime target for cuts.

The costs of the F-35 Joint Strike Fighter (JSF) have also vastly exceeded expectations, but even critics of the JSF such as Nick Schwellenbach, an investigator for the Washington watchdog group the Project on Government Oversight, concede that the JSF "has a bigger payload and fulfills close air-support missions" better than the costlier F-22.[45] These missions are more relevant for offensive operations, for example over Iraq and Afghanistan, but how will the JSF fare at controlling the skies over the United States? In all likelihood, rather well, especially when pitted against any possible competitor over the next fifteen to twenty years. The challenge for the JSF is in containing per unit costs and in maintaining its technological edge over time.

A relatively low-cost fighter is eventually needed to replace aging F-16s, but we don't need nearly as many F-35s as is currently planned, even if the program can achieve greater cost containment. The Air Force should be given a strict budget for procurement and maintenance, and be required to develop a suitable mix of aircraft that can maintain air superiority within these budget constraints, and without drawing money away from its other critical tasks.

A Much Smaller Nuclear Deterrent

One of these other critical tasks is nuclear deterrence. The Navy and the Air Force would continue to share the responsibility for deterring would-be attackers with nuclear weapons. A credible deterrent would be less than one-fifth the size of our current arsenal, and might number not more than 500 warheads. For example, four to five ballistic missile submarines, each carrying ninety-six thermonuclear warheads, would be sufficient to deter any leader foolish enough to even contemplate a strike on the United States. In the interest of ensuring a survivable second-strike capability, however, a roughly equal number of warheads might remain available for rapid deployment on Air Force bombers that can be dispersed at a moment's notice at one of hundreds of military or civilian airfields around the country, or deployed on Minuteman III ICBM's located in silos in the continental United States. We don't need both. The survival of the land-based deterrent might be attributed to the political influence of legislators and institutional resistance from within the Air Force. But to the extent that this is true, such parochial considerations should not influence the composition of our forces. As we continue to make deep cuts in our nuclear arsenal, the strategic triad should become a dyad, and we should debate the merits of bombers versus ICBMs.

Fighting Al-Qaeda and Other Non-State Actors

When the Taliban regime in Afghanistan refused to hand over al-Qaeda members after 9/11, the United States made them pay, driving them from their seat of power, and putting in their place a new class of leaders committed to governing a nation firmly ensconced within the international community.

But the Taliban were, thankfully, an exceptional case. In the future, few governments will be so foolish as to openly harbor anti-American terrorists, and any who do will get what's coming to them—via a 500-pound bomb dropped from a long-range bomber, or, increasingly, a Hellfire missile fired from an unmanned aerial vehicle. Beyond these rare cases when massive firepower and high-tech weapons can be brought to bear, neither the Navy nor the Air Force are well-suited to conduct counterterrorism operations. Al-Qaeda possesses neither a navy nor an air force, and the use of high explosives to kill or otherwise incapacitate individuals who hide among the civilian population will engender hostility toward the attackers if the bombs and bullets go astray, as they inevitably will. A much more discriminating approach is needed.

Some argue that the Army and Marine Corps are well-suited for counterterrorism missions, because they rely on precision firepower and they are more adept at separating terrorists and terrorist-sympathizers from innocent bystanders. On these grounds, some would substantially increase the size of the conventional Army and Marine Corps, in order to have the military become more involved in counterterrorism, as well as for conducting counterinsurgency and nation-building operations.[46]

But the belief that a larger military is necessary, or even effective, at reducing the threat of terrorism is mistaken. Counterterrorism is not an especially personnel-intensive endeavor, and, to the extent that it is, the people most heavily involved are not, and should not be, members of the military.

In many cases, in fact, when we try to use the U.S. military to fight terrorism it only makes the problem worse. For one, as already noted, military operations can result in civilian casualties, and those left behind will focus their ire on the people responsible for the loss of their loved ones. In some cases, they turn against the terrorists who invited the attacks; other times, the retaliation is directed against the attacker. Even non-kinetic military operations, however, including the stationing of ground troops in foreign lands, can serve as a central grievance around which terrorist organizations can mobilize new recruits.[47]

And what of the supposed need for more troops to conduct Iraq and Afghanistan-style conflicts? Many Americans believe that our failings there, especially in Iraq, are a function of our having "too few boots on the ground." From that flows the logical conclusion that we need more people in boots.[48] Republicans and Democrats both endorse the idea that our military is stretched too thin because our commitments exceeded our means to achieve them, and that the best way to resolve this imbalance is to increase the means, as opposed to rethinking the ends.[49]

No one disputes that our troops have been overtaxed by the wars in Iraq and Afghanistan, not to mention counterterrorism operations elsewhere around the world. But the problem of too few troops pursuing too many missions began even before 9/11. As noted throughout this book, we have asked the members of our military—and especially those in the Army and Marine Corps—to be the lead instrument of our interventionist foreign policies ever since the end of the Cold War. Our troops have responded honorably, but they cannot do everything, and they cannot be everywhere.

Current plans call for the Army to grow to over 547,000, perhaps by the end of 2010. The Marine Corps is also expected to grow over this same period to just over 200,000. But although adding more troops treats the symptoms, it does not address the root causes of the problem. On the contrary, it might make it worse; an expanded military would give us all the tools needed to fumble our way into another strategic disaster like Iraq. More U.S. troops are not the answer; a more judicious use of the troops that we already have is. The near-term solution for relieving the stresses on soldiers and Marines is to bring them home from Iraq. The long-term solution is a reappraisal of our flawed strategy for fighting terrorism and a reconsideration of the balance among the tools we use to implement that strategy. Rather than increase the size of the Army and Marine Corps, we should look to dramatically reduce the number of personnel in both services. ⟩

Fewer Missions, Fewer Boots (and Other Stuff)

As we cut the number of personnel in the active duty Army and Marine Corps, we will need fewer of their more expensive weapon systems. At least two of these programs—the Marine's V-22, and the Army's Future Combat Systems (FCS)—should be scaled back.

Critics take particular note of the V-22's high costs relative to other alternatives. The business of transporting Marines or special operations personnel and their equipment could just as easily be handled by purchasing new versions of the H-53s, the H-92s, or even by smaller helicopters such as the H-60 Black Hawk.[50] So far, the Pentagon has stuck with the program, despite the fact that the costs have nearly tripled, from an initial estimate of $24 million ($46 million, in 2008 dollars) per aircraft when the contract was first awarded in 1986, to its current per unit cost of $110 million, and despite lingering concerns about crew safety and comfort.

As of early 2008, Army planners did not expect FCS to be available for our military personnel until 2015, but Defense Secretary Gates and members of Congress prevailed upon the program's managers to accelerate that timeline by at least three years. Based on guidelines promulgated in June 2008, the FCS program now aims to have equipment available for use by men and women in the field by fiscal year 2011.[51]

But even if the program could achieve this new target, the high costs and still unproven technologies that are to be used in the FCS advise against moving forward with the program as is. The Center for American Progress's Lawrence Korb notes that within "the network of 53 crucial technologies, 52 are unproven." Korb therefore recommends cutting annual outlays by more than 60 percent, from $25 billion to $10 billion over the next five years.[52]

Beyond the V-22 and FCS, beyond the Virginia submarine and the DDG-1000, beyond the F-22 and the Joint Strike Fighter, we need a renewed emphasis in military procurement on cost containment. This can only occur within an environment of shrinking defense budgets. Defense contractors who are best able to meet stringent cost and quality standards will win the privilege of providing our military with the necessary tools, but at far less expense to the taxpayers. And those who cannot will have to find other business.

The Other Institutions We Need

We need institutions of government that are capable and empowered to work with others in a cooperative effort to round up known and suspected terrorists. But the truth is we already do. To the extent that our foreign policy professionals— diplomats and other civilians—seem overmatched against their uniformed colleagues, the problem is chiefly one of too much money going to the military. When one considers the many different functions of our government that are loosely grouped under the category of "foreign relations," the Pentagon's budget constitutes about 93 percent of the total. Reducing the military budget will begin to rectify this glaring imbalance between the military and non-military tools of statecraft.[53]

However, it is not clear that we need a far larger diplomat corps as we transition away from our hegemonic role. The State Department's budget is relatively small, and that is largely by design: its aim is to relate to foreign nations, not to run them. National security organizations are shaped by politics that reflect lasting national interests, namely a disinclination to subjugate foreign peoples and lose unnecessary wars. That disinclination is not simply accidental but rather derives from the lessons that Americans have learned from history. We have historically looked askance at the small wars European powers fought to maintain their imperial holdings, viewing these actions as illiberal and unjust. Our misadventures like Vietnam and Iraq are the exceptions that make the rule. It is no accident that U.S. national security organizations are not designed for occupation duties. When it comes to nation building, brokering civil and ethnic conflict and waging counterinsurgency, we are our own worst enemy, and that is a sign of our lingering common sense.[54]

Although the U.S. government will continue to maintain a diplomatic presence around the world, the primary object of U.S. policy should be to facilitate the peaceful, non-coercive interactions between Americans and non-Americans that occur tens of millions of times every day. For all the talk of the need for more public diplomacy, the fact remains that individuals, businesses, and NGOs are far better suited for these types of relations than are agents of the U.S. government. In most instances, the best thing for the government to do is to stay out of the way. For example, the U.S. higher education system has long been the envy of the world. Americans and non-Americans routinely work and study together in our colleges and universities, and it is precisely in these types of venues that misconceived notions of U.S. society and U.S. values can be ironed out. Unfortunately, our obsession with security following the 9/11 attacks discouraged some foreign students from coming to the United States. Government policies that are responsible for keeping the best and the brightest out of our institutions of higher learning can be recast with an eye toward greater openness without sacrificing security.[55]

To cite another example, government-sponsored foreign aid programs are an unmitigated failure. The esteemed economist Lord Peter Bauer once called foreign aid "a process by which poor people in rich countries help rich people in poor countries."[56] That may be, but it certainly doesn't help poor people in poor countries; an estimated $2.3 trillion spent over the course of five decades has had little if any impact on stimulating long-term economic growth.[57] Just as our military policies should be geared toward self-sufficiency for our allies around the world, so too should our approach to foreign assistance focus on empowering economic opportunity as opposed to an endless cycle of dependency. Poverty, disease, and violence go hand-in-hand. The best way to break this cycle in the developing world is by encouraging economic development through free trade and other economic policies that reward individual initiative and private enterprise.

A small portion of the savings from the defense budget could be directed to the State Department and to the intelligence services, but the lion's share should be returned to the country's 120 million households. Americans should be trusted to spend their money as they see fit. Given that we don't like to stuff our money into mattresses, most of the savings that Americans will achieve from cuts in our defense budget will make its way back into the private economy. Given that we are a generous and compassionate people, a considerable portion will be delivered to churches, charities, and NGOs. And given the abysmal track record of past foreign aid programs, it seems likely that this money will be far more targeted—and far more effective—than the most ambitious schemes cooked up at the World Bank and USAID.

A New Model for Intervention

Substantial force reductions will be impossible to effect in a responsible way if they are not matched with a major strategic realignment. When President Clinton accelerated the force reductions put in motion by President George H. W. Bush in the early 1990s, he did so even as he maintained virtually all the commitments of the Cold War era. Then, over the course of eight years, he added several new ones. The Clinton administration was unwilling to accept the trade-offs of the post–Cold War era, particularly in terms of encouraging regional powers to assume greater responsibility for maintaining order in the world—or, at a minimum, in their corner of the world—and our men and women in uniform paid the price.

Despite the evidence of the past two decades, however, most politicians—and most foreign policy experts—believe that the core grand strategy that would have the United States standing alone as the world's hegemon for the indefinite future can be sustained so long as competent managers in the White House are behind the controls.[58]

But this is a fool's game. Pretending that our military power is limitless, or that the public's distaste for intervention can be reversed by a skillful public relations campaign, does not make it so. We cannot so easily absolve ourselves of the need to prioritize when, and whether, to use our power. The governing presumption therefore should be that we will not.

It is naive to believe that our prodigious military has not deterred would-be attackers. It is unrealistic to believe that this deterrent will never fail, and that our military will never be called on to address extant threats. But it is even more unrealistic to believe that these forces are omnipotent. By carefully defining our vital security interests, and by making it necessary for other countries to step forward and assume responsibility for their own security, we can simultaneously reduce the occasions in which the U.S. military is expected to play a vital or even central role. Thus can we avoid the creation of a "hollow force," even as we retain our position as the world's preeminent military power, one fully capable of defending legitimate U.S. security interests for many years to come.

A new approach to foreign policy, based on the straightforward view that a government's primary obligations are to its own people, and that military intervention that does not serve that narrow purpose is dangerous, must address the hard cases. What about Rwanda? What about Darfur? Would we have sent troops into Bosnia before the slaughter at Srebrenica? Would U.S. troops be deployed today in the West Bank, standing between Israeli settlers and rock-throwing Palestinians? Would U.S. troops have sheltered the Marsh Arabs and the Kurds from Saddam Hussein?

In most of these cases, my answer is no. As a great and powerful nation, we are able to contemplate becoming involved in places far from our shores in ways that people in small, insular countries simply cannot fathom. But we must never forget that the U.S. military exists for one purpose, to protect and defend the physical territory of the United States, its citizens, and our way of life. If a mission cannot be shown to serve this purpose, then I don't believe that it should be undertaken. Period.

That does not mean, however, that no other country, or group of countries, will do so. In my ideal world, each country has primary responsibility for its own defense. Most, by extension, will have some capacity for taking action in their neighborhood, and a few, including the United States, will retain the ability to intervene far outside of their respective region.

The size and character of any nation's military is shaped by its obligations to its citizens, and this leads naturally to vast power disparities between different nation-states. In this context, the United States will most certainly have more military power than any other country on earth. Consider that the federal government in Washington, DC, has a constitutional obligation to provide the same measure of security to people living in Barrow, Alaska as it does to people in Key West, Florida. The citizens of Lubec, Maine (population 1,652), the easternmost town in the United States, live 5,450 miles away from Na'ahelu, Hawaii (population 919), and yet the people living in these two places are entitled to the same protections as those living within the shadow of the U.S. Capitol. The distribution of Americans across a vast swath of land and sea requires a vast military, far larger than that needed for any other country. Our military is much larger still because it is currently configured according to imperatives that go well beyond our government's constitutional obligations, chiefly imperatives that we have taken on ourselves, or that we have allowed others to place on our shoulders.

As it happens, the ability to address security challenges in the Western Hemisphere aligns quite well with our government's duties and obligations to the American people. The U.S. Navy's ability to police the open oceans off the coast of Chile is not much different from its ability to patrol the St. George's Bank in the North Atlantic. In our own hemisphere, security challenges should be addressed in a collaborative fashion with the many beneficiaries contributing in a manner commensurate with their ability to do so, and to the extent that their interests are at stake. However, even though the United States will continue to possess a military capable of operating throughout the Western Hemisphere, it is far harder to make the case for a similarly interventionist posture in Europe and Asia, and harder still to do so in the Middle East and Africa.

To return, then, to the hard cases: genocide, ethnic cleansing, massive human rights violations. These are horrible crimes. They are tragic. No one disputes this. The problem is clarifying who is responsible for averting or halting them. A person who falls ill on a city street, or who is the victim of a brutal beating in a dark alley, is more likely to be aided by a single passerby than if the attack is witnessed by dozens of people.[59]

The sovereign state in which the abuses are occurring has primary responsibility—a responsibility to protect. But in those cases where the government itself is complicit in the crimes, neighboring or nearby states may well intervene, in part on the basis of national interests. Most cases of extreme brutality and violence—such as the killings in Darfur, the ethnic cleansing in Bosnia and Kosovo, or the slaughter of millions in Cambodia—pose a direct threat to the safety and security of neighboring states. If a neighboring state chooses to intervene, citing its own security interests as justification, then the mission is more likely to enjoy domestic and regional support than if the intervening power is thousands of miles away and has no plausible national interest at stake. Sustaining such interventions over the long term, as is often necessary, likely requires some connection to a country's interests because it is unreasonable to expect average citizens to allocate precious resources, and risk the lives of their sons and daughters serving in the military, for purely altruistic ends.

In just the last ten years, countries other than the United States, unilaterally or as part of a coalition, undertook at least five military interventions in places far removed geographically from the United States with the object of protecting innocent civilians and advancing human rights.[60] Though the issues at hand did not rise to a level of great interest for most Americans, they were of primary concern for the states who did intervene. Few places on the planet are so remote such that massive disorder and wholesale violence will not pose a direct security threat to *some* outsiders.

The long and oftentimes bitter legacy of imperialism reminds us that the greater danger might be not that other countries don't intervene often enough, but rather that they choose to intervene too often. The Nigerian intervention in the Congo was both incompetent and criminal. We must never allow a vague "responsibility to protect" to become a cover for cross-border aggression. Gareth Evans of the International Crisis Group, and a co-author of the original responsibility to protect (R2P) report, explicitly warned that a too frequent application of R2P would demolish any international consensus in favor of the norm. Evans urged limiting the doctrine, and especially its "sharp military end" solely to addressing "mass atrocity crimes."[61]

There is also a risk that a welcome concern for the well-being of others transitions into unwelcome paternalism, a twenty-first century manifestation of neocolonialism. That some of the advocates of intervention invoke the language of "postmodern imperialism" and "neotrusteeships" reminds us why the norms prohibiting interventions in the internal affairs of sovereign states should be lifted only in rare instances.[62]

Conversely, we can't allow the perfect to be the enemy of the good, particularly when the alternative—the benevolent global hegemony of the United States—has proved so far from perfect both for Americans and the rest of the world. Fashioning a new model for global intervention to avert humanitarian disasters must begin with an understanding that the United States does not have an unlimited capacity for intervening in every case. But just as Americans place the highest priority on confronting direct threats to U.S. security, so too should other countries be encouraged and expected to do the same for threats to their security.

The promiscuous U.S. interventions of the 1990s too often contributed to global paralysis in the face of humanitarian crises. By intervening in a host of conflicts that had nothing to do with defending U.S. national security interests, beginning with the humanitarian operations in Somalia in 1993, and extending to the bombing of cities in Yugoslavia in 1999, the United States has repeatedly communicated a message to the rest of the international community: "stand back, we'll take care of this." Though some Americans might say this, and some might even believe it to be true, the United States has *not* always taken care of regional crises. Nor can we. Nor should we.[63]

The United States spends nearly $800 billion a year on its military and holds itself out as the world's indispensable nation, and yet there is violence and lawlessness in the world; there is suffering caused by neglect and by design. That is true today, and it will be true in the future, regardless of what we do. But if we choose a different course, if we devolve our responsibilities as global cop, there is a good chance that mendacious regimes and criminal gangs will not be able to perpetrate gross human rights abuses with impunity. Although it will not work every time, if the United States—by taking a step back from global hegemony—encourages regional actors to acquire greater capacity for addressing regional problems, we may yet establish a new model for dealing with some of the most urgent humanitarian crises. It is hardly perfect; but neither is our current course.

The U.S. Constitution empowers the federal government to provide for the common defense of the people of the United States. It grants Congress the power to declare war, and it assigns responsibilities as commander-in-chief to the president. But there is no such thing as a human-rights imperative under the Constitution. Private organizations, religious institutions, and even well-meaning individuals may feel compelled to aid others in need, and they should be free to do so. But the U.S. government has no such responsibility.

Washington in his Farewell Address and Jefferson in his First Inaugural both admonished their countrymen to steer clear of the internal affairs of foreign powers, and they were anxious for the United States to avoid unnecessary wars. But that does not mean that they didn't care about human rights. On the contrary, they cared deeply, and their greatest concern was for maintaining their new nation as a shining example, which they hoped would serve as a beacon for the world. The single best statement of the original intent of our Founders with respect to foreign policy, however, came not from a Founder, per se, but from a Founder's son. On July 4, 1821, John Quincy Adams declared, "[America] goes not abroad in search of monsters to destroy. She is the well-wisher to the freedom and independence of all. She is the champion and vindicator only of her own."[64]

Though the advocates of benevolent global hegemony scorned Adams's vision as synonymous with "cowardice and dishonor,"[65] we can see—given that *their* strategy has sapped our strength and undermined our security—what a wise standard it was. We would be richer, freer, and safer if we adhered to it more closely today.

CONCLUSION

It is possible that the United States could maintain its place at the top—alone at the top—of the global order for a very long time, but history teaches otherwise. It is more likely that as we struggle to stay ahead of others, we will live in a constant state of fear, and that we will never quite be able to overcome our nagging sense of insecurity. We will continue to spend more and more, convinced by our own rhetoric of an approaching near competitor. And as we spend, others will react. Some, our prospective adversaries, spurred by resentment, outright hostility, or merely fear, will develop the means to deter us from taking actions against them. Others, our allies and clients, or those who aspire to be, will cajole and connive us into taking risks on their behalf, while they remain content to dedicate resources to their own domestic pursuits. Thus it will become even harder for us to stay on the top of the heap. We will spend even more on our military, on the assumption that we must maintain our edge to discourage prospective adversaries from challenging us. And we will use our military power more frequently, in order to demonstrate our willingness to act on behalf of others, believing that this will reassure our allies, lest they be tempted to switch sides or chart their own course.

This is a fool's game. For too long, we have defined our strength as a nation by our capacity for waging war. We have come to believe, erroneously, that military power keeps us safe, and that more power will keep us safer. But the true strength of the United States, the true source of U.S. power, is its people. Our spirit, our generosity, our ingenuity, is expressed in countless ways, most of which have nothing to do with our military prowess. By reducing the size of our military to a level more consistent with our own needs, and by encouraging others to become more self-reliant, we can make space for the other forms of human interaction that facilitate security and prosperity over the long term.

This is neither naive nor utopian. The world is a dangerous place. It always has been. Although we aspire to a time when disputes are settled peacefully, we sometimes seem a long way from that noble goal. Some worry of a new cold war with Russia; others see a hot one with China in the offing, perhaps over Taiwan. Those prospects cannot be dismissed lightly, but the fact remains that the major powers have managed to avoid the very sorts of cataclysms that claimed the lives of an estimated 100 million people in the first half of the twentieth century. Perhaps we've all learned something?[1]

Even if major war between nations seems more remote than ever before, what of war between peoples, peoples disconnected from any particular nation-state, or peoples united by ideologies that transcend national boundaries? What if al-Qaeda and other terrorist organizations are but the tip of the iceberg? Newspapers and opinion journals are littered these days with apocalyptic predictions of an impending—or even ongoing—world war.[2]

How likely is it that the so-called war on terrorism will be looked upon through the long lens of history as comparable to the world wars of the twentieth century? Not very. The casualties caused by international terrorist incidents since September 11, 2001, and the prospects for future casualties, pale in comparison to the death and destruction that took place between August 1914 and November 1918, and again between September 1939 and August 1945. The violence and bloodshed that can be deployed by non-state actors is an order of magnitude smaller than what could be caused by even a medium-size modern industrial state.

Can it even be compared with the Cold War, which claimed far fewer lives but lasted nearly five times longer than the two world wars combined? Again, no. Both are ideological struggles, fought chiefly by non-military means, but the threat of global thermonuclear war hung over every aspect of Cold War diplomacy. And the scale of violence that would have been unleashed had U.S. or Soviet (or Chinese, French, or British) decision makers lost their cool would have caused far more death and destruction than Osama bin Laden can muster in the darkest reaches of his imagination.

What we need is a little perspective. This perspective should inform our strategy for the next generation. For if there is a historical analog for the radical Islamist terrorist threat of the early twenty-first century, it is the anarchist movement of the late nineteenth century. Like the modern-day terrorists, the anarchists spread chaos and disorder by blowing up bombs in crowded places and by inciting riots. Anarchists succeeded in assassinating a number of world leaders, including Czar Alexander II of Russia, Empress Elisabeth of Austria-Hungary, and even U.S. president William McKinley.

The killing of a single man, Archduke Franz Ferdinand in Sarajevo in June 1914, precipitated the global conflict that resulted in more than 30 million casualties. That provides a useful lesson for the present day, but not the one that the scaremongers want you to learn: namely, that the overreaction to comparatively minor incidents can have far-reaching, and often horrific, effects.

How well do policymakers understand this? On the one hand, we have tracked down, killed, or captured, a host of mass murderers and prospective mass murderers—including Khalid Sheikh Mohammed and Ramzi Bin al-Shibh, the chief plotters of the 9/11 attacks—without resorting to tactics that threatened the lives of innocent bystanders. On the other hand, and especially in the case of Iraq, we have lashed out, convinced of our right to do so based on our own security needs, and believing the military to be the best instrument for breaking that supposed state-terror nexus. On still other occasions, we have pointed to our sense of obligation to act, in the service of democracy promotion or the advancement of human rights, believing that those lofty goals would also undermine the terrorists' cause.

But surely if ever there was a case of means upsetting ends, this was it, because for every ten, or even one hundred, quiet successes against al-Qaeda and its ilk, it takes but one loud failure to set back our efforts, perhaps for many years. That is why much of the world looks upon the U.S. superpower as a bull in a china shop. The bull means no harm when it smashes priceless items, but it can't quite help itself. As far as the store proprietor and the customers go, the mere presence of the bull poses a problem—there is always the danger that some fool will run through the store waving a red flag. That is exactly what al-Qaeda did on 9/11, and millions of people around the world have been living in fear ever since. They worry not that we will direct our wrath at them, but rather that in our thirst for justice we will harm those unfortunate enough to be in the wrong place at the wrong time. It is no wonder, then, that we are having so much difficulty convincing others to follow our lead toward a tolerant social order, a liberal political order, and a freer economic order.

Nearly 200 years ago, John Quincy Adams declared that the Founders' accomplishments would stand forever as "a light of admonition to the rulers of men; a light of salvation and redemption to the oppressed."[3] Today we have difficulty convincing even those who agree with us, and who long ago escaped oppression.

The intellectual ferment taking place today within those parts of the world that haven't been touched by liberal democracy or free-market capitalism presents both a challenge and an opportunity for Americans. On the one hand, we have only a very limited capacity to shape the debate so that a modern, liberal vision of world order will prevail over a competing mind-set that seeks to roll back the tide of history.[4] On the other hand, and paradoxically, though we cannot ensure that the modernists prevail, we do have a great capacity for influencing the debate in a negative direction, empowering extremists and nihilists, and marginalizing the moderates. And that is why the strategy that we adopt to keep ourselves safe, and to encourage others to do the same, is so crucial.

For years, international relations scholars have stressed that the world would resist the emergence of a single global superpower.[5] The fact that we've managed to sustain our "unipolar moment" for nearly twenty years does not mean that an alternate path might not have delivered a comparable level of security at far less cost and risk. Even many who celebrate our hegemony admit that their approach is costly. They also admit that it cannot last forever. It was they, not their intellectual opponents, after all, who called it a "unipolar *moment*."[6]

The wisest course, therefore, is to adopt policies that will allow us to extricate ourselves from regional squabbles, while maintaining the ability to prevent a genuine threat to the United States from forming. This book has tried to set forth just some of the many reasons for doing this. The strongest reason of all might be that our current strategy doesn't align with the wishes of the American people. As the costs of our foreign adventures mount, and as the benefits remain elusive, Americans may push with increasing assertiveness for the United States to climb down from its perch as the world's sheriff.

For now, no clear consensus on an alternative foreign policy has emerged. Polls show that Americans are opposed to using the U.S. military to promote democracy abroad.[7] Similar majorities believe that the costs of the war in Iraq have not been worth the benefits.[8] There is now precious little enthusiasm for launching new military missions, and considerable skepticism that the United States must solve the world's problems, or even that these problems require solving.[9]

If the trends are moving away from a strategy of primacy, away from the United States as indispensable nation, and away from Uncle Sam as global sheriff, where might a new consensus on foreign policy end up? It is possible that it will coalesce around a strategy that is less dependent on the exercise of U.S. military power and more on other aspects of U.S. influence—including our vibrant culture, and our extensive economic engagement with the world. Another very different consensus could also coalesce, however, and move the country—and possibly the world—in a sad and ugly direction.

Surveying the high costs and dubious benefits of our frequent interventions over the past two decades, many Americans are now asking themselves, "what's the point?" Why provide these so-called global public goods if we will be resented and reviled—and occasionally targeted—for having made the effort? When Americans tell pollsters that we should "mind our own business" they are rejecting the global public goods argument in its entirety.

As noted in the introduction to this book, the defenders of the status quo like to describe such sentiments as isolationist, a gross oversimplification that has the additional object of unfairly tarring the advocates of an alternative foreign policy—*any* alternative—with an obnoxious slur.[10] There is, however, an ugly streak to the turn inward by the United States. It appears in the form of anti-immigrant sentiment and hostility to free trade. The policies that flow from these misguided feelings include plans to build high walls to keep unskilled workers out, and calls for mass deportations to expel those already here. And we already have a very different wall built with regulations and arbitrary quotas for skilled workers under the H1-B program.

For the most part, Americans want to remain actively engaged in the world without having to be in charge of it. We tire of being held responsible for everything bad that happens, and always on the hook to pick up the costs. We have grown even more skeptical of our current foreign policies when the primary benefit that they are supposed to deliver, namely greater security, fails to materialize. If "global engagement" is defined as a forward-deployed military, operating in dozens of countries, and if the costs of this military remain very high, then we should expect the public to object. And if the rest of the world looks upon this military power and our propensity to use it as a growing threat, and if Americans gain a fuller recognition that our great power and our willingness to use it *increases* the risks of terrorism directed against the United States, then many will demand that we change course. But if Washington refuses to do so, or simply tinkers around the margins while largely ignoring public sentiment, then we should not be surprised if many Americans choose to throw the good engagement out with the bad, opting for genuine isolationism, with all of its nasty connotations.

That would be tragic. It would also be dangerous. For to the extent that there is a global war brewing, it will not be won by closing ourselves off from the rest of the world. If Americans reject the peaceful coexistence, trade, and voluntary person-to-person contact that has been the touchstone of U.S. foreign policy since the nation's founding, the gap between the United States and the rest of the world will grow only worse, with negative ramifications for U.S. security for many years to come.

Our hyperactive foreign policy of the last twenty years has become an impediment to the spread of the ideas that make this country great. This should dictate a change in course toward a wise foreign policy that combines prudence and forbearance.

A similar warning was heard just after the end of the Cold War from the same man who had played an enormous role in shaping U.S. strategy in the earliest days of that long struggle. "The United States should conduct itself," wrote diplomat and historian George F. Kennan, "as befits a country of its size and importance." The qualities of U.S. foreign policy, Kennan wrote, should include "patience, generosity, and a uniformly accommodating spirit in dealing with small countries and small matters," and "reasonableness, consistency, and steady adherence to principle in dealings with large countries and large matters." "The greatest service this country could render to the rest of the world," Kennan concluded, "would be to put its own house in order and to make of American civilization an example of decency, humanity and societal success."[11]

Our challenge, and it is a challenge that other great nations have faced, is to match our power to our purpose; to see our power as a means to an end, and to shape our power to suit those ends. We should possess no more than we need, and we should husband what we have with extreme prejudice.

True wisdom comes in controlling power, and that begins with an appreciation for what power does, and what it does not do. It also requires an extraordinary degree of discipline. As the Chinese philosopher Lao-Tzu said, "He who controls others may be powerful, but he who has mastered himself is mightier still."

More than two millennia later, and half a world away, Thomas Jefferson voiced similar sentiments with respect not to one person, but to the nation that he helped establish. It was the summer of 1815, not long after the United States had prevailed over the British in the War of 1812. Never again would foreign troops set foot on U.S. soil. And if Jefferson sensed a measure of triumphalism in the air, that was all understandable. But he hoped that it wouldn't go to everyone's heads. He predicted that one day, in the not so distant future, Americans "may shake a rod over the heads of all, which may make the stoutest of them tremble. But I hope our wisdom will grow with our power, and teach us, that the less we use our power, the greater it will be."[12]

That we may "shake a rod" and make the world tremble is no longer in dispute. But whether we have the wisdom to control our power remains very much an open question.

I hope that we do. Some military power is necessary; too much is a problem. And it is a problem that we alone can solve, if only we choose to do so.

NOTES

Introduction

1. Leading advocates of this point of view include Joseph S. Nye, Jr., G. John Ikenberry, and Francis Fukuyama, but the point of view is widespread throughout the policy community. Stephen Walt makes a similar but more sophisticated argument in calling for an offshore balancing strategy, with a greater emphasis on regional allies, in part on the grounds that this will enable us to maintain our position "for as long as possible" and will "avoid giving other states additional incentives to build up their own power." With such a strategy, Walt predicts, "America will not be universally loved or admired, but it should get credit for the good that it does do, and it should not be blamed for misfortunes or evils that are not its fault." Stephen M. Walt, *Taming American Power: The Global Response to U.S. Primacy* (New York: W.W. Norton, 2005), 219, 229.

2. "Washington's Farewell Address 1796," http://avalon.law.yale.edu/18th_century/washing.asp.

3. Colin Powell, *My American Journey* (New York: Random House, 1995), 576.

4. Ibid. See also Thomas Blood, *Madame Secretary: A Biography of Madeleine Albright* (New York: Macmillan, 1999), 163–64.

5. For a discussion of how liberal ideology has shaped and occasionally misshaped U.S. foreign policy, see Christopher Layne, *Peace of Illusions: American Grand Strategy from 1940 to the Present* (Ithaca, NY: Cornell University Press, 2006); and Michael C. Desch, "America's Illiberal Liberalism: The Ideological Origins of Overreaction in U.S. Foreign Policy," *International Security* 32, no. 3 (Winter 2007–8): 7–43.

6. Quoted in Bob Woodward, *Plan of Attack* (New York: Simon and Schuster, 2004), 88 (emphasis in original). Michael Desch notes that "both the Clinton and Bush administrations embraced the democratic peace as their rationale for believing that the spread of democracy would both bolster U.S. security as well as advance U.S. ideals." Desch, "America's Illiberal Liberalism," 22.

7. In April 2008, the Government Accountability Office (GAO) concluded that the Army's plans through fiscal year 2013 for resetting and restructuring the force were likely to cost at least $190 billion. The GAO's estimate included the equipping of restructured modular units ($43.6 billion) and increasing the number of units ($18.5 billion), costs that were not directly

related to the Iraq War. Statement of Janet A. St. Laurent, Managing Director, Defense Capabilities and Management, "Force Structure: Restructuring and Rebuilding the Army Will Cost Billions of Dollars for Equipment but the Total Cost Is Uncertain," Testimony Before the Subcommittee on Tactical Air and Land Forces, Committee on Armed Services, House of Representatives, April 10, 2008, http://www.gao.gov/new.items/d08669t.pdf.

8. See Benjamin I. Page with Marshall M. Bouton, *The Foreign Policy Disconnect: What Americans Want from Our Leaders but Don't Get* (Chicago: University of Chicago Press, 2006); and Daniel Drezner, "Mind the Gap," *The National Interest,* no. 87 (January/February 2007): 47–53.

9. Eric Nordlinger noted that "the epithet was first used in the 1840s against those who opposed the breaking of diplomatic relations with Austria in support of Hungarian self-determination." Eric Nordlinger, *Isolationism Reconfigured: American Foreign Policy for a New Century* (Princeton, NJ: Princeton University Press, 1995), 7. Walter McDougall observes that Alfred Thayer Mahan used the term in the 1890s to tag critics as "old-fashioned curmudgeons" but the term "isolationist" did not appear in Webster's dictionary until 1921, and *Encyclopedia Britannica* made no reference to isolationism until after World War II. McDougall concludes that "our vaunted tradition of 'isolation*ism*' is no tradition at all, but a dirty word that interventionists, especially since Pearl Harbor, hurl at anyone who questions their policies." Walter A. McDougall, *Promised Land, Crusader State: The American Encounter with the World since 1776* (New York: Houghton Mifflin, 1997), 40.

10. Jim Rutenberg and Megan C. Thee, "Americans Showing Isolationist Streak, Poll Finds," *New York Times,* July 27, 2006.

11. Bill McInturff, Liz Harrington, and Geoff Garin, "The New American Consensus on International Cooperation: A Presentation of Key Findings from Focus Groups and a National Survey," Better World Campaign, United Nations Foundation, November 13, 2007, http://www.betterworldcampaign.org/assets/pdf/unf_national_survey2007.pdf.

12. Ibid., 27.

13. Indeed, President Obama is all but certain to increase the size of the military, further evidence of the bipartisan support for a continuation of the very foreign policies that most Americans reject. During the 2008 presidential campaign, both Obama and the Republican nominee John McCain, pledged to substantially increase the number of men and women in uniform, especially in the Army and Marine Corps. See Barack Obama, "Renewing American Leadership," *Foreign Affairs* 86, no. 4 (July/August 2007): 7; and John McCain, "An Enduring Peace Built on Freedom," *Foreign Affairs* 86, no. 6 (November/December 2007): 23.

14. Note that the ability to act does not imply the ability to succeed.

15. See, especially, Robert J. Art, *A Grand Strategy for America* (Ithaca, NY: Cornell University Press, 2004).

16. To reiterate, these requirements obviously apply *only* to wars of choice, not wars of necessity involving the defense of our physical homeland or the air and sea approaches to the United States. Public support is easily mobilized and sustained when a nation's survival is at stake. Exit strategies are meaningless when the enemy seeks unconditional surrender. The military object is clear when armies and navies clash on the field and at sea.

17. See, for example, Andrew Mack and Zoe Nielsen, "Dying to Lose: Explaining the Decline in Global Terrorism," in *Human Security Brief, 2007,* School for International Studies, Simon Fraser University, March 2008, http://www.humansecuritybrief.info/HSRP_Brief_2007.pdf, 8–21; and Max Abrahms, "Why Terrorism Does Not Work," *International Security* 31, no. 2

(Fall 2006): 42–78. On sensible strategies for containing terrorism that generally do not include the use of military force, see Seth G. Jones and Martin C. Libicki, *How Terrorist Groups End: Lessons for Countering al Qa'ida* (Santa Monica, CA: RAND, 2008); and Max Abrahms, "What Terrorists Really Want: Terrorist Motives and Counterterrorism Strategy," *International Security* 32, no. 4 (Spring 2008): 78–105.

18. James Fallows, "Declaring Victory," *The Atlantic Monthly*, September 2006, 62.

19. Ian Shapiro, *Containment: Rebuilding a Strategy against Global Terror* (Princeton, NJ: Princeton University Press, 2007).

Chapter One

1. As of January 2008, the United States had 3,575 strategic nuclear warheads in active status, plus another 1,260 held in reserve, plus 5,150 awaiting dismantlement. We also possess approximately 500 tactical warheads. Figures from Center for Defense Information, "United States Nuclear Forces," 2008, http://www.cdi.org/pdfs/USNuclearArsenal08.pdf. See also Sidney D. Drell and James E. Goodby, "What Are Nuclear Weapons For? Recommendations for Restructuring U.S. Strategic Nuclear Forces," An Arms Control Association Report, Revised and Updated October 2007, http://www.armscontrol.org/pdf/20071104_Drell_Goodby_07_new. pdf. After the United States, Russia has the second largest arsenal of strategic nuclear weapons, about 3,400; followed by France (350), the United Kingdom (180–200), China (130–200), Israel (100–200), Pakistan (40–70), India (50), and North Korea (5–12). All figures from Center for Defense Information, "The World's Nuclear Arsenals: Updated July 30, 2008," http://www.cdi. org/friendlyversion/printversion.cfm?documentID=2972. On the implications of U.S. primacy in nuclear weapons and the possibility of achieving a survivable first strike capability, see Keir A. Lieber and Daryl G. Press, "The End of MAD? The Nuclear Dimension of U.S. Primacy," *International Security* 30, no. 4 (Spring 2006): 7–44.

2. All figures in this section, except where otherwise noted, are from *The Military Balance 2008* (London: International Institute of Strategic Studies, 2008).

3. See Robert Kaplan, *Imperial Grunts: The American Military on the Ground* (New York: Random House, 2005).

4. Based on official defense budgets from *The Military Balance 2008*.

5. A Gallup poll conducted June 9–12, 2008, found that 71 percent of respondents expressed confidence in the military, as compared with only 12 percent who had confidence in Congress. The military as an institution polled higher than any other, including business, the police, and "The Church or organized religion." See "Confidence in Congress: Lowest Ever for Any U.S. Institution," Gallup.com, June 20, 2008, http://www.gallup.com/poll/108142/Confidence-Congress-Lowest-Ever-Any-US-Institution.aspx.

6. See Joseph Stiglitz and Linda Bilmes, *The Three Trillion Dollar War: The True Cost of the Iraq Conflict* (New York: W.W. Norton, 2008), 71.

7. Over the course of the first four BRAC rounds—1988, 1991, 1993, 1995—the Pentagon closed 97 major bases, conducted major realignments at 55 other facilities, and made 235 other minor changes. In the fifth and final BRAC round, completed in 2005, the commissioners approved 22 major closures and another 33 major realignments. Figures from Donna Miles, "BRAC Deadline Expires; DoD to Begin Closures, Realignments," American Forces Press Service, November 9, 2005, http://www.defenselink.mil/news/newsarticle.aspx?id=18352; and from the

Executive Summary of the "2005 Defense Base Closure and Realignment Commission Report," September 8, 2005, http://www.brac.gov/docs/final/ExecutiveSummary.pdf.

8. See, for example, the case of Fort McClellan, Alabama, closed under the 1995 BRAC round. Samantha L. Quigley, "BRAC: McClellan Loses 'Fort,' Gains 18,000-acre Community," American Forces Press Service, August 23, 2005, http://www.defenselink.mil/news/newsarticle. aspx?id=16820.

9. Figures from Department of Defense, "Active Duty Military Personnel Strengths by Regional Area and by Country (309A)," as of December 31, 2007. On U.S. overseas bases today, see Chalmers Johnson, *The Sorrows of Empire: Militarism, Secrecy, and the End of the Republic* (New York: Henry Holt, 2004). On the history of our overseas bases, see Christopher T. Sandars, *America's Overseas Garrisons: The Leasehold Empire* (New York: Oxford University Press, 2000); and Anni P. Baker, *American Soldiers Overseas: The Global Military Presence* (Westport, CT: Praeger, 2004).

10. Greg Bruno, "U.S. Security Agreements and Iraq," Council on Foreign Relations, June 6, 2008, http://www.cfr.org/publication/16448/us_security_agreements_and_iraq.html; Condoleezza Rice and Robert Gates, "What We Need in Iraq," *Washington Post*, February 13, 2008. In June 2008, a report by the Congressional Research Service put the number of agreements "that may be considered SOFAs" at over 100. R. Chuck Mason, "Status of Forces Agreement (SOFA): What Is It, and How Might One Be Utilized In Iraq?" CRS Report for Congress (RL34531), June 16, 2008, http://ftp.fas.org/sgp/crs/natsec/RL34531.pdf.

11. See, for example, Fareed Zakaria, *From Wealth to Power: The Unusual Origins of America's World Role* (Princeton, NJ: Princeton University Press, 1998); and Walter A. McDougall, *Promised Land, Crusader State: The American Encounter with the World since 1776* (New York: Houghton Mifflin, 1997).

12. Bruce D. Porter, *War and the Rise of the State: The Military Foundations of Modern Politics* (New York: Free Press, 1994), 250.

13. The Constitution also stipulated that appropriations for the Army would not be for more than two years; no similar restrictions applied to the Navy.

14. "Washington's Farewell Address 1796," http://avalon.law.yale.edu/18th_century/washing.asp.

15. Gaillard Hunt, ed., *The Writings of James Madison, Vol. 6* (New York: Putnam, 1900), 131–32.

16. James Wilson to the Pennsylvania Ratifying Convention, December 11, 1787, *The Founders' Constitution,* Volume 1, Chapter 7, Document 17, http://press-pubs.uchicago.edu/founders/documents/v1ch7s17.html.

17. Madison, writing as Helvidius, Letter No. 4, in *Liberty and Order: The First American Party Struggle,* ed. and with a preface by Lance Banning (Indianapolis: Liberty Fund, 2004). Also available at http://oll.libertyfund.org.

18. Thomas Jefferson, "Second Inaugural Address," March 4, 1805, http://avalon.law.yale.edu/19th_century/jefinau2.asp.

19. McDougall, *Promised Land, Crusader State,* 57–75.

20. In another fortunate twist of fate, British policy generally coincided with U.S. preferences in the Western Hemisphere.

21. Roosevelt quoted in "Crucible of Empire: The Spanish American War," PBS, http://www.pbs.org/crucible/tl7.html.

22. Roosevelt quoted in John B. Judis, "Imperial Amnesia," *Foreign Policy,* no. 143 (July/August 2004): 53.

23. Ibid., 54.

24. Dwight D. Eisenhower, "Farewell Radio and Television Address," January 17, 1961, http://www.eisenhowermemorial.org/speeches/19610117%20farewell%20address.htm.

25. Ibid.

26. Total defense outlays in constant (2000) dollars were $382.7 billion in 1990 and bottomed out at $282.4 billion in 1998. See "Table 6.1—Composition of Outlays: 1940–2012," *The Budget for Fiscal Year 2008, Historical Tables* (Washington, DC: Government Printing Office, 2007), 123–24.

27. Appearances, however, can be deceiving. See Michael Lind, *The American Way of Strategy: U.S. Foreign Policy and the American Way of Life* (New York: Oxford University Press, 2006), 127; and Andrew J. Bacevich, *The New American Militarism: How Americans Are Seduced By War* (New York: Oxford University Press, 2005), 163–64.

28. The story is told in the book (later a movie), Mark Bowden, *Black Hawk Down: A Story of Modern War* (New York: Pantheon, 2000).

29. For polls showing the lack of popular support for using the U.S. military to disarm rival warlords and general disapproval of involvement in Somalia, see Gary T. Dempsey, with Roger W. Fontaine, *Fool's Errands: America's Recent Encounters with Nation Building* (Washington, DC: Cato Institute, 2000), 43.

30. See Philip Gourevitch, *We Wish to Inform You That Tomorrow We Will Be Killed with Our Families: Stories from Rwanda* (New York: Farrar, Straus and Giroux, 1998). Regarding the United States failure to intervene, see Samantha Power, *"A Problem from Hell": America and the Age of Genocide* (New York: Basic Books, 2002).

31. "Interview with the French Media in Paris, June 7, 1994," *Public Papers of the Presidents of the United States, William J. Clinton III 1994, Book I–January 1 to July 31, 1994* (Washington, DC: Government Printing Office, 1995), 1056–57; William Ferroggiaro, "The U.S. and the Genocide in Rwanda 1994: Information, Intelligence and the U.S. Response," The National Security Archive, George Washington University, http://www.gwu.edu/~nsarchiv/NSAEBB/NSAEBB117/index.htm.

32. Derek Chollet and James Goldgeier explain that Clinton backed into this policy, having earlier promised to use U.S. troops to cover a withdrawal by European forces. Derek Chollet and James Goldgeier, *America Between the Wars: From 11/9 to 9/11* (New York: PublicAffairs, 2008).

33. For more on this episode, see Christopher Preble, "The Road Not Taken: The Republican National Security Strategy," in *The Republican Revolution 10 Years Later,* ed. Chris Edwards and John Samples (Washington, DC: Cato Institute, 2005), 228–29.

34. Dempsey, *Fool's Errands,* 88–89.

35. As of January 2004, there were 1,800 Americans serving as part of NATO's Stabilization Force. All but a few hundred were withdrawn over the course of the next three years.

36. Fred Kaplan notes, "In his first few years as president, Bill Clinton justified staying out of Slobodan Milosevic's brutal war in Yugoslavia by citing Robert Kaplan's book *Balkan Ghosts,* which argued that ethnic wars had consumed the region for centuries and there was nothing we could do about them. Later,... [Clinton] justified intervening after all by citing Michael Sells's *The Bridge Betrayed: Reform and Genocide in Bosnia,* which argued that ethnic conflict had ebbed and

flowed through the ages and that Western help could make a difference." Fred Kaplan, *Daydream Believers: How a Few Grand Ideas Wrecked American Power* (Hoboken, NJ: John Wiley & Sons, 2008), 140–41.

37. On the Defense Planning Guidance, see Stefan Halper and Jonathan Clarke, *America Alone* (New York: Cambridge University Press, 2004), 145–46; James Mann, *Rise of the Vulcans: The History of Bush's War Cabinet* (New York: Penguin, 2004), 209–15; and Tony Smith, *A Pact with the Devil: Washington's Bid for World Supremacy and the Betrayal of the American Promise* (New York: Routledge, 2007), 6–8, 11–12.

38. "Excerpts from Pentagon's Plan: 'Prevent the Re-Emergence of a New Rival,'" *New York Times,* March 8, 1992.

39. Patrick E. Tyler, "U.S. Strategy Plan Calls for Insuring No Rivals Develop," *New York Times,* March 8, 1992.

40. Ibid.

41. Mann, *Rise of the Vulcans,* 311.

42. Leslie H. Gelb, "Foreign Affairs; They're Kidding," *New York Times,* March 9, 1992.

43. James Chace, "The Pentagon's Superpower Fantasy," *New York Times,* March 16, 1992.

44. Patrick E. Tyler, "Pentagon Drops Goal of Blocking New Superpowers," *New York Times,* May 24, 1992.

45. "[Cheney] wanted to show that he stood for the idea," Khalilzad explained to James Mann. Quoted in Mann, *Rise of the Vulcans,* 211, 213.

46. For an excellent summary see Smith, *A Pact with the Devil.*

47. Elaine Sciolino, "Madeleine Albright's Audition," *New York Times,* September 22, 1996.

48. For more on the Weinberger-Powell Doctrine, see Jeffrey Record, *Beating Goliath: Why Insurgencies Win* (Dulles, VA: Potomac Books, 2007), 125–27; and Bacevich, *The New American Militarism,* 47–48.

49. Secretary of State Madeleine K. Albright, Interview on NBC's *Today* with Matt Lauer, Columbus, Ohio, February 19, 1998.

50. Quoted in Glenn Kessler, "Engagement Is Constant in Kerry's Foreign Policy," *Washington Post,* March 21, 2004.

51. On the ideology of neoliberalism and its application to humanitarian intervention see Smith, *A Pact with the Devil,* especially 163–94.

52. On the neoconservatives see Halper and Clarke, *America Alone,* 9–39.

53. Sciolino, "Madeleine Albright's Audition."

54. Mann, *Rise of the Vulcans,* 395, fn. 40.

55. Charles Krauthammer, "What's Wrong with the Pentagon Paper?" *Washington Post,* March 13, 1992.

56. Krauthammer published one of the first unabashed cases for U.S. unipolarity, and the DPG took its cues from Krauthammer's essay. See Charles Krauthammer, "The Unipolar Moment," *Foreign Affairs* 70, no. 1 (Winter 1990/91): 23–33.

57. William Kristol and Robert Kagan, "Toward a Neo-Reaganite Foreign Policy," *Foreign Affairs* 75, no. 4 (July/August 1996): 23, 26.

58. Ibid., 21, 22.

59. Ibid., 29.

60. Ibid., 31 (emphasis added).

61. William Kristol and Robert Kagan, "Introduction: National Interest and Global Responsibility," in *Present Dangers: Crisis and Opportunity in American Foreign and Defense Policy* (San Francisco: Encounter Books, 2000), 9.

62. Quote is from Bush during his third presidential debate with Vice President Al Gore, October 11, 2000, at Wake Forest University, North Carolina. Transcript available at: http://www.debates.org/pages/trans2000c.html.

63. President Bush's Graduation Speech at the U.S. Military Academy at West Point, June 1, 2002. Transcript available at: http://www.whitehouse.gov/news/releases/2002/06/20020601-3.html.

64. George W. Bush, *The National Security Strategy of the United States of America* (Washington, DC: The White House, September 2002), 30.

65. Ibid, 15.

66. See especially David Frum, *The Right Man: The Surprise Presidency of George W. Bush* (New York: Random House, 2003); and Fred Barnes, *Rebel in Chief: Inside the Bold and Controversial Presidency of George W. Bush* (New York: Crown Forum, 2006). Bush's harshest critics believe essentially the opposite: that his campaign stance was just a cover, and that he always intended to embark on a revolutionary course. The truth, which requires a certain knowledge of Bush's deepest intentions and motivations, is unclear, and ultimately unknowable.

67. See, for example, Ivan Eland, "Does U.S. Intervention Overseas Breed Terrorism? The Historical Record," Cato Foreign Policy Briefing no. 50, December 17, 1998. As the Defense Science Board wrote in 1997: "Historical data show a strong correlation between U.S. involvement in international situations and an increase in terrorist attacks against the United States." Defense Science Board, *The Defense Science Board 1997 Summer Study Task Force on DoD Responses to Transnational Threats* (Washington, DC: U.S. Department of Defense, October 1997), vol. 1, Final Report, 15.

68. Columbia University Professor Richard Betts explained that "American global primacy" "animates both the terrorists' purposes and their choice of tactics." Richard K. Betts, "The Soft Underbelly of American Primacy: Tactical Advantages of Terror," *Political Science Quarterly* 117, no. 1 (Spring 2002): 20. See also Anonymous (Michael Scheuer), *Imperial Hubris: Why the West Is Losing the War on Terror* (Washington, DC: Potomac Books, 2004). In addition, as former deputy chief of the CIA's Counterterrorist Center Paul Pillar explains, "More than anything else, it is the United States' predominant place atop the world order (with everything that implies militarily, economically, and culturally) and the perceived U.S. opposition to change in any part of that order that underlie terrorists' resentment of the United States and their intent to attack it." Paul R. Pillar, *Terrorism and U.S. Foreign Policy* (Washington, DC: Brookings Institution Press, 2003), 60.

Chapter Two

1. All figures calculated from International Institute for Strategic Studies, *The Military Balance, 2008* (London: International Institute for Strategic Studies, 2008).

2. The Office of Management and Budget's (OMB) assessment accurately captures an additional $2.9 billion that the Pentagon forgot to include, covering retirement and other nonhardware expenses, bringing OMB's budget to a total of $518.3 billion. See Winslow T. Wheeler, "What Do the Pentagon's Numbers Really Mean?" Strauss Military Reform Project, Center

for Defense Information, February 2, 2008, http://www.cdi.org/friendlyversion/printversion.cfm?documentID=4199.

3. Logic holds that the deficit can only be closed by tax increases, or spending cuts, or a combination of both. Additional tax revenues could be derived from economic growth, even if tax rates remain fixed. But if additional revenues created by economic growth are offset by increases in federal spending, as was the pattern during the Bush administration, then the deficits will persist. At some point in the future, all Americans are going to be forced to make some hard choices about what government buys, and how to pay for it. On Bush and the GOP's profligate spending, see especially Stephen Slivinski, *Buck Wild: How Republicans Broke the Bank and Became the Party of Big Government* (Nashville, TN: Nelson Current, 2006); and also Michael D. Tanner, *Leviathan on the Right: How Big-Government Conservatism Brought Down the Republican Revolution* (Washington, DC: Cato Institute, 2007), especially 139–63.

4. Wheeler makes a convincing case that the national security costs of just the interest portions of the federal deficit are actually far higher. Wheeler, "What Do the Pentagon's Numbers Really Mean?"

5. From the perspective of two economists on the question, see Todd Sandler and Keith Hartley, *The Economics of Defense* (New York: Cambridge University Press, 1995). Several studies of the political economy of defense procurement focus on one particular platform, including Robert J. Art, *The TFX Decision: McNamara and the Military* (Boston: Little, Brown, 1968); and Harvey M. Sapolsky, *The Polaris System Development: Bureaucratic and Programmatic Success in Government* (Cambridge, MA: Harvard University Press, 1972). Others focus on a class of weapons, for example, Edmund Beard, *Developing the ICBM: A Study in Bureaucratic Politics* (New York: Columbia University Press, 1976); and Michael Brown, *Flying Blind: The Politics of the U.S. Strategic Bomber Program* (Ithaca, NY: Cornell University Press, 1992). Still others focus on a particular industry, such as Gary E. Weir, *Forged in War: The Naval-Industrial Complex and American Submarine Construction, 1940–1961* (Washington, DC: Naval Historical Center, 1994).

6. See Dov S. Zakheim and Ronald T. Kadish, "One-Stop Defense Shopping," *Washington Post,* April 28, 2008; and Ivan Eland, "Reforming a Defense Industry Rife with Socialism, Industrial Policy, and Excessive Regulation," Cato Policy Analysis no. 421, December 20, 2001.

7. See James L. Payne, *The Culture of Spending: Why Congress Lives Beyond Our Means* (San Francisco: ICS Press, 1991); and idem, "Budgeting in Neverland: Irrational Policymaking in the U.S. Congress and What Can Be Done about It," Cato Policy Analysis no. 574, July 26, 2006.

8. A few of the exceptions include Taxpayers for Common Sense, the American Taxpayers Union and Americans for Tax Reform, as well as my employer, the Cato Institute, but these groups who generally argue for less government spending are dramatically outnumbered by those individuals and groups asking for more.

9. For a useful short summary, see Chris Edwards, *Downsizing Government* (Washington, DC: Cato Institute, 2005), 79–80; and David Boaz, *Libertarianism: A Primer* (New York: Free Press, 1997), 193–95. For more on how government spending tends to grow due to logrolling and the principle of universalism, see Dennis C. Mueller, *Public Choice III* (New York: Cambridge University Press, 2003), 213–15.

10. Winslow T. Wheeler, *The Wastrels of Defense* (Annapolis, MD: Naval Institute Press, 2004), especially, 31–94.

11. The single largest line item within the Strategic Modernization category will not purchase equipment for troops in the field, planes for pilots to fly, or ships for sailors at sea. Funding for

missile defense in FY 2009 weighs in at a whopping $9.4 billion, and the cumulative total allocated to this project in the eight years of the Bush administration tops $67.2 billion (if the FY 2009 request is fully funded). It might not be fully funded, however. Missile defense is one of the most contentious items within the Bush budget, and the debate largely breaks down along partisan lines, as it has since Ronald Reagan announced plans for a Strategic Defense Initiative in 1983. With few exceptions, Republicans tend to favor missile defense, whereas Democrats are opposed. Indeed, Democratic proposals for cutting the defense budget routinely target missile defense.

12. "Lockheed Martin Joint Strike Fighter Officially Named 'Lightning II,'" Official Press Release of Lockheed Martin, July 7, 2006, http://www.lockheedmartin.com/news/press_releases/2006/LOCKHEEDMARTINJOINTSTRIKEFIGHTEROFF.html.

13. On the TFX program, see Art, *The TFX Decision.*

14. "Lockheed Martin Team Wins Joint Strike Fighter: Pledges Full Commitment to This Cornerstone of Future Defense Capability," Official Press Release of Lockheed Martin, October 26, 2001, http://www.lockheedmartin.com/news/press_releases/2001/LockheedMartinTeamWinsJointStrikeFi.html.

15. In addition to the United Kingdom, the other participant countries are Italy, the Netherlands, Turkey, Australia, Norway, Denmark, and Canada. For more on the history of the Joint Strike Fighter program, see Christopher Preble, "Joint Strike Fighter: Can a Multiservice Fighter Program Succeed?" Cato Policy Analysis no. 460, December 5, 2002, 6–9.

16. See Franklin C. Spinney, "Defense Death Spiral," http://www.d-n-i.net/fcs/defense_death_spiral/contents.htm; and Spinney's interview with PBS Frontline, http://www.d-n-i.net/fcs/fcs_frontline_interview.htm. See also James Fallows, "Uncle Sam Buys an Airplane," *Atlantic Monthly,* June 2002, 66. Jacques Gansler, Under Secretary of Defense for Acquisition during the Clinton administration, is often credited with coining the term, but Spinney popularized and expanded on the concept.

17. For more on the JSF, see Anthony Murch and Christopher Bolkcom, "F-35 Lightning II Joint Strike Fighter (JSF) Program: Background, Status, Issues," Congressional Research Service, October 25, 2007.

18. Video of interview dated July 7, 2006, available at http://www.af.mil/tv/index.asp?showid=1227.

19. Christopher Bolkcom, "CRS Report for Congress: F/A-22 Raptor," Congressional Research Service, April 2004.

20. Hawley quoted in "The F-22 Debate," Online NewsHour with Jim Lehrer, July 27, 1999.

21. In 1993, the Department of Defense reviewed the progress of the F-22 and reduced the number of Raptors to be purchased to 442, citing rising costs. Over the years, the planned buy of F-22s continued to decline; in 1997, only 339 Raptors were in the budget, and the number dropped to 276 in 2001. Winslow Wheeler, Pierre Sprey, and James Stevenson, "F-22 Analysis: The Good, The Mad, and the Surly," Center for Defense Information, February 19, 2008, http://www.cdi.org/program/document.cfm?DocumentID=4212.

22. Wheeler, Sprey, and Stevenson note that in 1986 the Air Force estimated F-22 fly-away costs at $35 million.

23. Dave Montgomery, "Lawmakers Gird for Defense-Budget Battle," *Fort Worth Star-Telegram,* February 8, 2005.

24. Ibid.

25. Richard P. Hallion, "Why We Need the F-22," *Washington Post,* July 22, 1999.

26. Hawley quoted in "The F-22 Debate."

27. Winslow T. Wheeler, "Getting What We Pay For? Mangled Technology at Gigantic Cost," *Defense News*, March 31, 2008.

28. Wheeler, Sprey, and Stevenson, "F-22 Analysis: The Good, The Mad, and the Surly."

29. Mark Thompson, "Gates Down on the F-22," *Time*, February 7, 2008.

30. Wheeler, Sprey, and Stevenson, "F-22 Analysis: The Good, The Mad, and the Surly."

31. Thompson, "Gates Down on the F-22."

32. The third and final ship of the class, the USS *Jimmy Carter* (SSN-23), included a number of major modifications that ultimately rendered that boat very different from the first two vessels. These changes also contributed to a much longer development and construction cycle, and hence to increased costs.

33. "Virginia Class," General Dynamics-Electric Boat Web site, http://www.gdeb.com/programs/virginia/.

34. "Dodd, Lieberman Announce Appropriations for Connecticut's Defense, Submarine Industry," Senator Chris Dodd, September 29, 2006, http://dodd.senate.gov/index.php?q=node/3613.

35. "Lieberman Secures Funding for CT Defense Projects in Military Spending Bills," News Release, Senator Joe Lieberman, May 24, 2007, http://lieberman.senate.gov/newsroom/release.cfm?id=275124.

36. "Two Submarines per Year: Full Speed Ahead," Representative Joe Courtney, November 13, 2007, http://courtney.house.gov/News/DocumentSingle.aspx?DocumentID=78543.

37. Quoted in Lee Gaillard, "V-22 Osprey: Wonder Weapon or Widow Maker," Center for Defense Information, 2006, http://www.cdi.org/PDFs/Gailliard%20on%20V-22.pdf.

38. Quoted on the official Web site of the V-22, http://www.navair.navy.mil/v22/.

39. Ibid.

40. This brief history draws from Christopher Bolkcom, "V-22 Osprey Tilt-Rotor Aircraft," Congressional Research Service Report for Congress, RL 31384, updated March 13, 2007.

41. Ibid., 9–10. For more on safety concerns surrounding the V-22, see Gaillard, "V-22 Osprey."

42. Christopher J. Castelli, "Marine Commandant Predicts Additional V-22 Osprey Crashes," *Inside the Navy*, March 19, 2007.

43. Gaillard, "V-22 Osprey."

44. John J. Kruzel, "Osprey Aircraft to Make Combat Debut in Iraq," American Forces Press Service, April 13, 2007.

45. Bob Cox, "Pentagon to Buy 167 Tilt-Rotor Ospreys," *Fort Worth Star-Telegram*, March 29, 2008.

46. "Cornyn Statement on $10.4 Billion Contract for V-22 Aircraft Production," Senator Jon Cornyn, March 28, 2008.

47. "Weapons Pentagon Doesn't Want," *America's Defense Monitor*, December 27, 2002. Transcript available at http://www.cdi.org/adm/615/.

48. Gen. Cody quoted at "Future Combat Systems," official Web site of the FCS program manager, https://www.fcs.army.mil/.

49. Ibid.

50. Andrew Feickert, "The Army's Future Combat Systems (FCS): Background and Issues for Congress," Congressional Research Service Report for Congress, October 11, 2007, 4.

51. Boeing is the prime contractor, with SAIC designated as a sub-contractor, but both firms are actively managing the program, and working directly with a number of subcontractors. Ana

Marte and Elise Szabo, "Fact Sheet on the Army's Future Combat Systems," Straus Military Reform Project, Center for Defense Information, August 7, 2007, http://www.cdi.org/friendly version/printversion.cfm?documentID=4058.

52. Megan Scully, "Army Rewrites Plan for Deploying Future Combat Systems," *Congress-Daily*, June 26, 2008.

53. Feickert, "The Army's Future Combat Systems (FCS)"; see also United States Government Accountability Office, Testimony before the Subcommittee on Air and Land Forces, Committee on Armed Services, House of Representatives, "Defense Acquisitions: Future Combat System Risks Underscore the Importance of Oversight," GAO-07-672T, March 27, 2007.

54. Marte and Szabo, "Fact Sheet on the Army's Future Combat Systems."

55. Mackenzie Eaglen and Oliver Horn, "Future Combat Systems: Dispelling Widespread Myths of the US Army's Primary Modernization Program," Heritage Foundation Commentary, February 12, 2008, http://www.heritage.org/Press/Commentary/021208e.cfm.

56. Quoted in Greg Grant, "Fighting Folly," *Government Executive*, May 1, 2007.

57. Quoted in Alec Klein, "The Army's $200 Billion Makeover," *Washington Post*, December 7, 2007.

58. Critics contend that some of these ad campaigns are aimed at generating support for the individual service's spending requests before Congress, more than to attract potential recruits. In fact, they serve both functions. See, for example, Julian E. Barnes and Peter Spiegel, "Are Air Force Ads Recruiting, or Lobbying?" *Los Angeles Times*, March 30, 2008.

59. "Station Gives Free 'Spring Bling' Tickets at Army Recruiting Station," WBPF (West Palm Beach, Florida), March 27, 2008, http://www.wpbf.com/news/15722699/detail.html; and Nancy Bartley, "Here at Home, Army Battles to Attract Qualified Recruits," *Seattle Times*, March 21, 2008.

60. DoD report quoted in Michael Massing, "The Volunteer Army: Who Fights and Why?" *New York Review of Books*, April 3, 2008.

61. For more on "The Post-9/11 Veterans Educational Assistance Act," see "Facts about the Webb-Hagel-Lautenberg-Warner G.I. Bill: 'Post-9/11 Veterans Educational Assistance Act' (S.22)," May 2008, http://webb.senate.gov/pdf/factsheetgi52208.pdf.

62. The boot camps are located at Fort Benning, Georgia; Fort Jackson, South Carolina; Fort Leonard Wood, Missouri; Fort Sill, Oklahoma; Fort Knox, Kentucky; Camp LeJeune, North Carolina; Camp Pendleton, California; Naval Station Great Lakes, Illinois; and Lackland Air Force Base, Texas. Hollywood's vision of boot camp is decidedly distorted, and even more so since the boot camps for the draftee armies of World War II or Vietnam are very different from those adapted for the all-volunteer military. One of the best accounts of the Marine Corps' basic training program is Thomas Ricks, *Making the Corps: 10th Anniversary Edition with a New Afterword by the Author* (New York: Scribner, 2007).

63. Bryan Bender, "Army Cuts Time Spent on Training," *Boston Globe*, August 19, 2007.

64. Full disclosure, I earned my commission through the Naval ROTC unit at George Washington University. Cost to the taxpayer: about $40,000 in tuition expenses, books, and a $100 monthly stipend.

65. From David Isenberg, "Dogs of War: The Pay Gap Myth," *United Press International*, February 15, 2008. See also Cindy Williams, "Paying Tomorrow's Military," *Regulation* (Summer 2006): 26-31.

66. "New Navy Reenlistment Bonuses," Military.com, http://www.military.com/recruiting/bonus-center/news/new-navy-reenlistment-bonuses.

67. Lisa Burgess, "$150,000 Bonus Offered for Some Special Forces," *Stars and Stripes,* February 28, 2008.

68. Ibid.

69. Bryan Bender, "Military Scrambles to Retain Troops," *Boston Globe,* March 7, 2008. See also, Michael Massing, "The Volunteer Army: Who Fights and Why?" *New York Review of Books,* April 3, 2008.

70. There is a fairly widespread misunderstanding that supplemental war costs include an accounting for the depreciation of equipment already purchased, and also some personnel costs that would have been paid even in the absence of war. This is inaccurate. Although the White House and the Pentagon have inserted into the several supplemental requests items that might not be strictly associated with the wars in Iraq and Afghanistan, the vast majority of monies allocated within the supplemental budgets cover the costs of the wars, and would not be spent during peacetime.

71. This range was based on their "realistic-moderate" scenario. Their estimated costs of the war under their "best case" scenario, which would have had U.S. forces withdrawn from Iraq much faster, totaled more than $2 trillion. Joseph E. Stiglitz and Linda J. Bilmes, *The $3 Trillion War: The True Cost of the Iraq Conflict* (New York: W.W. Norton, 2008), 31.

72. And this is true even if you assume that some percentage might have fallen victim to peacetime accidents; these cannot offset the far higher accident rates in war zones, including accidents that are not directly combat related.

73. Linda Bilmes, "Another Year, Another $300 Billion," *Boston Globe,* March 16, 2008.

74. Stiglitz and Bilmes, *The $3 Trillion War,* 65–66.

75. Ibid., 86–87.

76. The O&M share of the supplemental appropriation totaled approximately 60 percent before 2005, and was focused on items directly related to the war effort. Congressional Budget Office (CBO), "Analysis of the Growth in Funding for Operations in Iraq, Afghanistan, and Elsewhere in the War on Terrorism," February 11, 2008. CBO's figures focus specifically on the national defense aspects of the supplemental/emergency spending requests, and exclude "funding for hurricane recovery, avian flu, border security, and other purposes not related to the war." Also left out are an additional $40 billion in war-related spending within other government agencies, including the State Department and Veterans Affairs.

77. Initial plans called for the increases to be completed by 2012, but Secretary of Defense Robert Gates approved the Army's request to complete the increase by the end of 2010. "Faster Army Expansion Plan Approved," *New York Times,* October 10, 2007.

78. "Army, Marines Give Waivers to More Felons," CNN, April 21, 2008, http://edition.cnn.com/2008/US/04/21/military.waivers/index.html?eref=edition.

79. Massing, "The Volunteer Army."

80. Michelle Tan, "Stuck on Stop-Loss," *Army Times,* May 5, 2008.

81. Quoted in Lee Hockstader, "Army Stops Many Soldiers from Quitting," *Washington Post,* December 29, 2003.

82. Tom Vanden Brook, "Bonuses Boost Reserve's Recruitment," *USA Today,* March 27, 2008.

Chapter Three

1. Jim Talent, "More: The Crying Need for a Bigger U.S. Military," *National Review,* March 5, 2007, 32. See also Baker Spring, "Defense FY 2008 Budget Analysis: Four Percent for Freedom," *Heritage Foundation Backgrounder,* no. 2012, March 5, 2007.

2. Gary J. Schmitt, "Of Men and Material: The Crisis in Defense Spending," National Security Outlook, American Enterprise Institute, November 2006, http://www.aei.org/publications/pubID.25097/pub_detail.asp.

3. Joseph Carroll, "Perceptions of 'Too Much' Military Spending at 15-Year High," Gallup News Service, March 2, 2007, http://www.gallup.com/poll/26761/Perceptions-Too-Much-Military-Spending-15Year-High.aspx.

4. See John McCain, "An Enduring Peace Built on Freedom," *Foreign Affairs* 86, no. 6 (November/December 2007): 23.

5. "Estimated Cost of the Administration's Proposal to Increase the Army's and the Marine Corps's Personnel Levels," Congressional Budget Office, April 16, 2007, www.cbo.gov/ftpdocs/80xx/doc8004/04-16-MilitaryEndStrength.pdf. Extrapolating such figures to McCain's proposal would add another $165 billion. Christopher Preble and Benjamin H. Friedman, "The Pentagon on Defense," The National Interest Online, October 31, 2008, http://www.national interest.org/Article.aspx?id=20168. See also Benjamin H. Friedman, "Fewer Missions, Not More Troops," Audit of Conventional Wisdom, July 2007, http://web.mit.edu/cis/pdf/Audit_07_07_Friedman.pdf; and Gordon Adams, "The Problem with Expanding the U.S. Military," *Bulletin of the Atomic Scientists,* April 30, 2007, http://www.thebulletin.org/web-edition/columnists/gordon-adams/the-problem-with-expanding-the-us-military.

6. China's official defense budget at market exchange rates totaled $35.3 billion in 2006; its defense expenditures, based on a purchasing power parity estimate, and including military expenditures that are outside of the official defense budget, totaled approximately $122 billion. Russia's official defense budget in 2006 was $24.7 billion, but equivalent to approximately $70 billion according to IISS estimates. Figures from International Institute for Strategic Studies, *The Military Balance, 2008* (London: International Institute for Strategic Studies, 2008), 376, 212. The Heritage Foundation's John J. Tkacik, Jr., concludes that Chinese defense spending topped $450 billion in 2007, more than four times greater than U.S. Department of Defense estimates at the time. See "A Chinese Military Superpower?" Heritage Foundation WebMemo, no. 1389, March 8, 2007, http://www.heritage.org/Research/AsiaandthePacific/wm1389.cfm. For a critique of Tkacik's methodology, see Justin Logan, "The Chinese Defense Budget: Myths and Reality," *Cato@Liberty,* April 23, 2007, http://www.cato-at-liberty.org/2007/04/23/the-chinese-defense-budget-myths-and-reality/.

7. *The World Factbook* does not include countries for which no reliable data is available, and that includes North Korea. Notably, the CIA relies on the base defense budget to calculate U.S. spending as 4.06 percent of GDP in 2005, whereas actual expenditures that year, including spending for the wars in Iraq and Afghanistan, plus other national security expenditures not covered under the Pentagon's budget, push the percentage closer to 4.5 percent.

8. See also Center for Arms Control and Non-Proliferation, "Tying U.S. Defense Spending to GDP: Bad Logic, Bad Policy," April 15, 2008; and Bernard Finel, "The 4 Percent Folly: Linking Defense Spending to GDP Could Backfire," *Defense News,* February 4, 2008.

9. See especially Arthur A. Stein, "The Hegemon's Dilemma: Great Britain, the United States and the International Economic Order," *International Organization* 38, no. 2 (Spring 1984): 355–86. Though focused on the financial costs that Great Britain and the United States incurred to sustain a liberal international trading regime, Stein's article includes a broader critique of the assumptions underlying hegemonic stability theory.

10. Some see merit in continuing to discourage Japan from developing sufficient military capability to defend itself, in deference to the concerns of its neighbors, especially China and the Koreas. On why these arguments might have been defensible in 1950 or 1960 or 1970, but are

no longer so today, see Christopher Preble, "Two Normal Nations: Rethinking the U.S.-Japan Strategic Relationship," Cato Policy Analysis no. 566, April 18, 2006, especially 9–12, 20–22.

11. Justin Logan and Ted Galen Carpenter, "Taiwan's Defense Budget: How Taipei's Free Riding Risks War," Cato Policy Analysis no. 600, September 13, 2007.

12. The table and chart appear in Jeffrey H. Birnbaum, "In the Loop: On K Street," *Washington Post*, April 15, 2008, A13.

13. "Lobbying Spending Database—Lockheed Martin, 2007," Center for Responsive Politics, http://www.fecwatch.org/lobby/clientsum.php?year=2007&lname=Lockheed+Martin.

14. "Technology of the Tiltrotor Aircraft," *Congressional Record*, July 12, 1990, H4640; and Elizabeth Donovan and David Steigman, "Gray: V-22 Substitute Scheme 'Ridiculous,'" *Navy Times*, March 5, 1990.

15. Sutton disputed ever having uttered the phrase, but the notion of attacking a problem where the potential payoff is greatest now has broad application, including in medicine, computer science, and financial accounting. See Willie Sutton, *Where the Money Was: The Memoirs of a Bank Robber* (New York: Viking, 1976).

16. For suggestions on reforming this process, including opening up defense contracts to foreign companies, and relaxing regulations on the purchase of commercial goods, see Ivan Eland, "Reforming a Defense Industry Rife with Socialism, Industrial Policy, and Excessive Regulation," Cato Institute Policy Analysis no. 421, December 20, 2001.

17. The two most notorious cases involved former Congressman Randy "Duke" Cunningham, who pled guilty to fraud, conspiracy to commit bribery, and tax evasion, after it was discovered that he had received cash and other benefits in exchange for steering contracts to several defense contractors; and Darleen Druyun, an Air Force official responsible for acquisition who admitted steering contracts to Boeing in return for a promise of employment for herself and other family members. The latter scandal involved Boeing's Chief Financial Officer, Michael Sears, who along with Druyun was sentenced to prison terms, and forced the resignation of Boeing CEO Phil Condit. On Cunningham, see Seth Hettena, "Former Congressman Gets Eight-Plus Years," *Associated Press*, March 3, 2006. On Druyun and Boeing, see Eric Rosenberg, "In Recent Years, Ties between Air Force, Boeing Strained," *Seattle Post-Intelligencer*, February 29, 2008.

18. Dana Hedgpeth, "GAO Blasts Weapons Budget," *Washington Post*, April 1, 2008. See also "Wasting and Wanting at the Pentagon," *New York Times*, April 2, 2008.

19. Jim Talent estimates savings of between $1 to $2 billion by cracking down on earmarks. Talent, "More: The Crying Need for a Bigger U.S. Military." A task force chaired by Foreign Policy in Focus and the Center for Defense Information estimated that improved efficiency at the Pentagon and elimination of as many as 3,000 earmarks in the defense budget would save about $7 billion. Miriam Pemberton and Lawrence Korb, "Unified Security Budget for the United States, 2008," Foreign Policy in Focus and the Center for Defense Information, April 2007, 25.

20. It is reasonable to speculate that a volunteer army lowers the *political* cost of military intervention by confining the burdens to a relatively small number of self-selected volunteers and their families, and that a government that relied on conscription to populate its ranks might be more constrained than one that had to employ incentives. I know of no empirical correlation between a country's propensity to become involved in foreign military campaigns and whether or not it relies on voluntarism or a draft. Anecdotally, the absence of constraints during the 1960s— policymakers were confident that the ranks would always be filled—contributed to a particular attitude toward the conduct of war that placed a lower priority on training and equipment and ultimately didn't prevent successive U.S. presidents from sinking deeper and deeper into the

Vietnam quagmire. By contrast, countries that operate under the resource constraints of a professional volunteer military will tend to spend more on training and advanced equipment to protect their precious "investments."

21. Doug Bandow, "Fighting the War against Terrorism: Elite Forces, Yes; Conscripts, No," Cato Policy Analysis no. 430, April 10, 2002.

22. Cindy Williams, "Draft Lessons from Europe," *Washington Post,* October 5, 2004.

23. A plan to phase out mandatory national service elicited howls of protest from the German health-care industry. In 2004, "more than 90,000 young men choose the community service option…and 80% of them end up in hospitals." Ben Aris, "German Hospitals Protest at Plan to End National Service," *Guardian* (UK), January 14, 2004, http://www.guardian.co.uk/world/2004/jan/14/germany.

24. See, for example, Stanley Kurtz, "Revive the Draft," *National Review Online,* September 12, 2001, http://www.nationalreview.com/contributors/kurtz091201.shtml; John Derbyshire, "Draft as Needed," *National Review Online,* October 4, 2001, http://www.nationalreview.com/derbyshire/derbyshire100401.shtml; and Charles Moskos and Paul Glastris, "Now Do You Believe We Need a Draft?" *Washington Monthly,* November 2001, http://www.washingtonmonthly.com/features/2001/0111.moskos.glastris.html.

25. John McCain and Evan Bayh, "A New Start for National Service," *New York Times,* November 6, 2001.

26. Quoted in Richard Just, "Suddenly Serviceable: Is This the Moment for National Service?" *American Prospect* 13, no. 1 (January 1–14, 2002).

27. Bandow, "Fighting the War Against Terrorism," 7.

28. Dean Baker, "The Economic Impact of the Iraq War and Higher Military Spending," Center for Economic and Policy Research, May 2007, http://www.cepr.net/documents/publications/military_spending_2007_05.pdf.

29. Robert R. Bowie and Richard H. Immerman, *Waging Peace: How Eisenhower Shaped an Enduring Cold War Strategy* (New York: Oxford University Press, 1998), 44.

30. From Congress, Senate, "Hearings Before the Committee on Foreign Relations and the Committee on Armed Services on S. Con. Res. 8, 82nd Cong., 1st Sess.," (1951), 2, cited in Bowie and Immerman, *Waging Peace,* 96.

31. John W. Sloan, *Eisenhower and the Management of Prosperity* (Lawrence: University Press of Kansas, 1991), 75. State of the Union Address reprinted from the *New York Times,* January 8, 1954.

32. Bowie and Immerman, *Waging Peace,* 34.

33. Eisenhower to Lucius Du Bignon Clay, February 9, 1952, *The Papers of Dwight D. Eisenhower,* ed. Louis Galambos, volume 13 (Baltimore: Johns Hopkins University Press, 1970), 963, cited in Richard Immerman, "Confessions of an Eisenhower Revisionist: An Agonizing Reappraisal," *Diplomatic History* 14 (Summer 1990): 328. On the Great Equation, see Sloan, *Eisenhower and the Management of Prosperity,* 76–77; and Bowie and Immerman, *Waging Peace,* 44, 47.

34. Yale sociologist Harold Lasswell coined the term. See Harold Lasswell, *Essays on the Garrison State,* ed. and with an introduction by Jay Stanley (New Brunswick, NJ: Transaction, 1997). On Eisenhower and the "garrison state," see Aaron Friedberg, *In the Shadow of the Garrison State: America's Anti-Statism and Its Cold War Grand Strategy* (Princeton, NJ: Princeton University Press, 2000), 133.

35. Dwight D. Eisenhower, "A Chance for Peace," Eisenhower speech to the American Society of Newspaper Editors, April 16, 1953, *Public Papers of the Presidents of the United States: Dwight D. Eisenhower, 1953* (Washington, DC: Government Printing Office, 1960), 182.

36. Ibid.

37. The B-2 costs about $2.2 billion per plane. The median cost of a new elementary school in 2007 was $12.8 million. See table 5, "Profile of New Schools Currently Underway," in Paul Abramson, "The 2008 Annual School Construction Report: More Dollars Spent, Less Construction Completed," *School Planning & Management,* February 2008, http://www2.peterli.com/spm/pdfs/constr_report_2008.pdf.

38. Road construction costs vary greatly by state and region, but this report includes a range of estimates. "Highway Construction Costs: Are WSDOT's Highway Construction Costs in Line with National Experience?" Washington State Department of Transportation, November 3, 2005, http://www.wsdot.wa.gov/biz/construction/CostIndex/CostIndexPdf/HighwayConstruction Costs2005.pdf.

39. On November 5, 2008, wheat futures for December delivery closed at $5.3725 per bushel, a 60 percent decline from its high of $13.495 in February. Tony C. Dreibus, "Wheat Falls as U.S. Exports May Decline With Bigger World Crop" Bloomberg, November 5, 2008.

40. This assumes four people in the average family. "Existing-Home Sales Rise on Improved Affordability," National Association of Realtors, October 24, 2008, http://www.realtor.org/press_room/news_releases/2008/ehs_rise_on_affordability.

41. For more, see David Boaz, "The Season of Taking," *Reason,* December 23, 2005. In September 2007, Alaska officials dropped plans to build the bridges, but kept the money. "Plans For 'Bridge to Nowhere' Killed; Alaska Scraps $398 Million Bridge Project, Keeps the Funding," Associated Press, September 22, 2007.

42. James Tobin, "Dollars, Defense, and Doctrines," *Yale Review* 47, no. 3 (March 1958): 328.

43. With respect to military spending, in particular, Dean Baker of the Center for Economic and Policy Research notes that "most models show that military spending diverts resources from productive uses, such as consumption and investment, and ultimately slows economic growth and reduces employment." Baker, "The Economic Impact of the Iraq War and Higher Military Spending," 5.

44. "IRAQ: Hillary's Remarks at The George Washington University," March 17, 2008, http://www.hillaryclinton.com/news/speech/view/?id=6553.

45. "Full Text of Obama's Speech 'The Cost of War,'" Time.com, March 20, 2008, http://thepage.time.com/full-text-of-obamas-speech-the-cost-of-war/.

46. Thomas Jefferson to Edward Carrington, May 27, 1788, from *The Writings of Thomas Jefferson,* http://etext.virginia.edu/jefferson/quotations/jeff1800.htm.

47. James Madison, "Political Observations," April 20, 1795, in Philip R. Fendall, ed, *Letters and other Writings of James Madison,* vol. 4 (Philadelphia, 1865), 491, quoted in Andrew J. Bacevich, *The New American Militarism: How Americans Are Seduced by War* (New York: Oxford University Press, 2005), 7.

48. "Washington's Farewell Address 1796," http://avalon.law.yale.edu/18th_century/washing.asp.

49. Bruce Porter, *War and the Rise of the State: The Military Foundations of Modern Politics* (New York: Free Press, 1994), 280 (emphasis in original). See also Robert Higgs, *Crisis and Leviathan: Critical Episodes in the Growth of American Government* (New York: Oxford University Press, 1989).

50. McLellan and Bradford, *The Debates,* cited in Gene Healy, *The Cult of the Presidency: America's Dangerous Devotion to Executive Power* (Washington, DC: Cato Institute, 2008), 24.

51. Alexander Hamilton, "The Federalist Papers: No. 69," http://avalon.law.yale.edu/18th_century/fed69.asp. Emphasis in original.

52. James Madison, writing as Helvidius, Letter No. 4, in *The Letters of Pacificus and Helvidius (1845) with The Letters of Americanus,* with an introduction by Richard Loss (Delmar, NY: Scholars' Facsimiles & Reprints, 1976), 89 (emphasis in original). Notably, although Alexander sided with Washington and the executive, and nominally against Madison and the Congress, in this dispute, he never challenged the fundamental premise that the power to initiate war rested solely with the legislature. Healy, *Cult of the Presidency,* 24.

53. Lincoln to William Herndon, February 15, 1848, in *Lincoln: Selected Speeches and Writings,* ed. Don E. Fehrengbacher (New York: Vintage Books, 1989), 67–68, cited in Healy, *The Cult of the Presidency,* 41.

54. See Ted Galen Carpenter, "Global Interventionism and a New Imperial Presidency," Cato Policy Analysis no. 71, May 16, 1986.

55. In July 2008, a commission led by former secretaries of state James Baker and Warren Christopher recommended changes to the War Powers Act, but the Congress has, as yet, taken no action. See Karen DeYoung, "Ex-Secretaries Suggest New War Powers Policy," *Washington Post,* July 9, 2008.

56. See, especially, Richard Posner, *Not a Suicide Pact: The Constitution in a Time of National Emergency* (New York: Oxford University Press, 2006). This phrase derives from Supreme Court Justice Robert H. Jackson's dissenting opinion in *Terminiello v. Chicago* (1949), and was repeated in Justice Arthur Goldberg's majority opinion in the case *Kennedy v. Mendoza-Martinez* (1963).

57. Healy, *The Cult of the Presidency,* 21.

58. John Yoo, *The Powers of War and Peace: The Constitution and Foreign Affairs after 9/11* (Chicago: University of Chicago Press, 2005), x.

59. *Report of the Defense Science Board Task Force on Strategic Communication* (Washington, DC: U.S. Department of Defense, September 2004), 40, www.acq.osd.mil/dsb/reports/2004-09-Strategic_Communication.pdf.

60. *The 9/11 Commission Report* (Final Report of the National Commission on Terrorist Attacks upon the United States), Official Government Edition (Washington, DC: Government Printing Office, 2004), 375–77.

61. Robert Kagan, *Of Paradise and Power* (New York: Knopf, 2003), 34.

62. Michael Mandelbaum, *The Case for Goliath: How America Acts as the World's Government in the 21st Century* (New York: Public Affairs, 2005), 218–19. See also Ivo H. Daalder and James M. Lindsay, "The Globalization of Politics: American Foreign Policy for a New Century," *Brookings Review* 21, no. 1 (Winter 2003): 12–17, http://www.brookings.edu/articles/2003/winter_diplomacy_daalder.aspx; and Richard K. Betts, "The Soft Underbelly of American Primacy: Tactical Advantages of Terror," *Political Science Quarterly* 117, no. 1 (Spring 2002): 20.

Chapter Four

1. The formulation is from Michael Mandelbaum, *The Case for Goliath: How America Acts as the World's Government in the 21st Century* (New York: Public Affairs, 2005), xvi.

2. Ibid., 223.

3. See, for example, Keir A. Lieber and Gerard Alexander, "Waiting for Balancing: Why the World Is Not Pushing Back," *International Security* 30, no. 1 (Summer 2005): 109–39. Stephen

Walt correctly describes the U.S. position as "primacy" as opposed to hegemony "because [the United States] cannot physically control the entire globe and thus cannot compel other states to do whatever it wants." Stephen M. Walt, *Taming American Power: The Global Response to U.S. Primacy* (New York: W.W. Norton, 2005), 31. On the definition of hegemony, see John J. Mearsheimer, *The Tragedy of Great Power Politics* (New York: W.W. Norton, 2001), 40–42. However, although the United States is not a hegemon, in the strict sense, I am using the term as it was adopted and used by the advocates of our current course, who called for "benevolent global hegemony" believing it to be both achievable and sustainable.

4. Mandelbaum explains "a world without America would be the equivalent of a freeway full of cars without brakes." Mandelbaum, *The Case for Goliath,* 188.

5. Michael Ignatieff, "The American Empire; The Burden," *New York Times,* January 5, 2003. Ignatieff chooses to ignore a number of order-inducing interventions conducted over the past twenty years that have not involved the U.S. military. The practice of other countries acting in their own self-defense, but also advancing human rights in their neighborhood, or in countries of special concern, is discussed in chapter 5.

6. "Text of Blair's Speech," BBC News, July 17, 2003, http://news.bbc.co.uk/2/hi/uk_news/politics/3076253.stm.

7. This logic is consistent with one of Jack Snyder's central "myths of empire": that the best defense is a good offense. This conceit includes overconfidence in offensive action, and a strong preference for preventing falling dominoes by stopping the first one from toppling over. See Jack Snyder, *Myths of Empire: Domestic Politics and International Ambition* (Ithaca, NY: Cornell University Press, 1991), 4, 22–24.

8. Quoted in Matthew Yglesias, "The Militarist," *American Prospect* 19, no. 5 (May 2008). Other examples include the U.S. government's continued attempts to bring down Fidel Castro's regime. Although various assassination gambits failed, Washington persists in trying to starve the Cuban government, but in the end the horribly short-sighted embargo succeeds only in starving the Cuban people. Likewise do hawks in Washington, drawing comparisons between Castro and his wannabe successor, Hugo Chavez in Venezuela, loudly suggest that we "liberate" the people of Venezuela from Chavez's tyranny. See, for example, Frank Gaffney, "Liberate Venezuela," Fox News.com, April 25, 2002.

9. Robert D. Kaplan, "The Coming Anarchy," *Atlantic Monthly,* February 1994, 48.

10. William Kristol and Robert Kagan, "Toward a Neo-Reaganite Foreign Policy," *Foreign Affairs* 75, no. 4 (July/August 1996): 23.

11. This section draws heavily from Justin Logan and Christopher Preble, "Failed States and Flawed Logic: The Case against a Standing Nation-Building Office," Cato Institute Policy Analysis no. 560, January 11, 2006.

12. The White House, "President's Remarks at the United Nations General Assembly," September 12, 2002, http://www.whitehouse.gov/news/releases/2002/09/20020912-1.html.

13. "President Bush Delivers Graduation Speech at West Point," June 1, 2002, http://www.whitehouse.gov/news/releases/2002/06/print/20020601-3.html.

14. Bush was speaking here not of *preemption,* operations launched in anticipation of an imminent attack from an adversary, a threat that could only be dealt with by military means, but rather an attack conducted *before* the adversary has the capacity to attack. History includes cases of both preemptive and preventive wars, but the latter are generally regarded as inconsistent with modern norms of international behavior.

15. See Richard Betts, "Suicide from Fear of Death," *Foreign Affairs* 82, no. 1 (January/February 2003): 34–43. See also *Bismarck: The Man and the Statesman,* trans. A. J. Butler, vol. 2 (New York: Harper & Brothers, 1898), 103.

16. It would have to be a considerable improvement. After all, wars often consume vast sums of treasure, and cost thousands or tens of thousands of lives. From a moral perspective, no one should argue that those losses could be justified by merely modest gains. For more on preventive war, see Robert Jervis, *American Foreign Policy in a New Era* (New York: Routledge, 2005), 84–86.

17. Robert Kagan, *The Return of History and the End of Dreams* (New York: Knopf, 2008), 90.

18. Ken Adelman, "Cakewalk in Iraq," *Washington Post,* February 13, 2002.

19. See, for example, Pentagon adviser Richard Perle's comments to an interviewer for the PBS program *Frontline:* "having destroyed the Taliban, having destroyed Saddam's regime, the message to the others is, 'You're next.' Two words. Very efficient diplomacy." Quoted in Thomas Power, "Tomorrow the World," *New York Review of Books,* March 11, 2004, http://www.nybooks.com/articles/16953.

20. Niall Ferguson, "A World without Power," *Foreign Policy,* no. 143 (July–August 2004): 38.

21. Robert Kagan freely admits that, "Given America's willingness to spend so much money protecting them," it is hardly surprising that "Europeans would rather spend their own money on social welfare programs, long vacations, and shorter workweeks." Kagan, *Of Paradise and Power,* 54.

22. Mandelbaum, *The Case for Goliath,* xx–xxi.

23. Ibid., 218 (emphasis added).

24. See especially Kagan, *Of Paradise and Power,* 68.

25. Machiavelli's Discourses are available at http://xenophon-mil.org/milhist/renaissance/machdisc.htm#2twentyseven.

26. I expropriated this term from my colleague Ted Galen Carpenter. See his *Smart Power: Toward a Prudent Foreign Policy for America* (Washington, DC: Cato Institute, 2008), 6.

27. This is a variation on traditional hegemonic stability theory, which holds that a stable international economic order must be policed by a single hegemonic power. See, especially, Charles P. Kindleberger, "Dominance and Leadership in the International Economy: Exploitation, Public Goods, and Free Rides," *International Studies Quarterly* 25 (June 1981): 242–54; Robert Gilpin, "Economic Interdependence and National Security in Historical Perspective," in *Economic Issues and National Security,* ed. Klaus Knorr and Frank N. Trager (Lawrence: Regents Press of Kansas, 1977), 19–66; and Stephen Krasner, "State Power and the Structure of International Trade," *World Politics* 28 (April 1976): 317–47.

28. Geir Lundestad, "Empire by Invitation? The United States and Western Europe, 1945–1952," *Journal of Peace Research* 23 (September 1986): 263–77. See also Robert O. Keohane, "The United States and the Postwar Order: Empire or Hegemony?" *Journal of Peace Research* 28, no. 4 (November 1991): 435–39; and John Lewis Gaddis, *We Now Know: Rethinking Cold War History* (New York: Oxford University Press, 1997), 285–86.

29. Kagan, *Of Paradise and Power,* 35–36.

30. See "Northfield Raid and the James-Younger Gang," Minnesota Historical Society, http://www.mnhs.org/library/tips/history_topics/16northfield.html.

31. Mandelbaum, *The Case for Goliath,* 8–9. Richard N. Cooper uses the same analogy in a comment on the Olson-Zeckhauser thesis. See Richard N. Cooper, Comment on "Collective Goods, Comparative Advantage and Alliance Efficiency," in *Issues in Defense Economics,* ed. Ronald McKean (New York: National Bureau of Economic Research, 1967), 55.

32. Mandelbaum, *The Case for Goliath,* 10.

33. I am especially grateful to my colleagues Jagadeesh Gokhale, William Niskanen, and Peter Van Doren for their helpful comments on this section; any subsequent errors in interpretation are strictly my own.

34. Mancur Olson, *The Logic of Collective Action: Public Goods and the Theory of Groups* (Cambridge, MA: Harvard University Press, 1971), 14, fn. 21.

35. Ibid.

36. Note: *The Logic of Collective Action* focused chiefly on domestic organizations and lobbies. Olson mentions NATO in passing, but suggests that, to the extent that alliances provided public goods, the theory as applied in the domestic context must be modified. This was done in Mancur Olson, Jr., and Richard Zeckhauser, "An Economic Theory of Alliances," *Review of Economics and Statistics* 48, no. 3 (August 1966): 266–79; and idem, "Collective Goods, Comparative Advantage and Alliance Efficiency," in *Issues in Defense Economics,* ed. McKean, 25–48.

37. Wallace Thies notes that optimality is itself "an elusive concept." Wallace J. Thies, "Alliances and Collective Goods: A Reappraisal," *The Journal of Conflict Resolution* 31, no. 2 (June 1987): 301.

38. Jacques Van Ypersele De Strihou, Comment on "Collective Goods, Comparative Advantage and Alliance Efficiency," in *Issues in Defense Economics,* ed. McKean, 59. See also Thies, "Alliances and Collective Goods," 303; and Todd Sandler and Keith Hartley, "Economics of Alliances: The Lessons for Collective Action," *Journal of Economic Literature* 39, no. 3 (September 2001): 872.

39. The beneficiaries include, for example, shipyard workers, aeronautical engineers, and others directly employed in the manufacture of military hardware. Of course, the particularized benefits that flow to these workers are paid by all taxpayers.

40. Other problems of extended deterrence will be discussed in the next section.

41. Cooper, in *Issues in Defense Economics,* ed. McKean, 56.

42. It might be true that involvement in a distant war is preferable to a war on one's borders, or in one's own territory, particularly if one assumes that a distant threat that is not stopped will eventually become a proximate threat. But in most cases that assumes too much.

43. George F. Will, "Russia's Power Play," *Washington Post,* August 12, 2008, A13; Fred Kaplan, "Lonely Night in Georgia," *Slate,* August 11, 2008, http://www.slate.com/id/2197281/. For more on NATO's eroding credibility, see Stanley Kober, "Cracks in the Foundation: NATO's New Troubles," Cato Institute Policy Analysis no. 608, January 15, 2008.

44. Economists have noted that a declining share of U.S. taxpayers are subject to federal income taxation. Still, all wage earners in the legal economy are subject to federal tax withholding for social security (FICA) and Medicare, and even wage earners who are paid in cash (and who therefore avoid payroll taxes) pay state and local sales taxes whenever they spend their hard-earned wages. Only an individual operating *entirely* in the gray- or black-market economy could avoid paying any taxes, but such a condition seems possible only on a theoretical level.

45. Olson, *The Logic of Collective Action,* 13.

46. Christopher Coyne and Steve Davies also discuss the positive and negative effects of order-imposing empires. See Christopher J. Coyne and Steve Davies, "Empire: Public Goods and Bads," *Econ Journal Watch* 4, no. 1 (January 2007): 3–45.

47. Kagan, *Of Paradise and Power*, 36.

48. This is a major theme in Stephen Walt's work. Walt contends that other states seek to "tame" U.S. power because they fear it, even when it is not directed at them. Because Americans should be finding ways to encourage greater cooperation from allies, and greater tolerance for our dominant position in the world, Walt argues that we should consciously constrain our own power, and go out of our way to accommodate the wishes of others. See Walt, *Taming American Power*.

49. In some cases, the hegemonists are trying to have it both ways: claiming that others will not do more to defend themselves, or alternately worrying that they will.

50. Mandelbaum, *The Case for Goliath*, 40.

51. Robert Art notes the "deep fear that, if the United States were to withdraw its nuclear umbrella, regional powers would, one after another, seek nuclear weapons." Robert Art, *A Grand Strategy for America* (Ithaca, NY: Cornell University Press, 2003), 164. Robert Kagan is more ambivalent, noting that a multipolar world with several regional powers in possession of nuclear weapons "could make wars between them less likely, or it could make them more catastrophic." Robert Kagan, *The Return of History and the End of Dreams* (New York: Knopf, 2008), 94.

52. Defenders of the Bush Doctrine who claim that Libya's decision to divest itself of its nascent nuclear weapons program (which amounted to not much more than some drawings and some disassembled machines) was driven by U.S. actions against Iraq overstate their case. Libyan leader Muammar Qaddafi had been attempting to negotiate an end to international sanctions for years, but had failed to reach an agreement with U.S. officials before the invasion of Iraq. See Bruce Jentleson and Christopher A. Whytlock, "Who 'Won' Libya?" *International Security* 30, no. 3 (Winter 2005/6): 47–86. For more on preventive war and non-proliferation, see Jeffrey Record, "Nuclear Deterrence, Preventive War, and Counterproliferation," Cato Institute Policy Analysis no. 519, July 8, 2004.

53. Layne, *Peace of Illusions*, 166.

54. Quoted in David Alan Rosenberg, "The Origins of Overkill: Nuclear Weapons and American Strategy, 1945–1960," *Strategy and Nuclear Deterrence: An International Security Reader*, ed. Steven E. Miller (Princeton, NJ: Princeton University Press, 1984), 137.

55. Henry A. Kissinger, *Nuclear Weapons and Foreign Policy* (New York: Harper & Brothers, 1957), 10.

56. Thomas Schelling, *Arms and Influence* (New Haven, CT: Yale University Press, 1966), 36 (emphasis in original), cited in Layne, *Peace of Illusions*, 272.

57. Robert Jervis, "What Do We Want to Deter and How Do We Deter It?" in *Turning Point: The Gulf War and U.S. Military Strategy*, ed. L. Benjamin Ederington and Michael J. Mazar (Boulder, CO: Westview Press, 1994), 130, cited in Layne, *Peace of Illusions*, 166.

58. Chris Layne makes a similar argument. See, Layne, *Peace of Illusions*, 164–68.

59. Taiwan's more fervent defenders in the United States might dispute such claims, but the pledges inherent within the Taiwan Relations Act and the Shanghai Communiqué are highly contingent. See Ted Galen Carpenter, *America's Coming War with China: A Collision Course over Taiwan* (New York: Palgrave Macmillan, 2005), 172–76.

60. See Richard L. Russell, "Military Planning for a Middle East Stockpiled with Nuclear Weapons," *Military Review* (November–December 2006); and Kate Amlin, "Will Saudi Arabia Acquire Nuclear Weapons?" Nuclear Threat Initiative Issue Brief, August 2008, http://www.nti.org/e_research/e3_40a.html.

61. The U.S. Department of Energy annual budget for nuclear weapons is approximately $17 billion; the United Kingdom spends just under $2 billion; France about $4 billion; and Russia just under $1 billion.

62. See also the collection of essays surrounding the question of Japan and nuclear weapons in Benjamin L. Self and Jeffrey W. Thompson, eds., *Japan's Nuclear Option: Security, Politics, and Policy in the 21st Century* (Washington, DC: Henry L. Stimson Center, 2003). On the U.S.-Japan strategic relationship more broadly, see Christopher Preble, "Two Normal Nations: Rethinking the U.S.-Japan Strategic Relationship," Cato Institute Policy Analysis no. 566, April 18, 2006; and Michael Mastanudo, "Incomplete Hegemony and Security Order in the Asia-Pacific," in *America Unrivaled: The Future of the Balance of Power,* ed. G. John Ikenberry (Ithaca, NY: Cornell University Press, 2002), 201–2.

63. Mandelbaum, *The Case for Goliath,* 94. See also Joseph McMillan, "U.S. Interests and Objectives," *The United States and the Persian Gulf: Reshaping Security Strategy for the Post-Containment Era,* ed. Richard D. Sokolsky (Washington, DC: National Defense University, 2003), 15, 18.

64. As of October 2008, the Energy Information Administration (EIA) projected that the average retail price for regular grade gasoline would be $3.56 per gallon ($3.40 inflation-adjusted) in 2008, up from $1.56 ($1.76 inflation-adjusted) in 2003. Prices fell precipitously, however, to near 2003 levels in the final two months of 2008.

65. Among major European and Asian countries, Japan, Germany, the Netherlands, South Korea, and Italy are all completely dependent on imported oil. Ninety-four percent of consumption in France is supplied by oil imports; 86 percent in India. By way of comparison, approximately 65 percent of the oil consumed in the United States comes from foreign sources.

66. I am deeply indebted to my colleague Jerry Taylor for his patient explication of the relevant facts, and for his insightful comments pertaining to this section.

67. Figures are from the EIA. Thanks to research assistants Craig Principe, Charles Rice, and Charles Zakaib for their help in compiling these statistics and keeping them up to date.

68. Donald Losman, "Economic Security: A National Security Folly?" Cato Institute Policy Analysis no. 409, August 1, 2001.

69. Eugene Gholz and Daryl G. Press, "Energy Alarmism: The Myths That Make Americans Worry about Oil," Cato Institute Policy Analysis no. 589, April 5, 2007. See also Robert L. Bradley, *The Mirage of Oil Protection* (Lanham, MD: Rowman and Littlefield, 1988), 4. Bradley notes that "domestic price ceilings artificially increased world prices by increasing domestic demand (which constituted one-third of world demand), discouraging production, and preventing countercyclical inventory strategies by majors and independents alike. Regulated domestic prices, coupled with the refinery entitlements program, which lowered the effective price of foreign crude for domestic refiners, also enhanced demand for foreign oil and raised the world prices above the levels an unhampered market would have set."

70. Jerry Taylor and Peter Van Doren, "The Energy Security Obsession," *Georgetown Journal of Law & Public Policy* 6, vol. 2 (Summer 2008): 477–78. See also M.A. Adelman, *The Genie Out of the Bottle: World Oil Since 1970* (Cambridge, MA: MIT Press, 1996), 109–17; and idem, "Coping with Supply Insecurity," in *The Economics of Petroleum Supply* (Cambridge, MA: MIT Press, 1993), 510–11.

71. These costs are not zero, but they are not very large. Consumers typically respond as though there were an actual cutoff, engaging in a wave of panic buying to stock up on the embargoed resource. This boost in short-term demand often sets off a temporary price spike, but market forces respond by increasing supply, which ultimately satisfies demands, and prices stabilize. I am indebted to Peter Van Doren for his helpful comments on this point.

72. Indeed, several writers then and since made the case for an offshore balancing strategy. See, for example, Stephen M. Walt, *The Origins of Alliances* (Ithaca, NY: Cornell University Press,

1986), 152; idem, *Taming American Power,* 222–23; Christopher Layne, "From Preponderance to Offshore Balancing: America's Future Grand Strategy," *International Security* 22, no. 1 (Summer 1997): 86–124; Leon Hadar, *Sandstorm: Policy Failure in the Middle East* (New York: Palgrave Macmillan, 2005), 6–9, 35–42; and Daryl G. Press, Eugene Gholz, and Benjamin Valentino, "Time to Offshore Our Troops," *New York Times,* December 12, 2006.

73. The low-point for the price of oil within the past ten years occurred in December 1998, when a barrel of oil cost just $12.47 a barrel in 2008 dollars. Data from the Energy Information Administration, July 2008.

74. Alan Clendenning, "Brazil Oil Field Could Be Huge Find," *Associated Press,* April 14, 2008.

75. On oil from shale, see James T. Bartis, Tom LaTourrette, Lloyd Dixon, et al., "Oil Shale Development in the United States: Prospects and Policy Issues," RAND Corporation, 2005, http://www.rand.org/pubs/monographs/2005/RAND_MG414.pdf. Regarding the Bakken formation, see Catrin Einhorn, "Billions of Barrels of Oil May Lie under Northern Plains," *New York Times,* April 11, 2008; and "Report Says up to 4.3 Billion Barrels of Oil in Bakken Shale," *International Herald Tribune,* April 11, 2008. On how technological advances affect estimates of recoverable oil, see Gholz and Press, "Energy Alarmism," 6.

76. See, for example, Kurt Campbell and Michael O'Hanlon, *Hard Power: The New Politics of National Security* (New York: Basic Books, 2006), 164–84; and Thomas L. Friedman, "Fly Me to the Moon," *New York Times,* December 5, 2004.

77. "In the international economy," writes Michael Mandelbaum, "much of the confidence needed to proceed with transactions and the protection that engenders this confidence come from the policies of the United States." Mandelbaum, *The Case for Goliath,* 88.

78. At the time, this amounted to about $112 per person, per year. David Henderson, "Do We Need to Go to War for Oil?" Cato Institute Foreign Policy Briefing no. 4, October 24, 1990.

79. Graham E. Fuller and Ian O. Lesser, "Persian Gulf Myths," *Foreign Affairs* 76, no. 3 (May/June 1997), 43.

80. Figures from Losman, "Economic Security: A National Security Folly?" 9.

81. Mark A. Delucchi and James J. Murphy, "U.S. Military Expenditures to Protect the Use of Persian Gulf Oil for Motor Vehicles," *Energy Policy* (2008), doi:10.1016/j.enpol.2008.03.006.

82. Figures from the EIA in nominal dollars, http://www.eia.doe.gov/emeu/aer/txt/ptb0520.html.

83. As discussed in chapter 3, these direct costs do not account for the long-term costs of the war, which could total more than $2 trillion. I have not even attempted here to account for the many other costs of our foreign policies stressed throughout this book, including the changes to the character of our government, and the increased risk from terrorism, for example.

84. Americans consume 388.6 million gallons of gasoline every day, about 1.29 gallons per person per day, or 472 gallons per person, per year. Figures compiled from EIA.

85. Wolfowitz quoted in Karen DeYoung and Walter Pincus, "Despite Obstacles to War, White House Forges Ahead," *Washington Post,* March 2, 2003. Others, including strong advocates of the war, disputed Wolfowitz's suggestion, and argued instead that our interests in the region would increase following Saddam's removal from power, and that we must plan on a long-term military presence there. See, for example, Tom Donnelly, "There's No Place Like Iraq...," *Weekly Standard,* May 5, 2003; and Max Boot, "American Imperialism? No Need to Run Away from That Label," *USA Today,* May 6, 2003.

86. U.S. forces were moved out of Saudi Arabia, but merely shifted to other countries in the region, not removed from the region as a whole.

87. Quoted in George Herring, "America and Vietnam: The Unending War," *Foreign Affairs* 70, no. 5 (Winter 1991/92): 104.

88. John Mueller, "The Iraq Syndrome," *Foreign Affairs* 84, no. 6 (November/December 2005): 53–54.

Chapter Five

1. George H. W. Bush, Address Before a Joint Session of the Congress on the State of the Union, Washington, DC, January 28, 1992. See also Christopher Layne, *Peace of Illusions: American Grand Strategy from 1940 to the Present* (Ithaca, NY: Cornell University Press, 2006), 140.

2. Condoleezza Rice, Remarks at the International Institute for Strategic Studies, London, United Kingdom, June 26, 2003, http://www.whitehouse.gov/news/releases/2003/06/20030626. html.

3. Inveterate skeptics who are inclined to infer nefarious intent whenever the U.S. government acts, tend to dismiss such stated rationales as pure cover for actions that are, in fact, intended to advance narrow U.S. interests. Sometimes that is the case. But to the extent that the U.S. government acts to advance U.S. interests, it need not rely on cover and subterfuge to justify such acts. They should be understood by other countries as legitimate expressions of our sovereign rights of self-defense, and they should enjoy the support of the American people who expect their government to protect them. Americans can, and should, scrutinize whether such acts are likely to accomplish the stated aims, and in many cases the policies do not. That is a legitimate and necessary critique, as discussed in chapter 6.

4. On the origins of the United Nations, see Stephen C. Schlesinger, *Act of Creation: The Founding of the United Nations: A Story of Superpowers, Secret Agents, Wartime Allies and Enemies, and Their Quest for a Peaceful World* (Boulder, CO: Westview Press, 2003).

5. On the evolution of this concept during the 1990s, see Penelope C. Simons, "Humanitarian Intervention: A Review of Literature," Ploughshares Working Paper 01–2, http://www.ploughshares.ca/libraries/WorkingPapers/wp012.html.

6. Kofi A. Annan, "We the Peoples: The Role of the United Nations in the 21st Century," UN Doc. No. A/54/2000, April 3, 2000. Full text of the report available at http://www.un.org/millennium/sg/report/full.htm.

7. International Commission on Intervention and State Sovereignty, *The Responsibility to Protect* (Ottawa: International Development Research Centre, December 2001), 8.

8. Ibid., xi.

9. Article 2.7 of the UN Charter reaffirms the basic principle of non-intervention in purely domestic matters, but adds the crucial caveat that "this principle shall not prejudice the application of enforcement measures under Chapter VII." The principle of a responsibility to protect affirms and clarifies a number of other international legal norms for intervention, including the Hague Convention of 1907, which stated that nationals of non-belligerent states are considered neutral; the Geneva Conventions, particularly the Fourth, which relates to the protection of civilians during times of war; Protocol II of 1977, which further established the protection of victims in non-international armed conflicts; the Genocide Convention, which was signed and ratified by the General Assembly on December 9, 1948, and went into force in 1951; and the International Criminal Court, particularly the Rome Statute adopted by the General Assembly in 1998, which went into force on July 1, 2002.

10. The erosion of the concept of sovereignty, in turn, might encourage other states to seek new means for preserving their independence, including the development of a nuclear deterrent.

11. The intervention in Afghanistan after the 9/11 attacks was in keeping with the spirit of this norm, even if some might challenge the particulars.

12. For the argument that the Iraq War was legitimate on those grounds, see Jose Ramos-Horta, "Sometimes, A War Saves People," in *A Matter of Principle: Humanitarian Arguments for War in Iraq*, ed. Thomas Cushman (Berkeley: University of California Press, 2005), 281–84. Others vociferously disagree. See, for example, Ken Roth, "War in Iraq: Not a Humanitarian Intervention," Human Rights Watch, January 2004, http://www.hrw.org/wr2k4/3.htm.

13. "Iraq War Illegal, Says Annan," BBC, September 16, 2004, http://news.bbc.co.uk/2/hi/middle_east/3661134.stm.

14. See, for example, Ramos-Horta, "Sometimes, A War Saves People."

15. "A More Secure World: Who Needs to Do What?" Interview with Brent Scowcroft, Richard N. Haass, and Kofi Annan, Council on Foreign Relations, December 16, 2004, http://www.cfr.org/publication.html?id=7569.

16. Tony Smith, *A Pact with the Devil: Washington's Bid for World Supremacy and the Betrayal of the American Promise* (New York: Routledge, 2007), 175.

17. Most countries possess the ability to intervene militarily on their borders, as Russia dramatically demonstrated with its invasion of Georgia in August 2008, but only the United States has regularly engaged in major military operations in distant regions.

18. "A multiplicity of geographically and functionally overlapping institutions will permit the United States and other powers to 'forum shop' for an appropriate instrument to facilitate international cooperation." Francis Fukuyama, *America at the Crossroads: Democracy, Power and the Neoconservative Legacy* (New Haven, CT: Yale University Press), 172.

19. This certainly does not apply to all, or even most, members of the international community. Russia, China, and India—with a combined population of more than 2.5 billion people—do not endorse U.S. activism in most cases.

20. Michael Ignatieff, "The Burden," *New York Times*, January 5, 2003.

21. Anne-Marie Slaughter and Lee Feinstein, "A Duty to Prevent," *Foreign Affairs* 83, no. 1 (January/February 2004): 136, 137, 138 (emphasis added). In a similar vein, Slaughter and her Princeton colleague G. John Ikenberry sought ways to overcome the "impediments to collective action" that constrained multilateral institutions such as the United Nations and NATO. See G. John Ikenberry and Anne-Marie Slaughter, "Forging a World of Liberty under Law: U.S. National Security in the 21st Century," Final Report of the Princeton Project on National Security, September 27, 2006, 27.

22. George W. Bush, Second Inaugural Address, Washington, DC, January 20, 2005, http://www.whitehouse.gov/news/releases/2005/01/20050120-1.html, emphasis added.

23. Ibid.

24. Alex de Waal notes that this "was an important finding, not least because it broadens the usage of the term 'genocide' to include ethnically targeted killings, rapes and displacement perpetrated in the course of counter-insurgency, a significant expansion on the customary usage of the term to refer to attempts to eliminate entire populations." Alex de Waal, "Darfur and the Failure of the Responsibility to Protect," *International Affairs* 83, no. 6 (2007): 1041–42.

25. William G. O'Neill, "The Responsibility to Protect Darfur," *Christian Science Monitor*, September 28, 2006.

26. Nicholas D. Kristof, "Prosecuting Genocide," *New York Times*, July 17, 2008.

27. De Waal, "Darfur and the Failure of the Responsibility to Protect," 1043, 1045.

28. Victoria Holt and Tobias Berkman, *The Impossible Mandate? Military Preparedness, the Responsibility to Protect and Modern Peace Operations* (Washington, DC: Henry L. Stimson

Center, 2006), 71. The Brahimi Report accurately anticipated these challenges. "Promising to extend such protection establishes a very high threshold of expectation," the report noted, and it warned that the "large mismatch between desired objective and resources available" would contribute to "continuing disappointment with United Nations follow-through in this area." UN General Assembly and Security Council, *Report of the Panel on United Nations Peace Operations* (the "Brahimi Report"), A/55/305-S/2000/809, August 2, 2000, para. 63.

29. See, for example, Timothy W. Crawford and Alan J. Kuperman, eds., *Gambling on Humanitarian Intervention: Moral Hazard, Rebellion and Civil War* (New York: Routledge, 2006).

30. De Waal, "Darfur and the Failure of the Responsibility to Protect," 1046. The reference is to Anthony Lake, Susan Rice, and Donald Payne, "We Saved Europeans. Why not Africans?" *Washington Post,* October 2, 2006.

31. "Experts to Assess Myanmar Cyclone Survivors' Needs," *Associated Press,* June 10, 2008.

32. Kouchner's views quoted in Seth Mydans, "Myanmar Faces Pressure to Allow Major Aid Efforts," *International Herald Tribune,* May 8, 2008.

33. Madeleine K. Albright, "The End of Intervention," *New York Times,* June 11, 2008.

34. Matthew Continetti, "UN to Burma: Drop Dead: Let's Airdrop Aid to the Cyclone Victims," *Weekly Standard,* May 26, 2008, 9. Interest in intervention in Burma continued long after the immediate humanitarian crisis caused by Cyclone Nargis abated. See, for example, Max Boot, "What to Do about Burma?" *Contentions,* August 28, 2008, http://www.commentarymagazine.com/blogs/index.php/boot/23381.

35. Gareth Evans, "Facing Up to Our Responsibilities," *Guardian* (UK), May 12, 2008. The Commission Report made allowances for interventions based on natural disasters when the state is unwilling or unable to provide relief, but the UN World Summit did not adopt that language.

36. Michael Walzer, "The Argument about Humanitarian Intervention," *Dissent* 49, no. 1 (Winter 2002): 31.

37. Quoted in Michael Ignatieff, "Why Are We in Iraq? (And Liberia? And Afghanistan?)," *New York Times,* September 5, 2003.

38. Many other European countries have a colonial legacy including Spain, Portugal, the Netherlands, Belgium, and France.

39. Meanwhile, unlike former colonial powers, our rationales for intervening or not intervening cannot be based on historical or cultural connections; we did not establish a formal empire, and had only minimal involvement outside of the Western Hemisphere before 1945. The U.S. acquisition of the Philippines from Spain following the Spanish-American War is the exception to the rule. No other sovereign country can claim to have been a former U.S. colony. Some, however, pointed to the "special relationship" of the United States with Liberia to make the case for U.S. military intervention there in 2003. See, for example, James S. Robbins, "The Liberian Opportunity," *National Review Online,* July 8, 2003, http://www.nationalreview.com/robbins/robbins070803.asp.

40. Rice, Lake, and Payne, "We Saved Europeans. Why Not Africans?"

41. C. S. Lewis invoked a similar metaphor in discussing his support for British involvement in World War II, but made an equally sophisticated argument for why such interventions could not be considered the norm:

I believe our cause to be, as human causes go, very righteous, and I therefore believe it to be a duty to participate in this war. And every duty is a religious duty, and our obligation to perform every duty is therefore absolute. Thus we may have a duty to rescue a drowning man, and perhaps, if we live on a dangerous coast, to learn life-saving so as to be ready for any drowning man when he turns up. It may be our duty to lose our own lives in saving him. But if anyone devoted himself to life-saving in the sense of giving it his total attention—so that he thought and spoke of nothing else and demanded the cessation of all other human activities until everyone had learned to swim—he would be a monomaniac. The rescue of drowning men is, then, a duty worth dying for, but not worth living for. It seems to me that all political duties (among which I include military duties) are of this kind. A man may have to die for our country: but no man must, in any exclusive sense, live for his country. He who surrenders himself without reservation to the claims of a nation, or a party, or a class is rendering unto Caesar that which of all things most emphatically belongs to God: himself.

In *The Essential C. S. Lewis,* edited by Lyle W. Dorsett (New York: Macmillan, 1988), 373.

42. "Myanmar Says U.S. Aid Can't Be Trusted," *Associated Press,* June 13, 2008.

43. Mandelbaum, *The Case for Goliath,* 219.

44. Quoted in Michael R. Gordon, "Bush Would Stop U.S. Peacekeeping in Balkan Fights," *New York Times,* October 21, 2000.

45. Condoleezza Rice, "Rethinking the National Interest: American Realism for a New World," *Foreign Affairs* 87, no. 4 (July/August 2008): 24.

46. A more nuanced concern is that an inordinate focus on a particular threat, or a particular type of mission, will undermine the military's ability to deal with a wide range of missions and threats.

47. On the "hegemon's dilemma" in the context of international trade, see Arthur A. Stein, "The Hegemon's Dilemma: Great Britain, the United States, and the International Economic Order," *International Organization* 38, no. 2 (Spring 1984): 355–86.

48. Claes G. Ryn, *America the Virtuous: The Crisis of Democracy and the Quest for Empire* (New Brunswick, NJ: Transaction, 2004), 3.

49. Daniel W. Drezner, "Mind the Gap," *The National Interest,* no. 87 (January/February 2007): 49.

50. Chicago Council on Global Affairs and WorldPublicOpinion.org, "World Publics Reject US Role as the World Leader," April 2007, http://www.worldpublicopinion.org/pipa/pdf/apr07/CCGA+_ViewsUS_article.pdf. See also, Bill McInturff, Liz Harrington, and Geoff Garin, "The New American Consensus on International Cooperation: A Presentation of Key Findings from Focus Groups and a National Survey," Better World Campaign, United Nations Foundation, November 13, 2007, http://www.betterworldcampaign.org/assets/pdf/unf_national_survey2007.pdf.

51. Andrew Kohut and Bruce Stokes, *America against the World: How We Are Different, and Why We Are Disliked* (New York: Times Books, 2006), 49–50.

52. Michael Mandelbaum predicts that "the American role in the world may depend in part on Americans not scrutinizing it too closely." Mandelbaum, *The Case for Goliath,* 223–24.

Chapter Six

1. "Excerpts from Pentagon's Plan: 'Prevent the Re-Emergence of a New Rival,'" *New York Times,* March 8, 1992.

2. Patrick E. Tyler, "Pentagon Drops Goal Of Blocking New Superpowers," *New York Times,* May 24, 1992.

3. For more on the 1992 DPG, see Stefan Halper and Jonathan Clarke, *America Alone: The Neo-Conservatives and the Global Order* (New York: Cambridge University Press, 2004), 145–46; James Mann, *Rise of the Vulcans: The History of Bush's War Cabinet* (New York: Penguin Books, 2004), 209–15; and Tony Smith, *A Pact with the Devil: Washington's Bid for World Supremacy and the Betrayal of the American Promise* (New York: Routledge, 2007), 6–8.

4. George W. Bush, *The National Security Strategy of the United States of America* (Washington, DC: The White House, September 2002), 30.

5. Stockholm International Peace Research Institute's (SIPRI) figures for 2006 are not the same as those compiled by the International Institute for Strategic Studies (IISS) and cited in chapter 2, but only SIPRI compares defense expenditures over time and holding constant for inflation. The different estimates surrounding especially China's budget are significant, but probably not from the perspective of increases over time. For example, China's official defense budget at market exchange rates totaled $35.3 billion in 2006; its defense expenditures, based on a PPP estimate, and including military expenditures that are outside of the official defense budget, totaled approximately $122 billion. International Institute for Strategic Studies, *The Military Balance, 2008* (London: International Institute for Strategic Studies, 2008), 376. IISS did not have figures for the 2007 budget at the time this manuscript went to press. On the debate over estimating defense spending in China, see John J. Tkacik, Jr., "A Chinese Military Superpower?" Heritage Foundation WebMemo, no. 1389, March 8, 2007, and Justin Logan, "The Chinese Defense Budget: Myths and Reality," Cato@Liberty, April 23, 2007, http://www.cato-at-liberty. org/2007/04/23/the-chinese-defense-budget-myths-and-reality/.

6. All figures are in constant 2005 U.S. dollars, compiled by the Stockholm International Peace Research Institute, and published in *SIPRI Yearbook 2008: Armaments, Disarmaments, and International Security* and in The SIPRI Military Expenditure Database, http://milexdata. sipri.org/result.php4.

7. Patrick E. Tyler, "U.S. Strategy Plan Calls for Insuring No Rivals Develop," *New York Times,* March 8, 1992.

8. Benjamin Franklin to Sir Joseph Banks, July 27, 1783. *The Writings of Benjamin Franklin,* ed. Albert Henry Smyth, vol. IX (New York: Macmillan, 1907), 74.

9. Joseph J. Ellis, *His Excellency: George Washington* (New York: Vintage Books, 2005), 235–36.

10. From "The Uses of Military Power," speech before the National Press Club, Washington, DC, November 28, 1984, reprinted in Caspar W. Weinberger, *Fighting for Peace: Seven Critical Years in the Pentagon* (New York: Warner Books, 1990), 433–48 (emphasis added).

11. On Somalia, a study by the RAND Corporation of public attitudes toward foreign military operations found that two-thirds of poll respondents favored withdrawal from Somalia *before* the Black Hawk Down incident. The report concluded, "the reason that most preferred withdrawal was the widespread belief that the United States had only modest stakes in the situation." See Eric V. Larsen and Bodgan Savych, *American Public Support for U.S. Military Operations from Mogadishu to Baghdad* (Santa Monica, CA: RAND Corporation, 2005), xx. For a timeline showing changing public attitudes toward the war in Iraq juxtaposed against major events there, see Ben Arnoldy, "US Public's Support of Iraq War Sliding Faster Now," *Christian Science Monitor,* March 20, 2007.

12. Edward S. Corwin et al., *The President: Office and Powers 1787–1984*, 5th rev. ed. (New York: New York University Press, 1984), 201, cited in Ted Galen Carpenter, "Global Interventionism and a New Imperial Presidency," Cato Policy Analysis no. 71, May 16, 1986.

13. See for example Arthur Schlesinger, Jr., "Back to the Womb," *Foreign Affairs* 74, no. 4 (July/August 1995): 3.

14. Stanley Kober, "James Madison vs. Madeleine Albright: The Debate over Collective Security," in *NATO Enlargement: Illusions and Reality*, ed. Ted Galen Carpenter and Barbara Conry (Washington, DC: Cato Institute, 1998), 257.

15. The poorly considered decision to expand NATO in two successive rounds, ratified by Congress with almost no dissent, demonstrates that too few people contemplate the risks associated with such decisions, and reveals how far we must go to restore Congress's proper role in the decision to go to war. The bipartisan enthusiasm for admitting Ukraine and Georgia into NATO, despite the very real risks of war with Russia made manifest in the dispute over Abkhazia and South Ossetia in August 2008, is but the latest manifestation of this problem. For just some of the arguments against NATO enlargement, offered over a decade ago, but still relevant today, see Carpenter and Conry, eds., *NATO Enlargement: Illusions and Reality*.

16. The notion that democracies are inherently less warlike than autocracies does not survive close scrutiny. See, especially, Christopher Layne, "Kant or Cant: The Myth of the Democratic Peace," *International Security* 19, no. 2 (Autumn 1994): 5–49; Layne, *Peace of Illusions*, 121–22; and Smith, *A Pact with the Devil*, 96–114. See also Edward D. Mansfield and Jack Snyder, *Electing to Fight: Why Emerging Democracies Go to War* (Cambridge, MA: MIT Press, 2005), which endorses the broad notion of a democratic peace, but points out that immature democracies are no less prone to war than autocracies.

17. James Madison, "Universal Peace," *National Gazette*, February 2, 1792, in *The Mind of the Founder*, ed. Marvin Meyers, rev. ed. (Hanover, NH: University Press of New England, 1981), 192, cited in Kober, "James Madison vs. Madeleine Albright," 258.

18. Of course, historians have subsequently learned that Roosevelt and Truman might have been willing to accept something short of that; and it could be reasonably asserted that allowing the Japanese to retain the emperor, even in a much diminished capacity, violated the spirit of unconditional surrender.

19. Bob Woodward, *Plan of Attack* (New York: Simon & Schuster, 2004), 150.

20. Quoted in Rick Atkinson, "The Long, Blinding Road to War," *Washington Post*, March 7, 2004. See also Christopher Dickey, "The Story of O," *New York Times*, April 4, 2004.

21. Michael Isikoff and David Corn, *Hubris: The Inside Story of Spin, Scandal, and the Selling of the Iraq War* (New York: Crown, 2006), 15.

22. Dwight D. Eisenhower, "Farewell Radio and Television Address," January 17, 1961, http://www.eisenhowermemorial.org/speeches/19610117%20farewell%20address.htm.

23. See, for example, Conrad C. Crane and W. Andrew Terrill, "Reconstructing Iraq: Insights, Challenges, and Missions for Military Forces in a Post-Conflict Scenario," Strategic Studies Institute, U.S. Army War College, February 2003, http://www.strategicstudiesinstitute.army.mil/pdffiles/PUB182.pdf, vi; Ted Galen Carpenter, "Missing the Point: Bush's Speech to the U.N.," *Orange County Register*, September 15, 2002; William Niskanen, "U.S. Should Refrain from Attacking Iraq," *Chicago Sun-Times*, December 7, 2001; "War with Iraq is *Not* in America's National Interest," advertisement published on the op-ed page of the *New York Times*, September 26, 2002, http://mearsheimer.uchicago.edu/pdfs/P0012.pdf; and John J. Mearsheimer and

Stephen M. Walt, "An Unnecessary War," *Foreign Policy* (January–February 2003): 51–59. A survey of 1,084 international relations scholars found that nearly 80 percent opposed the war in Iraq from the outset. Susan Peterson, Michael J. Tierney, and Daniel Maliniak, "Inside the Ivory Tower," *Foreign Policy* (November–December 2005): 64.

24. Among the many examples, see especially Douglas J. Feith, *War and Decision: Inside the Pentagon at the Dawn of the War on Terrorism* (New York: HarperCollins, 2008). See also, Kenneth M. Pollack, "The Seven Deadly Sins of Failure in Iraq: A Retrospective Analysis of the Reconstruction," *The Middle East Review of International Affairs* 10, no. 4 (December 2006): article 1/7; Larry Diamond, *Squandered Victory: The American Occupation and the Bungled Effort to Bring Democracy to Iraq* (New York: Times Books, 2005); and David L. Phillips, *Losing Iraq: Inside the Postwar Reconstruction Fiasco* (Boulder, CO: Westview Press, 2005).

25. Ivo Daalder and Robert Kagan, "The Next Intervention," *Washington Post*, August 6, 2007.

26. David C. Hendrickson and Robert W. Tucker, "Revisions in Need of Revising: What Went Wrong in the Iraq War," Strategic Studies Institute, U.S. Army War College, December 2006, http://www.strategicstudiesinstitute.army.mil/pdffiles/pub637.pdf, vii. See also Stephen M. Walt, "The Blame Game," *Foreign Policy* (November–December 2005): 44–46; and Benjamin H. Friedman, Harvey M. Sapolsky, and Christopher Preble, "Learning the Right Lessons from Iraq," Cato Policy Analysis no. 610, February 13, 2008.

27. David Edelstein, *Occupational Hazards: Success and Failure in Military Occupation* (Ithaca, NY: Cornell University Press, 2008). See also Christopher J. Coyne, *After War: The Political Economy of Exporting Democracy* (Palo Alto, CA: Stanford University Press, 2007), 45–78.

28. See, especially, Jeffrey Record, "The American Way of War: Cultural Barriers to Successful Counterinsurgency," Cato Policy Analysis no. 577, September 1, 2006. See also Colin S. Gray, "The American Way of War: Critique and Implications," in *Rethinking the Principles of War*, ed. Anthony D. McIvor (Annapolis, MD: Naval Institute Press, 2005): 13–40; and Andrew Mack, "Why Big Nations Lose Small Wars: The Politics of Asymmetric Conflict," *World Politics* 27, no. 2 (1975): 175–200.

29. Brigadier Nigel Aylwin-Foster, British Army, "Changing the Army for Counterinsurgency Operations," *Military Review* (November–December 2005): 2–15.

30. Secretary of Defense Rumsfeld did this in December 2004, and then tried to foist the blame on faulty intelligence, despite the fact the National Intelligence Council warned *before* the war, as reported in the *New York Times*, "of a possible insurgency against the new Iraqi government or American-led forces, saying that rogue elements from Saddam Hussein's government could work with existing terrorist groups or act independently to wage guerrilla warfare." Douglas Jehl and David E. Sanger, "Prewar Assessment on Iraq Saw Chance of Strong Divisions," *New York Times*, September 28, 2004. In November 2003, President Bush told members of his cabinet not to refer to the violence in Iraq as "insurgency." Nearly two years later, Rumsfeld refused to use the word "insurgents" to describe the enemy our troops were facing. See Fred Kaplan, *Daydream Believers: How a Few Grand Ideas Wrecked American Power* (Hoboken, NJ: John Wiley & Sons, 2008), 160.

31. Eliot Cohen, Conrad Crane, Jan Horvath, and John Nagl, "Principles, Imperatives, and Paradoxes of Counterinsurgency," *Military Review* (March–April 2006): 53.

32. Ben Farmer, "Afghanistan President Hamid Karzai Hopes Barack Obama Will Bring 'Peace,'" *Telegraph* (UK), November 5, 2008, http://www.telegraph.co.uk/news/newstopics/uselection2008/barackobama/3385388/Afghanistan-President-Hamid-Karzai-hopes-Barack-Obama-will-bring-peace.html.

33. *The U.S. Army Marine Corps Counterinsurgency Field Manual* (Chicago and London: University of Chicago Press), xxviii–ix.

34. Andrew P. N. Erdmann, "The U.S. Presumption of Quick, Costless Wars," in *America the Vulnerable: Our Military Problems and How to Fix Them,* ed. John Lehman and Harvey Sicherman (Philadelphia: Foreign Policy Research Institute, 2000), 71. The article first appeared, in slightly different form, in *Orbis* 43, no. 3 (Summer 1999): 363–81.

35. Quoted in Ann Scott Tyson, "The Curtain Is Drawn on the Rumsfeld Era," *Washington Post,* December 16, 2006.

36. Adm. Mike Mullen, "We Can't Do It Alone," *Honolulu Advertiser,* October 29, 2006, http://www.nwc.navy.mil/cnws/marstrat/docs/library/Articles/We_Can't_do_it_Alone_by_ADM_Mullen.doc. Navy officials briefed journalists on the outlines of the plan during the summer of 2006. For a complete discussion of the origins of the plan, as well as some expert reaction, see Christopher P. Cavas, "The Thousand-Ship Navy," *Armed Forces Journal* (December 2006): 26–39.

37. Mullen, "We Can't Do It Alone."

38. Robert M. Gates speaking before the Navy Flag Officers Conference, U.S. Naval Academy, Annapolis, Maryland, April 25, 2007, http://www.defenselink.mil/speeches/speech.aspx?speechid=1149.

39. The fleet as of July 2008 numbered approximately 280 ships. With respect to the Navy's long-range shipbuilding plan, the Congressional Budget Office determined that the Navy's annual shipbuilding budget would have to total $25 billion over thirty years, more than double what the service has been spending, on average, in recent years. See Dale Eisman, "Navy's Shipbuilding Wish List Sails into Troubled Waters," *Virginian-Pilot* (Norfolk, VA), March 15, 2008.

40. In 2001, the Congressional Budget Office estimated that this option, combined with buying three fewer Virginia's than the Navy had planned at the time, would save $3.4 billion over a ten-year period. See Congressional Budget Office, "Budget Options 2001," February 2001, http://www.cbo.gov/ftpdocs/27xx/doc2731/ENTIRE-REPORT.PDF, 140–41. Lawrence Korb, senior fellow at the Center for American Progress and a senior advisor to the Center for Defense Information, estimates that refueling the LA class and scrapping the Virginia program would generate net savings of more than $60 billion over a fifteen-year period. See Lawrence Korb, "The Korb Report: A Realistic Defense for America," Business Leaders for Sensible Priorities, http://www.sensiblepriorities.org/pdf/Korb_2007.pdf, 8.

41. As happened when the Suez Canal was out of service, shippers will simply go around. The additional costs associated are not zero, but they are not very large, either.

42. "World Oil Transit Chokepoints," Energy Information Administration, updated January 2008, http://www.eia.doe.gov/cabs/World_Oil_Transit_Chokepoints/Full.html.

43. For more on the Navy's role, see Barry Posen, "Command of the Commons: The Military Foundations of U.S. Hegemony," *International Security* 28, no. 1 (Summer 2003): 11–12, 20, 42.

44. On the merits of unmanned aerial vehicles launched from sea, see Thomas P. Ehrhard and Robert O. Work, *Range, Persistence, Stealth, and Networking: The Case for a Carrier-Based Unmanned Combat Air System* (Washington, DC: Center for Strategic and Budgetary Assessments, 2008).

45. Quoted in Richard Burnett, "Joint Strike Fighter Costs Could Hit Home," *Orlando Sentinel,* April 7, 2008.

46. See, for example, "The Army We Need," *Washington Post,* December 19, 2006; and "A Real-World Army," *New York Times,* December 24, 2006. See also Frederick W. Kagan

and Thomas Donnelly, *Ground Truth: The Future of U.S. Land Power* (Washington, DC: AEI Press, 2008).

47. On the many different grievances and other risk factors that can drive an individual or group to employ terrorism, see Marc Sageman, *Leaderless Jihad: Terror Networks in the 21st Century* (Philadelphia: University of Pennsylvania Press, 2007); Louise Richardson, *What Terrorists Want: Understanding the Enemy, Containing the Threat* (New York: Random House, 2006); Mia Bloom, *Dying to Kill: The Allure of Suicide Terrorism* (New York: Columbia University Press, 2005); Robert Pape, *Dying to Win: The Strategic Logic of Suicide Terrorism* (New York: Random House, 2005); and Jessica Stern, *Terror in the Name of God: Why Religious Militants Kill* (New York: HarperCollins, 2003). Earlier studies noted the correlation between U.S. military intervention and incidents of terrorism against Americans. See Ivan Eland, "Does U.S. Intervention Overseas Breed Terrorism? The Historical Record," Cato Foreign Policy Briefing no. 50, December 17, 1998; and *The Defense Science Board 1997 Summer Study Task Force on DoD Responses to Transnational Threats,* vol. 1, Final Report (Washington: U.S. Department of Defense, October 1997).

48. See, for example, Frederick Kagan and Michael E. O'Hanlon, "The Case for Larger Ground Forces," The Stanley Foundation, April 2007, http://stanleyfoundation.org/publications/other/Kagan_OHanlon_07.pdf. For a skeptical view, see Benjamin H. Friedman, "Fewer Missions, Not More Troops," MIT Center for International Studies, Audit of Conventional Wisdom, July 2007, web.mit.edu/CIS/pdf/Audit_07_07_Friedman.pdf.

49. For example, Barack Obama called for increasing the Army and the Marine Corps to be "better prepared to put boots on the ground in order to take on foes that fight asymmetrical and highly adaptive campaigns on a global scale." Barack Obama, "Renewing American Leadership," *Foreign Affairs* 86, no. 4 (July/August 2007): 7. See also John McCain, an outspoken advocate for a considerably larger force. "On the Issues: National Security," Official John McCain 2008 Campaign Web site, www.johnmccain.com; and idem, "An Enduring Peace Built on Freedom," *Foreign Affairs* 86, no. 6 (November/December 2007): 23.

50. See, especially, Charles Peña, "V-22: Osprey or Albatross?" Cato Institute Foreign Policy Briefing no. 72, January 8, 2003; and Korb, "The Korb Report: A Realistic Defense for America," 9.

51. Megan Scully, "Army Rewrites Plan for Deploying Future Combat Systems," Congress-Daily, June 26, 2008.

52. Korb, "The Korb Report: A Realistic Defense for America," 11–12.

53. See, for example, *A Unified Security Budget for the United States, 2007,* Report of the Joint Task Force, Foreign Policy in Focus and the Center for Defense Information, May 2006; and Cindy Williams, "Beyond Preemption and Preventive War: Increasing U.S. Budget Emphasis on Conflict Prevention," Policy Analysis Brief, The Stanley Foundation, February 2006, http://www.stanleyfoundation.org/publications/pab/pab06budget.pdf. Although not calling for cuts to the defense budget, Secretary of Defense Gates did say that *increases* in the State Department's budget were more important than increases in his own department. See Julian E. Barnes, "Defense Chief Urges Bigger Budget for State Department," *Los Angeles Times,* November 27, 2007. In a similar vein, Gates warned in July 2008 of the "creeping militarization" of U.S. foreign policy, and urged the State Department to take the lead when it came to engaging with other countries, with the military in support. See Ann Scott Tyson, "Gates Warns of Militarized Policy," *Washington Post,* July 16, 2008.

54. This passage draws from Friedman, Sapolsky, and Preble, "Learning the Right Lessons from Iraq." See also Justin Logan and Christopher Preble, "Failed States and Flawed Logic: The Case against a Standing Nation-Building Office," Cato Policy Analysis no. 560, January 11, 2006.

55. Harvard's Stephen Walt makes a similar case. See Stephen M. Walt, *Taming American Power: The Global Response to U.S. Primacy* (New York: W.W. Norton, 2005), 231.

56. P[eter] T. Bauer, *Dissent on Development* (Cambridge, MA: Harvard University Press, 1971), 115.

57. See, especially, William Easterly, *The White Man's Burden: Why the West's Efforts to Aid the Rest Have Done so Much Ill and so Little Good* (New York: Penguin, 2006); and also Deepak Lal, *The Poverty of "Development Economics"* (Cambridge, MA: MIT Press, 2000).

58. Layne calls them the "unipolar agnostics," *Peace of Illusions*, 138–40. Several scholars discount the notion that U.S. hegemony can be extended indefinitely. See, for example, Rajan Menon, *The End of Alliances* (New York: Oxford University Press, 2007); Barry R. Posen, "The Case for Restraint," *American Interest* 3, no. 2 (November–December 2007): 6–17; Richard Betts, "A Disciplined Defense," *Foreign Affairs* 86, no. 6. (November/December 2007): 67–80; and Michael Lind, *The American Way of Strategy: U.S. Foreign Policy and the American Way of Life* (New York: Oxford University Press, 2006).

59. The analogy is from David Miller, "The Responsibility to Protect Human Rights," Centre for the Study of Social Justice Working Paper SJ006, May 2007, 4.

60. The cases, as discussed in chapter 1, were Italy and other states in Albania (1997); the intervention of a coalition of African states in the Central African Republic (1997); the British in Sierra Leone (1999); Australia, New Zealand, and other Pacific nations in the Solomon Islands (2003); and Australia, Malaysia, New Zealand, and Portugal in East Timor (2006).

61. Gareth Evans, "Facing Up to Our Responsibilities," *Guardian*, May 12, 2008.

62. For more on this see, Logan and Preble, "Failed States and Flawed Logic," 12–15.

63. In rare cases, the United States might choose to become involved in an operation led by some other country or group of countries that have a more direct national security interest at stake. This involvement might include logistical and technical assistance. But proposals to include U.S. ground troops in such missions should meet the stringent criteria outlined above.

64. John Quincy Adams, "Address Delivered at the Request of the Committee of Arrangements for Celebrating the Anniversary of Independence," Washington, DC, July 4, 1821, http://digital.library.umsystem.edu/cgi/t/text/text-idx?c=jul;cc=jul;sid=bb8e6dc69251643968f204be49e91dac;rgn=main;view=text;idno=jul000086.

65. William Kristol and Robert Kagan, "Toward a Neo-Reaganite Foreign Policy," *Foreign Affairs* 75, no. 4 (July/August 1996): 31.

Conclusion

1. Ohio State University Professor John Mueller thinks so. He first made the argument nearly twenty years ago, and has since revised his thesis. See, John Mueller, *Retreat from Doomsday: The Obsolescence of Major War* (New York: Basic Books, 1989); and idem, "The Demise of War and of Speculations about the Causes Thereof," Paper presented at the National Convention of the International Studies Association, Chicago, Illinois, February 29, 2007.

2. See, for example, Norman Podhoretz, *World War IV: The Long Struggle against Islamofascism* (New York: Doubleday, 2007). For a critical appraisal see Ian Buruma, "His Toughness Problem—and Ours," review of Podhoretz, *World War IV,* in *New York Review of Books,* September 27, 2007. On the supposed threat to Western Civilization from Radical Islam, see, for example, Lee Harris, *The Suicide of Reason: Radical Islam's Threat to the West* (New York: Basic

Books, 2007); and Bruce Bawer, *While Europe Slept: How Radical Islam is Destroying the West from Within* (New York: Doubleday, 2006).

3. John Quincy Adams, "Address Delivered at the Request of the Committee of Arrangements for Celebrating the Anniversary of Independence," Washington, DC, July 4, 1821, http:// digital.library.umsystem.edu/cgi/t/text/text-idx?c=jul;cc=jul;sid=bb8e6dc69251643968f204be4 9e91dac;rgn=main;view=text;idno=jul000086, 23.

4. The 9/11 commissioners recommended that the United States "encourage reform, freedom, democracy, and opportunity," but conceded that "our own promotion of these messages is limited in its effectiveness simply because we are its carriers." *The 9/11 Commission Report* (Final Report of the National Commission on Terrorist Attacks upon the United States), Official Government Edition (Washington, DC: Government Printing Office, 2004), 375–77.

5. See, for example, Christopher Layne, "The Unipolar Illusion: Why New Great Powers Will Rise," *International Security* 17, no. 4 (Spring 1993): 5–51.

6. Charles Krauthammer, "The Unipolar Moment," *Foreign Affairs* 70, no. 1 (Winter 1990/91): 23–33 (emphasis added).

7. Pollster Daniel Yankelovich explained that only 20 percent of survey respondents ranked promoting democracy as a "very important" goal for the U.S. government—the lowest support noted for any goal asked about in a survey conducted in January 2006. Daniel Yankelovich, "The Tipping Points," *Foreign Affairs* 85, no. 3 (May/June 2006): 121. A follow-up study explained why the U.S. public ranks democracy promotion at the bottom of the list: 74 percent say that democracy promotion is "something other countries can only do on their own." This general belief that democracy must be homegrown, the survey found, had risen 20 percent in two years. Public Agenda, "Confidence in U.S. Foreign Policy Index," Spring 2007.

8. "Poll: Most Americans Say War Not Worth It," CBS News, March 18, 2008, http://www. cbsnews.com/stories/2008/03/18/iraq/main3946663.shtml.

9. See, for example, a survey conducted by the Chicago Council on Global Affairs in July 2006, which found that 75 percent of respondents believed that the United States "should do its share to solve world problems together with other countries" and only 10 percent wanted the United States to "remain the preeminent world leader... in solving international problems." Chicago Council on Global Affairs and WorldPublicOpinion.org, "World Publics Reject US Role as the World Leader," April 2007, http://www.worldpublicopinion.org/pipa/pdf/apr07/CCGA+_ ViewsUS_article.pdf.

10. For more on the use, and misuse, of the term, see Justin Logan, "The 'Isolationism' Canard," *San Diego Union-Tribune,* February 9, 2006.

11. George Frost Kennan, *Around a Cragged Hill: A Personal and Political Philosophy* (New York: W.W. Norton 1993), 64–65, 223–24.

12. Thomas Jefferson, letter to Thomas Leiper, June 12, 1815, in *The Writings of Thomas Jefferson* (Memorial ed.), vol. 14, 308, republished online at http://harpers.org/archive/2008/03/ hbc-90002075.

INDEX